Jap   *ance*

CORNELL EAST ASIA SERIES
108

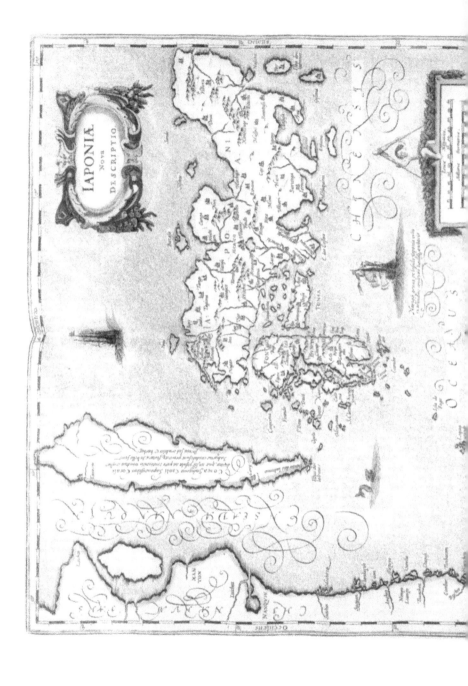

JAPAN'S RENAISSANCE

The Politics of
the Muromachi Bakufu

KENNETH ALAN GROSSBERG

East Asia Program
Cornell University
Ithaca, New York 14853

To my parents
Solomon Samuel and Elsie Leitner Grossberg,
who taught me that nothing is impossible.

The Cornell East Asia Series is published by the Cornell University East Asia Program (distinct from Cornell University Press). We publish reasonably-priced books on a variety of scholarly topics relating to East Asia as a service to the academic community and the general public. Standing orders, which provide for automatic billing and shipping of each title in the series upon publication, are accepted.

If after review by internal and external readers a manuscript is accepted for publication, it is published on the basis of camera-ready copy provided by the volume author. Each author is thus responsible for any necessary copy-editing and for manuscript formatting. Address submission inquiries to CEAS Editorial Board, East Asia Program, Cornell University, Ithaca, New York 14853-7601.

Frontispiece: An Early European View of Japan and East Asia. *Amsterdam Chez Ian Ianſson 1640,* Le nouveau théâtre du monde ou nouvel atlas tome 3ème. *Courtesy of the Harvard Map Collection.*

New paperback edition first published by East Asia Program, Cornell University, 2000. Originally published in 1981 by the Council on East Asian Studies, Harvard University, as no. 99 in the Harvard East Asian Monographs series.

Number 108 in the Cornell East Asia Series
Copyright © 2001 Kenneth Alan Grossberg. All rights reserved
ISSN 1050-2955
ISBN 1-885445-08-3 pb
Library of Congress Card Number: 00-107653

15 14 13 12 11 10 09 08 07 06 05 04 03 02 01   9 8 7 6 5 4 3 2 1

Contents

Figures

Preface

This small book was influenced in many ways by numerous individuals over a period of seven years, starting from the time I first began researching the topic as a doctoral dissertation for Princeton University until the completion of the book manuscript while I was a Junior Fellow at Harvard. The original suggestion to study the Muromachi Bakufu came from Marion J. Levy, Jr., who has been a constant inspiration to me and who transmitted to me his sense of the period's significance in Japan's political development. I confess that, when I first decided to study the Muromachi period, I was unaware of the frustrations that awaited me, and it is to the credit of my advisors, Harry Eckstein, Marius Jansen, and Lynn White III, that they waited patiently and encouragingly for the vague notions in my mind to take shape.

Generous fellowship support from the National Science Foundation enabled me to spend three years at Tokyo University, during which time I read voraciously in Japanese about the Muromachi period and began to study the medieval documents which were to provide the raw data for this study. In Japan I was privileged to receive guidance and instruction from two of that country's most respected medieval scholars, Ishii Susumu and Momose Kesao. I was also helped by my fellow students at Todai, Chijiwa Itaru and Kanamoto Nobuhisa. I owe them all a debt which words alone cannot express. During those exciting years in Tokyo, and on subsequent visits, Kanai Madoka of the Tokyo University Historiographical Institute offered his help and good advice unsparingly. If ever there was an unsung hero of Japanese studies in the West it would have to be Professor Kanai, since there is hardly a single Japanologist—young or old—who has not benefited from his kindness.

I would like to add a special word of thanks to several people who have contributed in major ways to refining the format of this book. First: to John M. Rosenfield who gave generously of his time and his vast knowledge of Muromachi art in helping me to select rarely seen paintings as illustrations depicting the period; to the Harvard Map Collection for their assistance in locating the antique maps which adorn this volume; to Pat McDowell for doing such a fine job on the graphic illustrations; to my beloved Keiko for doing the calligraphy and other unsung drudgery involved in producing a book; and to my wonderful editor, Mary Ann Flood, without whose patience and attention to detail this book could never have seen the light of day.

I owe a final debt of gratitude to the Harvard Society of Fellows, whose generous support between 1974 and 1977 allowed me to rethink and revise this work and to include comparative material on European Renaissance systems.

Cambridge, Mass.
August 1981

Towns and Ports Dotting the Rivers from Sakai to Kyoto
Carte de la route depuis Nagasaki jusqu'à . . . Jedo (Amster-
dam, R. & J. Ottens 173-?).
Courtesy of the Harvard Map Collection

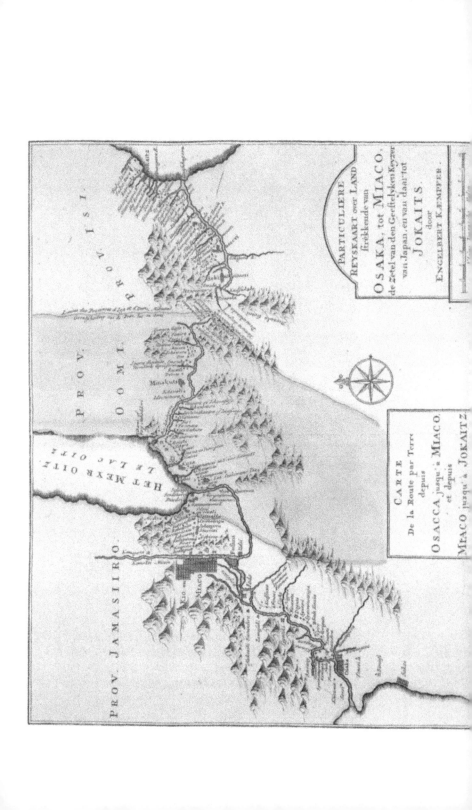

PROV. ISI.

PROV. OOMI. PROV.

PARTICULIERE
REYSKAART over LAND
strekkende van
OSAKA, tot MIACO,
de Zetel van den Geestelyken Keyzer
van Japan, en van daar tot
JOKAITS,
door
ENGELBERT KEMPFER.

HET MEYR OITZ
LE LAC OITZ

Minaksuts

PROV. JAMASIIRO.

CARTE
De la Route par Terre
depuis
OSACCA jusqu'à MIACO,
et depuis
MIACO jusqu'à JOKAITZ

MIACO

ONE

The Muromachi Period in Japanese History

Certain periods of history reveal only enough about themselves to confuse us. The Muromachi period (1336–1573) is one of these, having long defied attempts to discover in it orderly patterns of political and social life. Many traditional historians simply dismissed it as an age of political and economic instability, social anarchy, and inordinate civil violence. While these evaluations are not totally inaccurate, the era that produced the very zenith of Japan's high culture in the visual and performing arts surely offers more to the student of institutional development. This paradox inevitably led Japanese scholars to draw contradictory conclusions about what they found and about what the Muromachi contribution was to Japanese history. This volume will try to present a synthetic reinterpretation of Muromachi politics and society in the light of their detailed researches, which in their several ways have helped to demystify the pall of confusion surrounding the era. Our focus will be on the Muromachi Bakufu, the military regime that governed Japan during the fourteenth and fifteenth centuries, and on the shogun who headed that government. Although the Muromachi Bakufu existed from its founding by Ashikaga Takauji in 1336 until the last shogun Ashikaga Yoshiaki was overthrown by Oda Nobunaga in 1573, it ceased to exert real national influence from the early sixteenth century. This book will concentrate only on that part of the Muromachi age (c. 1336–

1490) when the Ashikaga shoguns actually ruled and their Bakufu was a viable central government.

The Ashikaga family was a samurai clan which had its roots in the Kantō region not far from modern Tokyo. Descended from the noble Minamoto house and related by marriage to the Hōjō who ruled the previous Kamakura Bakufu, the Ashikaga were no mere upstarts but had long been a prominent warrior (*bushi*) family in the eastern part of Japan. Ashikaga Takauji had himself declared shogun—military dictator—and established his Bakufu in the old imperial capital of Kyoto, from which he and his descendants exercised their power in the name of an emperor who reigned in that city but did not rule. The Ashikaga shoguns of the first half-century of the dynasty constructed a political synthesis which embraced aristocratic elements from the imperial court, feudal elements from their own samurai heritage, and bureaucratic elements which they adopted from the Kamakura Bakufu (1185–1333) and the Heian state. These various sources of legitimate authority had always overlapped, but the Ashikaga Bakufu was the first government in Japanese history to combine them successfully in one regime deriving its support from every tradition of political legitimacy then current. Despite their military weakness and increasing political ineffectuality from 1500 on, the Ashikaga shoguns up to that time were feudal monarchs striving toward a postfeudal autocracy which is recognizably similar to that of the Valois in France or the York-Lancaster in England.[1]

Subordinated to the Ashikaga shoguns were the shugo, later to become the *shugo-daimyō*, great provincial military governors whose participation in the Bakufu system was necessary for its continued effectiveness, and who were in turn dependent on the Bakufu for their own legitimation. Among these shugo, three Ashikaga-related families—the Shiba, Hosokawa, and Hatakeyama—came to monopolize the office of *kanrei*. The *kanrei* was the shogun's chief minister who presided over the great council of shugo in the Bakufu and transmitted the shogun's orders to them for implementation. It is concerning the issue of where final authority actually rested within the Bakufu—with the shogun or with his *kanrei-shugo* cabinet—that a major controversy arose among postwar Japanese scholars. One school of thought is best represented by Satō Shin'ichi, who maintains that the shogun was supreme in the Bakufu and exercised his power on the basis of a fusion of two different types of authority. One dimension was private, individual and personal, while the other was public and territorial. This interpretation is countered by those like Naga-hara Keiji who regard the locus of Bakufu power to be in the collective decision-making authority of the shugo and *kanrei*. In fact, both views are partially correct, but advocates of each fail to see them as complementary aspects of the same historical de-velopment. It is true that, at times between the Bakufu establish-ment and its final demise in 1573, the *shugo-daimyō* were in control and the shogun's authority was severely circumscribed. But it is equally true that at other periods, particularly during the late fourteenth and first half of the fifteenth century, the shogun's preeminence was unchallenged and his prerogatives were kingly ones. In addition to reconciling these two conflict-ing images of the Muromachi government, Satō's formulation of the duality of shogunal authority as embracing a personal "feu-dal" component and a public "monarchical" one should also be modified. Rather than his static and unwavering combination of these two dimensions, this book describes a shift between them. This occurred during the reign of the third shogun, Ashikaga Yoshimitsu, and involved a turning away from the reliance on feudal bonds between the shogun and his shugo *qua* vassals, and toward an increasing assertion of his authority as a monarch over his shugo *qua* loyal subjects and officials. When this trend was reversed after the death of the eighth shogun, Ashikaga Yoshi-masa, and the private element of shogunal authority became pre-dominant once more, the shogunal office had already lost much of its regal stature, although the monarchical model then became the sought-after goal of their competitors, the *sengoku-daimyō* of the sixteenth century.

These political shifts did not occur in a vacuum, and the sho-gun's evolution into a kinglike figure was accompanied by an unprecedented change in the economic underpinnings of the Bakufu system—away from the previous Kamakura regime's overwhelming dependence on land ownership and the income to be derived from agriculture in an autarkic setting and toward a greater reliance on the revenue that could be gotten from milking the nascent capitalist-agrarian economy then emerging in the Home Provinces around Kyoto. These two sets of changes, that of the Ashikaga shogun from feudal chieftain to secular monarch and that of the economy from autarkic to capitalist-agrarian, and the relationship between them in the urban environment of the capital, defined the emergence of a shogunal autocracy in fifteenth-century Japan.

There were corollaries to these two primary changes which also influenced the course of events. After shugo took up residence in Kyoto toward the end of the fourteenth century, they began to entrust the administration of their provinces largely to their subordinates, the *shugo-dai*. The *shugo-dai* abused this delegated authority to build their own personal power bases in those very provinces. As happened during the late Heian period, those entrusted with responsibility for collecting revenue for their superiors expropriated both revenue and authority for themselves. The growth of surplus income in the countryside helped the growth of another group which also undermined the shugo's position. These were the *kokujin*, provincial squires whose property was usually concentrated in one contiguous or geographically proximate bloc, thereby facilitating the consolidation of their physical control over such lands. The *kokujin* were often made direct retainers of the Ashikaga shoguns, who used them as pawns to counterbalance shugo power, with such success that the shugo were effectively prohibited from entering the lands of such enfranchised *kokujin*. *Kokujin* and the independent yeoman-farmers beneath them called *myōshu* formed leagues (*ikki*) to defend themselves against the excesses of *shugo-daimyō* rapacity and of a financial elite in the capital whose interests received prior consideration from the shogun's government. This financial elite consisted of moneylenders (*dosō*) and sake manufacturers (*sakaya*) whose enterprises formed the basis for Kyoto's economic expansion during the Muromachi age and who exerted a disproportionate influence over the livelihood of almost everyone in the Kinai region surrounding the capital—samurai, aristocrat, and commoner alike. Major revolts, spearheaded by the leagues of *kokujin,* were joined by indebted peasants and townsmen demanding "virtuous government" decrees (*tokusei*), edicts to cancel their repayment obligations to the Kyoto moneylenders. The fifteenth century witnessed recurrent uprisings of this sort, sometimes preceded by onerous exactions of new supplementary levies devised by spendthrift shoguns or aggravated by prolonged famine and poor harvests.

For all the misfortune it caused, simple rapacity on the part of the Bakufu or *shugo-daimyō* would not by itself have caused such repeated explosions by the populace. But the Muromachi period was a time of greater than average social mobility (upward and downward) for all classes, with fewer effective constraints on geographic mobility than would come to be the case in the seventeenth century. The price of this uncontrolled social movement was a high incidence of sporadic warfare and random violence, an atmosphere which may have provided Hideyoshi with one of his strongest incentives to disarm the populace, and the collective memory of which may have accounted for the severity of the system of social controls instituted by the Tokugawa Bakufu early in the seventeenth century.

All the elements that have been mentioned thus far—the social unrest, economic expansion, shogunal ambitions, samurai greed, itinerance, and peasant strivings toward greater autonomy—were parts of a unity. The Muromachi period was blessed with its share of creativity and innovation in its various institutions, but condemned to constant turmoil by an inability to curb the negative consequences of the very liberality that allowed those innovations to take place. In Muromachi Japan the freedom of movement and opportunities for personal advancement by the sword resulted in an anarchy which ultimately benefited neither the most gifted nor the most creative, but only the most ruthless. Nevertheless, the worst effects of this growing decentralization of authority did not reach full strength until after the Ōnin War (1467–1477), and meanwhile the Bakufu's innovations in administrative technology, economic policy, and military organization during the century and a half preceding this breakdown set the pattern for all subsequent samurai regimes. The growth of the shogun's personal authority over his shugo cabinet, and the ways in which he accomplished this, parallel strikingly the expansion of the Renaissance monarchies in western Europe. As occurred in the West, the attempt to create in the capital a magnet for powerful feudatories in order to keep them under surveillance, the various stratagems employed to reap the profits of a growing commerce, and the ruler's drive to expand the jurisdiction of his bureaucracy and the final authority of his courts, all bespeak a nascent Ashikaga kingship.

THE MUROMACHI PERIOD IN JAPANESE SCHOLARSHIP

Until the end of World War II, interpretations of the Muromachi period by Japanese scholars were largely colored by the fact that Ashikaga Takauji had been an imperial usurper who overthrew the reigning Emperor Go-Daigo and installed his own puppet emperor instead. The focus for most historical analysis was the political struggle between the loyalist supporters of Go-Daigo's Southern Court and the Northern Court in Kyoto, which was an instrument of Ashikaga ambitions. Few students of the period went beyond either condemnation of Takauji for his treachery or detailed narrative description of the dynastic struggle between the two factions during this so-called Northern and Southern Courts (Nambokuchō) period (c. 1336–1392). Matsumoto Shimpachirō was the first postwar Japanese historian to detect something more than simply mayhem and perfidy in the Nambokuchō period and to identify this early stage of Ashikaga hegemony as a social transition between ancient and medieval society. His major prewar influence, Tanaka Yoshinari, had taken the first hesitant steps in the direction of a deeper understanding of this era when he attributed the Emperor Go-Daigo's Kemmu Restoration (1333–1335) to warrior dissatisfaction with the monopoly of power in the Kamakura Bakufu then held by the Hōjō family. He saw these samurai as exploiting the imperial court's prestige to restore their own clan fortunes. Matsumoto viewed the warfare that overthrew the Hōjō in 1333 as a battle between a reactionary emperor and his court aristocrats (*kuge*) on the one hand and the old samurai ruling class on the other, both of whom were buttressed by a class of warriors whose actions were motivated by a desire for a more favorable redistribution of land and income for themselves. Matsumoto, reflecting the spirit of his own times and his personal political preferences, chose to emphasize the self-liberation aspect of this conflict, as exemplified by what he considered to be a united revolutionary action by yeoman-proprietors (*jinushi*), free peasants (*nōmin*), and serfs (*nōdo*). In his analysis, the Nambokuchō period was marked by two important changes: (1) the failure of Go-Daigo's restoration government signaled the end of a dual courtier-warrior power structure and of the ancient Japanese state, with power now surrendered entirely to the warrior clans; and (2) the dividing line between "ancient" and "medieval" Japan, the beginning of Japanese feudalism and the establishment of serfdom, with the driving force provided by lesser samurai chieftains. Matsumoto saw Ashikaga Takauji as an intermediate figure, progressive in comparison with the *ancien régime* of emperor and Hōjō regent, but destructive of "revolutionary" elements in rural society. Civil war resulted because such elements formed leagues to establish their own regional power bases and ceased to give positive support to Takauji and the "reactionary" Bakufu. Shugo were installed to head these leagues and built up their own organizations in the countryside, leading to their becoming new provincial magnates, the *shugo-daimyō*.

The most significant Muromachi scholar since Matsumoto is Satō Shin'ichi, whose theory of the dual nature of shogunal power has been the primary influence on almost all scholarship during the last twenty years. In his earlier research, Satō gave the fourteenth century a threefold importance: (1) it was the century when the principle of blood relationship among the warrior clans declined to be replaced with the principle of territorial unity or union; (2) it witnessed the rise of classes of small and medium peasant producers; and (3) it saw a trend toward the establishment of a regional feudal system under the shugo. Two primary areas of scholarly investigation branched at this point, and led to a bifurcation of opinion which prevails to this day. Growing out of Matsumoto's and his own earlier work, Satō wrote a seminal essay called "On the Muromachi Bakufu," in which he enunciated the dual nature of shogunal authority, divided into private-feudal and public-territorial components, and linked this authority to the primacy of the central government in fifteenth-century Japan. In contrast to this interpretation, Nagahara Keiji began a prolific series of investigations of the shugo system and the indigenous *kokujin* proprietors who formed the shugo's grassroots organization. His conclusions are in direct opposition to Satō's and are based on the thesis that the Bakufu was the tool of its great *shugo-daimyō* who used and abused it almost at will.

Both Satō and Nagahara accepted the same fourfold division of the Nambokuchō period: (1) Go-Daigo's Kemmu Restoration government; (2) the decline of the Southern Court's military power; (3) Ashikaga infighting; and (4) Yoshimitsu's concentration of power in his own hands. But their focus was predictably different. Nagahara was interested in the ramifications of the struggle between the shogun Takauji and his brother Tadayoshi in policy regarding manorial (*shōen*) proprietors. Takauji's steward, Kō no Moronao, tried to organize manorial officials and squires in the Home Provinces as his own retainers and inevitably came into conflict with the proprietors of those *shōen*. Tadayoshi received his support from Ashikaga-related shugo with land bases in eastern Japan who challenged Moronao and were in a position to thwart his ambitions. Satō saw this division between the supporters of Takauji and Tadayoshi in a different light, based on spheres of jurisdiction in the Bakufu itself. Takauji secured military command of all warriors and the right to appoint and dismiss shugo. Tadayoshi had control over civil litigation and land confirmation. Unlike Tadayoshi's supporters, who as Ashikaga relatives had their original base in the east and possessed lands widely scattered throughout the country, Takauji's samurai were yeoman-farmers (*jizamurai*) from the Kinai whose holdings tended to be more concentrated. Their leader Moronao was himself a house vassal of the Ashikaga main line, not a collateral like the shugo.

Nagahara categorically defined the Muromachi period as the end of the *shōen* and denied the possibility of *shōen* proprietors becoming feudal proprietors. Satō emphasized less the outright seizure of manorial properties by warriors than he did the legal absorption and reduction of the authority of such *shōen* proprietors by the subordination of *kuge* law and the establishment of Bakufu legal and jurisdictional supremacy. By analyzing the legal system, Satō clarified the difference between the way in which the Kamakura and Ashikaga Bakufu dealt with the imperial court, and the difference between the Kamakura clan chief and the Muromachi shugo. Unlike the Kamakura clan head (*sōryō*), the Muromachi shugo possessed land-granting and order-implementing authority and was in fact an administrative official of the central government, not just a private warlord. Sugiyama Hiroshi amplified Satō's shogunal authority thesis by adding information concerning the shogun's military and financial base. He established the existence of the shogun's bodyguard and direct retainer bands, and differentiated them from Ashikaga blood-related shugo. He also demonstrated the contribution made by the shogunal domain to the shogun's economic resources.

As for the decline of the clan headship system based on blood ties and its replacement during the Nambokuchō period by territorial unions among *kokujin* squires under shugo domination, Kawai Masaharu had a different view of this development. He interpreted this change not as the elimination of the *sōryō* system, but its transformation, with the Muromachi Bakufu exploiting the authority to grant or withhold approval of appointment to a clan headship. If the Bakufu could directly decide *sōryō* appointments, then it could not be just a rubber stamp accepting the corporate will of the *shugo-daimyō*, but must have its own independent sphere of competence. Kawai's research thus cast doubt on Nagahara's thesis which equated shugo collective authority with final

Bakufu authority, and lent credence to the theory of shogunal supremacy.

By the mid-1960s there were three major schools of thought concerning the Muromachi Bakufu. Nagahara's theory of *shugo-daimyō* corporate authority was opposed by two Satō theories. The early Satō thesis treated Bakufu power as a coalition of the shogunal house, Ashikaga-related and non-related (*tozama*) shugo. The later Satō thesis opposed both of these corporate authority theses with the concept of the dual nature of shogunal authority: the rule of men on the one hand, and the rule of land on the other. In this view Takauji and Tadayoshi were, respectively, the concrete symbols of these two dimensions of shogunal power. Nagahara's rebuttal was that shogunal authority was not based on two dimensions at all, but that the one, private-feudal authority, was a means for realizing the other, public-territorial authority.

Elaborating on Satō's and Sugiyama's idea of a shogunal army, Fukuda Toyohiko and Satō Ken'ichi studied that army, known as the *hōkōshū,* and in a related area Kobayashi Hiroshi demonstrated how the shogun supported members of that army by prohibiting shugo entry into their estates. Momose Kesao further established the existence of a separate tax-collecting route from the shugo's, called the *kyōsai* system, which enabled members of the shogun's army to pay taxes directly to the Bakufu without a shugo intermediary. In the area of taxation and economic policy, Kuwayama Kōnen's research has shed light on the financial basis of Ashikaga power. He located the economic center of gravity not in the shogunal domain or the Kyoto moneylenders, but in the taxes which the Bakufu levied on shugo and land stewards (*jitō*). His research became one more thrust at the Nagahara thesis of a shugo-dominated Bakufu in the fifteenth century. Concerning taxing authority, Tanuma Mutsumi and Momose Kesao separately verified that, between the second half of the fourteenth and the beginning of the fifteenth century, the imperial court's authority to appoint and expel trustees from imperial estates (*kokugaryō*) was absorbed by the Muromachi shogun, illustrated by the shift to the Bakufu of tax and exemption authority over the Ise shrine levies (*yakubutakumai*). With respect to the manorial system in general, for Nagahara the Bakufu began by attempting to compromise with *shōen* proprietors but ended up by causing the outright erosion of those proprietors' rights. With respect to the economic system in general, Sasaki Gin'ya saw the fifteenth century as the great divide between the medieval Japanese economy and the early modern one. He described this as a change from geographically limited specialization and distribution to the circulation of specialized products over widely distant areas, in other words, a highly commercialized preindustrial economy. The resulting social differentiation, according to Sasaki, led directly to an urban-rural confrontation.[2]

These fundamental themes and controversies are the starting point for this volume. It is hoped that the following chapters will place them coherently within an intellectual structure which permits the reader to grasp the importance of the Muromachi period for Japan's political development and, in the larger context, to perceive similarities between this epoch and the evolution of Renaissance monarchies in the European West. This book has been written with two very different audiences in mind. It is on the one hand a monograph designed for the benefit of Orientalists who already possess substantial knowledge about Japan. But it has been written in such a way that those who have not mastered the esoterica of Japanese studies may also enjoy it and learn from it. A comparative chapter and reference aids in the appendix have been included to enable the general reader to use the book productively and to place the information presented here in a more easily recognizable frame of reference. Despite the specific particulars of Muromachi government, the phenomena discussed are universal ones, and it is the author's wish that such aids as are provided will make the Muromachi period both comprehensible and interesting not only to the specialist but to the general reader as well.

TWO

The Ashikaga Shogun in Muromachi Japan

In Japan during the Muromachi age, similar to occurrences in Europe during the quattrocento, a society arose which viewed the state as, if not exactly a work of art, at least a guided creation of human effort, "the fruit of reflection and careful adaptation."[1] During this period the Ashikaga shoguns who ruled Japan, like the Renaissance kings of western Europe, had classical models which they claimed to be following at the very instant they were in fact creating new ways of exercising political authority. When Ashikaga Takauji, the founder of the shogunate, asked his legal experts for political advice, they responded rhetorically, "Does one follow in the path of an overturned wagon?"[2] Although they carefully qualified this caveat with the proviso that precedent must not be violated, the message was clear. Expediency and practicality were the lessons the Ashikaga learned from their scholars. Within the matrix of an occasionally constructive but usually brutal realpolitik, the Muromachi Bakufu introduced the bulk of Japan's major political innovations for the next three centuries. How this happened and why this period deserves to be called Japan's Renaissance are the subjects of this book.

Strictly speaking, the Japanese Renaissance (like its European namesake) was not a rebirth at all, but the result of a conscious act of political creation. As in the West, this Renaissance was also animated by the change from an overwhelmingly autarkic-agrarian

economy to an increasingly capitalist-agrarian one, causing reper-
cussions in governing the country.³ An autarkic-agrarian society is
one in which the great majority of members are engaged in agriculture as their major occupation, the objective of which is self-suffi-
ciency, that is, to meet as many of their material needs as possible
from local resources with minimal recourse to interregional commerce and trade. Manufacturing exists primarily to meet local
needs or those of a very small societal elite. In a capitalist-agrarian
society, the predominant activity remains agriculture, but cash
crops become an important component of agricultural production,
and animate energy—human and animal—is increasingly used to
manufacture goods not just for local consumption. A growing portion of the population becomes engaged in the sale and distribution of such manufactures and cash crops, and they in turn become
dependent on the flow of these crops for their livelihood. There is
a concomitant growth of banking and credit facilities (and indebtedness), halting and primitive at first, but increasingly indispensable
to the society and, most especially, to the ruler and his government. While capitalist agriculture is ultimately augmented by in-
dustrialization, most of the organizational technology—the ways
of organizing human effort to carry on these economic activities
and to govern the societies in which they are being carried on—is
the creation not of the industrializing society but of its predecessor, the Renaissance state with its capitalist-agrarian economy.
These are, after all, the governments which first experiment with
professional bureaucracies and armies free of conflicting loyalties,
fiscalism and the exploitation of commerce, absolutist ideology,
and the idea of the state's primacy over its subunits.

In later medieval Japan, a capitalist-agrarian economy developed
in the Home Provinces, the Kinai region centering on Kyoto, and
the Ashikaga shoguns changed from rustic feudal warlords into
urban princes. Like his Kamakura predecessors and Tokugawa
successors, the Muromachi shogun remained answerable in theory
to the emperor, very much as the European monarchs were to
the pope. Just as the Babylonian captivity caused an irretrievable
loss in the papacy's authority, however, the failure of Emperor

Go-Daigo's restoration government in 1336 and the ensuing conflict between senior and junior lines of the imperial family caused
a disastrous downturn in the court's fortunes. On the ruins of Go-
Daigo's ill-fated *imperium* the Ashikaga family established itself
as the ruling dynasty and, by the turn of the fourteenth century,
the shogun had become a king in everything but name.

Kamakura had been the seat of the Bakufu since Minamoto no
Yoritomo moved there in 1185 to assert his independence from
the imperial court in Kyoto and to shield his retainers from the
baleful influence of the luxuries to be found in the ancient capital.
Political turmoil and civil war following Go-Daigo's ouster led the
Ashikaga to move the Bakufu back to Kyoto, in spite of the fact
that their own home was in the Kantō region north of Kamakura.
As a result of this move by an eastern warrior family, Kyoto
emerged from its post-Heian slumber to become the real political
capital of Japan once more. Thrice blessed: as the center of a rich
and fertile region, as the ancient home of the imperial court and
Japan's metropolitan culture, and from 1336 as the new home of
the government which would come to be known as the Muromachi
Bakufu, Kyoto regained its former preeminence.

Despite the political seesaw of the first fifty years of Ashikaga
rule, marked by the vigorous opposition of Kitabatake Chikafusa
and the loyalists who fought for Go-Daigo's cause, the capital
managed to enjoy a period of rapid expansion as great mansions
were erected to house the shugo, and the Bakufu took on a veneer
of permanence. An urban economy arose based on free wage labor,
a high level of itinerance, and credit institutions, developing the
industries Kyoto has been famous for ever since: textiles, sake
brewing, skilled handicrafts, and the plastic and visual arts. The
Zen branch of Buddhism became the patronized religion of the
shoguns, and Zen clerics attained great political influence within
the Bakufu. In agriculture, the Kinai region surrounding the capital was the nation's most advanced, and manorial markets, which
made their appearance in the thirteenth century, thrived by providing the raw materials to feed both the Kyotoites and their commercial ventures. These markets had originally provided the

moneychanging facilities for commuting the annual tax rice (*nengu*) and other commodities into cash equivalents for transmission to the proprietors in the capital. By the fifteenth century, however, rice could often demand a higher price in the city than in the countryside and, since the Kyoto and Nara markets were better equipped to convert large quantities than they had been a century before, landlords no longer had all of their *nengu* converted into cash at the local market exchanges. Great *shōen* proprietors like the Tōji temple were sensitive to such fluctuations and changed the form of revenue payments from cash to kind accordingly.[4]

As Kyoto prospered first from historical accident and later from the favors of shogunal patronage, so the Muromachi Bakufu was reciprocally the gift of a city. Without the wealth, the aura of legitimacy, and the diversity of the capital, this Bakufu would not have been so different from the Kamakura government as it turned out to be. The union of samurai politics with the imperial capital carried the Japanese political experience into the early modern age and transformed the Bakufu from a decentralized feudal regime into the prototype of preindustrial autocracy embodied in the Tokugawa settlement of the seventeenth century. This fundamental shift was influenced partly by the political institutions the Ashikaga inherited from their Minamoto and Hōjō predecessors, partly by the social and economic changes which swept Japan during the fourteenth and fifteenth centuries, and partly by the personalities of the Ashikaga rulers themselves. Unlike the great samurai progenitor Yoritomo, the Muromachi shogun was more than a feudal lord, and, unlike the samurai administrator Hōjō Yasutoki, more than a dictatorial bureaucrat, for by the time of Yoshimitsu he had become a princely ruler possessing the trappings of power and legitimacy which have come to be identified as the marks of Renaissance kingship.

COMPONENTS OF SHOGUNAL AUTHORITY

The Ashikaga were heirs to several conceptions of legitimate rulership, and their success was determined by the degree to which they were able to absorb these and convert them into a single coherent basis for exercising political authority. The primary elements of such a synthesis were: (1) bureaucratic authority which had its origins in the early eighth-century Ritsuryō state and which was transmitted to the Ashikaga via the imperial court and the Hōjō regency; (2) feudal-military authority for which the prototype was Yoritomo's appointment as shogun; and (3) aristocratic authority transmitted through the *kuge* (court aristocrats), important for the prestige which their pedigree could bestow on a regime. These three strands in the Japanese political tradition—bureaucratic, feudal, and aristocratic—coexisted when Takauji founded his Bakufu, but their synthesis into a unitary system of political legitimation was not completed until the end of the fourteenth century.

The bureaucratic structure bequeathed by the Ritsuryō system had originally been based on Japan's adoption during the early eighth century of the T'ang civil and penal codes. This structure was the basic raw material out of which medieval government would be formed. But the system of public land and public power, of official bureaucratic ranks and hereditary officeholding in the service of the emperor which the Ritsuryō government represented, was put increasingly on the defensive, first by the Fujiwara regents and later by the two great military clans—the Taira and Minamoto. By the founding of the Kamakura Bakufu, the imperial court had been displaced by the military houses as the dominant force in Japan. But the ideal of bureaucratic government that the Ritsuryō represented continued to exert an influence on the details of feudal politics, especially after the Hōjō regents seized control in Kamakura during the thirteenth century. The third and perhaps most formidable of these, Hōjō Yasutoki (regent 1224-1242), went so far as to employ legal experts to write out the Ritsuryō codes for his reference. Although not entirely suitable to the needs of a government of military barons and stewards, after considerable modification they were applied in Yasutoki's administration.[5] The code finally promulgated by the Hōjō, known as the Jōei Formulary (*Jōei shikimoku; Goseibai shikimoku*) of 1232, became

the fundamental law for the military houses. Its successor promulgated by Ashikaga Takauji, the seventeen-article Kemmu Formulary (*Kemmu shikimoku*) of 1336—ostensibly the basic law of the
Ashikaga Bakufu—was declared in its preamble to be an addendum
to the basic Jōei Code. This placed it firmly within the orthodox
limits of legal precedent ultimately traceable back to the Ritsuryō
standard.[6] In this way, a respect for the precedents established by
the Ritsuryō codes, and especially its civil law, was inherited by
the Muromachi Bakufu and perpetuated by the active presence in
the early Ashikaga government of many of the original Hōjō
bureaucrats.[7]

Another development that was conceivably inspired by the
bureaucratic ideal was the creation of the office of *kanrei,* or chief
minister, which replaced the older office of shogunal steward
(*shitsuji*) as the shogun's most powerful deputy. Unlike the steward, who was a non-shugo official of the Ashikaga house with
primarily feudal obligations to his master, the *kanrei* was a great
shugo and an independent agent in his own right. His primary
function was to supervise the various government organs, including
the shugo cabinet, and to mediate between them and the shogun.
Because the *kanrei* was also always a shugo, the new office may be
seen as a fusion of feudal and bureaucratic elements, although it
was largely a bureaucratic role insofar as daily administration was
concerned. How much this was so became apparent when the third
and sixth shoguns both tried to attach some of the *kanrei's* authority to themselves by removing him from the chain of decision-
making in whole classes of civil suits. The Muromachi shoguns
retained and cultivated the spirit of public, bureaucratic authority
because it was in their own best interest to do so, confronted as
they were by *shugo-daimyō* who represented a constant threat to
shogunal prerogatives.

Bureaucratic authority may be described as ruling over a territorial and legal landscape; feudal authority, then, may be character-
ized as rule over a human landscape, over individual men rather
than over the state they comprise. The shogun's feudal authority
in this sense, of first among lords—*primus inter pares*—dated from

the establishment of the first Bakufu in Kamakura by Yoritomo. The legitimacy of the shogun's right to demand obedience and service from all warriors throughout the empire likewise stems from Yoritomo's precedent. Similar to the custom in feudal Europe, the bond between lord and retainer was sealed by the granting of a *beneficium* or *gewere* (*ryō* or *shiki,* respectively, in Japan) to a vassal in return for a pledge of loyalty and service to the lord. The shogun stood at the apex of a huge pyramid of such bondings, the ultimate grantor of all *beneficia* and the final recipient of all pledges of loyalty and service. As in the West, the system in practice never approached the perfection of its idealized conception, and betrayal, treachery, and disloyalty were almost more the rule than the exception throughout Japan's medieval period. But the assertion of a political bond based on the private acquisition of the right to wage war, and the legitimacy that the shogun received as a result of his power to control the allocation of estates and feudal rents, became an important innovation in the political life of the country and remained a significant determinant of political power in Japan until the modern age.

The early Muromachi shogun thus stood at the pinnacle of two hierarchies: one civil-bureaucratic and the other feudal-military. The shogun was both chief administrator and generalissimo, the ultimate decision-maker in matters of state and the final arbiter of vassal conflicts. As long as agriculture remained basically autarkic, with a non-free peasantry and weak squirearchy, feudal ties were of primary importance but, once capitalist agriculture stimulated the growth of alternative sources of revenue and political legitimacy, the feudal coloration of the shogun's office became considerably diluted.

Unlike most of Eurasia, Japan suffered no successful foreign invasion until the twentieth century, and the roles of conqueror and vanquished, of "barbarian" and "civilized" were both played on a microcosmic scale by the Japanese themselves. The confrontation between *bushi* (warrior) and *kuge* (courtier) and the adoption by the former of the lifestyle, the culture, and the pretensions of the latter elite, were substantially the same as those repeated

countless times elsewhere in the world. The identical ethnicity of
conqueror and conquered in Japan, however, makes the "aristocratization" of the Ashikaga samurai elite almost unique in history.
The intermingling of the Japanese equivalents of courtier and
knight in Muromachi Kyoto had an unmistakable leavening influence on the samurai for, though they remained fighters and generals, the scions of the military houses were not averse to indulging
in the refined pastimes of the capital. At the same time, their
parvenu enthusiasm for all that the city had to offer helped to
preserve cultural forms of the aristocratic society which had been
jeopardized by the decline of imperial court influence since the
Kamakura period. In place of the respect which had once been
accorded their aesthetic canons, there arose the austere, almost
morbid predisposition of a warrior class never very far from the
battlefield and possible death. Kamakura became the concrete
embodiment of this state of mind, and it is small wonder that,
despite its religious importance, it never grew to be more than an
administrative town. It is probably also true that the samurai as
a class were not as well-off financially during the Kamakura period
as they were to become by the fifteenth century after their wholesale land grabs of the early Muromachi period and the rise in the
level of economic productivity.[8]

While the shugo were active participants in cultural activities
promoted by the court aristocrats, the shogun's individual use of
kuge prestige to enhance his own authority took the form of
accepting court titles of progressively higher rank. Takauji and
his son Yoshiakira did not rise beyond the honorific title of *gon
dainagon* (Great Counselor under the old system of court offices),[9]
but Yoshimitsu rose from *gon dainagon* (1378) to *sadaijin* (Minister of the Left) in 1382, and finally in 1394 to *daijōdaijin* (Chancellor), the highest rank of all.[10] The taking of aristocratic rank
was a time-honored practice and, although the custom did not by
itself demilitarize the shogun, in combination with the other two
types of authority, the Ashikaga increasingly sought such *kuge*
trappings to broaden the base of their legitimacy.

FEUDAL-BUREAUCRATIC CONFRONTATION:
TAKAUJI VERSUS TADAYOSHI

The founder of the Ashikaga shogunate was eminently a man of his time. Unprincipled, audacious, and belligerent, Takauji's rise to political prominence was founded on a triple betrayal: of the Hōjō in Kamakura when he threw in his lot with Go-Daigo; of the emperor's restoration government which he replaced with his own Bakufu; and of his brother and chief deputy, Tadayoshi, whom he had murdered.[11] In his rivalry with Tadayoshi was expressed the fundamental conflict between two different ways of conceiving the political order. Neither brother considered himself a political innovator; neither initially intended to create a new basis for shogunal legitimacy. And yet precisely because each tried at the same time to base his authority on a different model from the past— Takauji the feudal pyramid, Tadayoshi the Bakufu bureaucratic corps—that exclusive reliance on either became impossible. Out of their personal and ideological conflict, and the imperatives of a totally new urban setting, arose the Muromachi synthesis. Takauji for his part was a paragon of the military strongmen of his age. James Murdoch damned him with faint praise a half century ago when he quipped that "Takauji may indeed have been the greatest man of his time; but that is not saying very much, for the middle of the fourteenth century in Japan was the golden age not merely of turncoats, but of mediocrities."[12]

Murdoch's hyperbole notwithstanding, Takauji was more than anything else a military chieftain, the leader of the Seiwa Genji clans in the Kantō. He practiced an informal, ad hoc governance and tried to consolidate his strength in the Kinai by basing his rule on the loyalty of his retainers, the military acumen of his lieutenants the Kō brothers,[13] and his final authority to grant lands and feudal rents. If he intellectualized his role at all, he probably saw himself as the inheritor of an idealized Kamakura tradition, of a system of feudal government which had existed briefly at the end of the twelfth century and which very early ceased to function according to its original guidelines. He may have thought of himself as a second Yoritomo, but the shugo were more formidable than they had been under Yoritomo, the imperial court poorer and weaker, and the economy of the Home Provinces was no longer autarkically agrarian.

In spite of his identity crisis as a reactionary leader living in rapidly changing times, he was nonetheless an effective and successful figure during his lifetime. Through his position as commander-in-chief of all samurai (*bushi tōryō*) he controlled three major organs of the central government: the Board of Administration (*mandokoro*) which managed the shogun's lands; the Board of Retainers (*samuraidokoro*) which had responsibility for warrior discipline; and the Awards Office (*onshōgata*) which during the early years of the Bakufu handled the receipt and processing of vassal claims and requests for enfeoffment. These three organs reflected Takauji's preoccupation with building a government like Yoritomo's, based on personal ties of loyalty to himself as the grantor of award fiefs. Tadayoshi, on the other hand, who was just as important in the Bakufu, strove instead to strengthen the influence of the bureaus that dealt with lawsuits and land disputes. These offices (*bugyō*) were staffed by the hereditary bureaucrats who had served the Hōjō and whose primary functions in both governments were those of legal specialists and magistrates. Among them were the very drafters of the Kemmu Formulary, which was Takauji's manifesto. Two of them in particular, Zeen—who is generally given primary responsibility for drafting the document—and his brother Shin'e were of the Nikaidō family and former members of the Kamakura Bakufu's Council of State (*hyōjōshū*), that regime's highest corporate body.[14] Tadayoshi utilized this ready-made magistracy to protect the *shōen* lands of the imperial court and of temple and shrine proprietors, who were known collectively as *jisha honjo,* from the inroads effected by Takauji's program of feudal investiture.

The confrontation between Takauji's and Tadayoshi's spheres of influence occurred primarily in two specific areas of policy.

Those two were: the appointment and dismissal of shugo; and the treatment of *jisha honjo* estates, especially half-tax *(hanzei)* decrees in which Takauji made outright gifts of *shōen* land to his vassals. In the case of shugo, they were military governors who represented the Bakufu on the provincial level and who were regional hegemons in their own right. In his capacity as shogun, Takauji had the personal power to issue orders of appointment *(shugo buninjō)*, and he used this privilege to distribute shugo posts as rewards for loyal service in battle. The Kemmu Formulary, however, stated that the shugo was a regional administrator comparable to the governor *(kokushi)* of the old Ritsuryō state, and therefore the duties of the office and the right to its income *(shiki)* should only be given to those well qualified and able, and under no condition should it be used to reward a vassal for performance on the battlefield.[15] A supplementary law promulgated two years after Kemmu elaborated on this principle, specifying that unworthy shugo must be replaced, including those who received their posts as rewards for military or partisan reasons, and those who illegally appropriated *jisha honjo* estates. This decree also reiterated the Jōei Formulary injunction that had limited the shugo's powers to three duties *(daibon sankajō)*: tax collection, maintenance of public order, and apprehension of criminals.[16] Since the Kemmu Formulary was drafted by Hōjō magistrates who belonged to the Council of State, one of the Bakufu organs most closely identified with Tadayoshi's authority,[17] it is fairly clear that the document provides us with a forthright statement of his basic position on the issue.

In the second major area of conflict, that of *shōen* policy, Takauji used the half-tax *(hanzei)* laws to gain the support of local samurai in Yamashiro province surrounding Kyoto. Original *hanzei* decrees had applied to one-half of the annual produce of selected estates, but the shogun instead gave to these warriors in permanent tenure one-half of the land itself of manors which had been declared subject to the order. He then declared those samurai to be his own housemen *(gokenin)*, thereby guaranteeing them Bakufu protection. The· *jisha honjo* proprietors quite rightly considered these *hanzei* grants illegal seizures, and Tadayoshi championed their cause in the government.[18]

Takauji's stand on this issue in particular amounted to a direct affront to the imperial court, for it implied that both samurai and *kuge* families were equally under the shogun's heel. Tadayoshi, on the other hand, took a stand similar to Hōjō Yasutoki's, the third Kamakura regent, who had firmly maintained a posture of non-interference in court affairs even as he strengthened his family's control over the military houses. Yasutoki had even joined forces with *shōen* proprietors against the rising local military squires.[19] It remains to be seen whether Tadayoshi's solicitude for the *jisha honjo* proprietors was purely altruistic, since the confrontation between himself and the shogun was not just an antagonism between two philosophies of government but also the personal struggle for supremacy between two equally ambitious siblings. Fratricide was not uncommon in medieval Japan, and the rivalry between these two ended with Tadayoshi's murder at Kamakura in 1352. The reconciliation of the two philosophies of government was not as easily achieved, however, and it was left to Yoshiakira, Takauji's son and successor, to accomplish.

Ashikaga Yoshiakira replaced Tadayoshi as Takauji's chief deputy in 1349 and became shogun on his father's death in 1358. His shogunate was a hybrid, a way station between the feudal-bureaucratic dualism of his father's and the shogunal autocracy of his son Yoshimitsu's. His uncle's influence was evident in his reliance on the bureaucracy, while the growing power of the shugo within the Bakufu, and particularly of the Ashikaga-related families, led him to create the position of *kanrei* in 1362, when Shiba Yoshimasa (1350–1410) was appointed its first occupant.[20]

Even before his father's death, Yoshiakira's own role had been that of reconciling the feudal and bureaucratic components of shogunal authority. He reduced the five bureaus of the Board of Coadjutors (*hikitsuke*) to three. The *hikitsuke* handled all civil property suits from court hearings to drafting judgments, which they then sent up to the Council of State for final pronouncement. Yoshiakira inaugurated a parallel, shorter petition procedure. Begun while Tadayoshi was still alive, it was expanded after his death. Instead of the "three petitions and three responses" (*sanmon santō*) of plaintiff and defendant, the one who had seized land illegally would be immediately ordered to return it. This simplified samurai justice was most welcome to the *jisha honjo* proprietors, for whom it meant the speedy return of their property, but at the same time it also strengthened the shogun's authority over the military houses.[21]

Bakufu *hanzei* decrees issued in 1355/8th month and 1357/9th month indicate an even more direct attempt by the shogun to limit samurai expropriation of manorial property.[22] Yoshiakira's most important act in trying to control the warriors, however, was to establish the *kanrei* office. Shiba Yoshimasa was only thirteen years old when the shogun made him the first *kanrei,* but the real purpose for this title at this time was to enlist his father, the formidable shugo Shiba Takatsune, in Yoshiakira's cause. Unlike the Kō and others who had served the shogun as steward (*shitsuji*) the Shiba were not Ashikaga retainers, but were shogunal relatives of the highest lineage. Takatsune was lured into helping the shogun by giving the position of *kanrei* broader powers than the shogunal steward had possessed. Takatsune was also able to extend his influence in the Board of Coadjutors, since a year after Yoshimasa became *kanrei* Takatsune's grandson Yoshitaka became head of one of the three *hikitsuke* bureaus (*hikitsuke tōnin*).[23]

In 1363 Yoshiakira moved one step farther toward a stable Bakufu by reconciling powerful Ōuchi and Yamana shugo to Ashikaga hegemony, but at the price of accepting their "condition" that he adopt a laissez-faire attitude toward them in their provincial domains.[24] But in the constant tug of war between shogunal initiative and shugo resistance to centralization, one phase of shugo dominance was coming to an end, and ironically it was a fellow shugo who helped to bring it about. Although the shugo continued to strengthen their hand in provincial affairs by the enfranchisement of local *shōen* officials and yeoman-samurai (*myōshu*), in the central government the rise of Hosokawa Yoriyuki to the office of *kanrei* in 1367 marked a change for the better in Ashikaga fortunes.

Almost immediately after Yoriyuki became *kanrei,* Yoshiakira died, leaving the child Yoshimitsu as his successor. Throughout Yoriyuki's long tenure as chief minister and shogunal regent, he took steps to provide the Ashikaga heir with an effective government. Yoriyuki's regency was conservative and moralistic, and one of the first laws promulgated under his regency was a sumptuary edict calling for frugality on the part of the military houses.[25] At the same time he took great pains to surround the young shogun-to-be with the ceremonial signs of deference and engineered Yoshimitsu's rapid rise in the hierarchy of imperial court ranks. Yoshimitsu was still only twenty-one years of age when he attained the second rank (*junii*), as compared with his father, who did not attain the same rank until he was already thirty-four years old.[26] Also during Yoriyuki's regency the shogun's new palace, the "Palace of Flowers" (Hana no gosho), was constructed (c. 1377–1378) at Kitanokōji Muromachi in a district of the capital which was much closer to the emperor's palace than the former shogunal residence at the Sanjōbōmondai had been. This physical reduction in distance between shogun and emperor, Bakufu and court, was symbolically expressed in a gesture made by the Emperor Go-En'yū (r. 1371–1382) at a court banquet in the first month of 1379, when he offered his own cup to Yoshimitsu in a toast, an unprecedented reversal of traditional protocol.[27]

Yoriyuki's zealous support of shogunal advancement was not totally disinterested, for he too had much to gain from controlling his shugo rivals in his capacity as the shogun's mouthpiece. His official duty and his self-interest merged in the policy of protection for temple, shrine, and *kuge* lands which appeared in Bakufu laws regulating the operation of the *hanzei* system. In these he opposed illegal appropriation of land and crops by shugo and restricted the types of lands that could lawfully be subjected to division between samurai and *kuge*.[28] Whatever Yoriyuki's real motivations may have been, he stood opposed to the breakneck growth of power by the *shugo-daimyō* and their deputies the *shugo-dai,* and he thus contributed to a centripetal tendency which became pronounced during Yoshimitsu's adult reign. To suppress the diehards who still supported the cause of the Southern Court, the *kanrei* appointed a former head of the Board of Retainers and the Board of Coadjutors—Imagawa Ryōshun—as Kyushu commissioner (*Kyūshū tandai*) in 1370.[29] Imagawa was another loyal and gifted servant of the Bakufu and, within four years, he managed to turn the tide in favor of the central government. From that time on, the Bakufu's authority in northern Kyushu was secured.

THE MUROMACHI SYNTHESIS OF ASHIKAGA YOSHIMITSU

Yoshimitsu's reign as shogun accomplished the synthesis of bureaucratic, feudal, and aristocratic authority and, in the process, created a political figure who was undeniably both head of government and de facto head of state. At the same time, his reign saw the formation of a stabler group of *shugo-daimyō* who enjoyed longer tenures and greater authority over their provincial domains. Yoshimitsu had been fortunate in having a regent of Yoriyuki's ability to guide his wardship, but the *kanrei's* severity and apparent high-handedness made him extremely unpopular with the shugo and led to his dismissal in 1379.[30] From this date on, Bakufu policies bore the shogun's personal stamp.

The more than three decades which span Yoshimitsu's public life witnessed a dynasty's maturation and the first period of genuine political stability that Japan had enjoyed in more than a century. Initially under the guidance of his regent, and after 1379 as a ruler in his own right, Yoshimitsu succeeded where his predecessors had failed. He subdued the shugo and firmly established the Ashikaga house as the center of national politics. His reign was punctuated by two major disturbances, the Meitoku (1391) and Ōei (1399) rebellions, both of which were shugo efforts to weaken his government and both of which he pacified unequivocally. Yoshimitsu stood midway between the feudal regime of his grandfather Takauji and the culturally efflorescent but politically enervated rule of his grandson Yoshimasa. Thoroughly Kyoto bred, Yoshimitsu was in every respect a civilian prince but, unlike his grandson, he still retained the warlord's toughness and, unlike his grandfather, he was above all a political innovator. Whereas his Ashikaga forebears had attempted to apply models of government inherited from the past to makeshift arrangements, wherever possible Yoshimitsu created his own precedents. His main objective was the establishment of his family's dynastic power on the basis of a legitimacy far broader than the one he had inherited, with a corresponding expansion of the shogun's exclusive prerogatives. In pursuit of this goal, Yoshimitsu adroitly balanced the society's conflicting forces to his own advantage by pitting shugo against shugo, Northern against Southern Court, and new mercantile elements eager for trade against hard-line conservatives who took umbrage at Japan's new status as a tributary of the Ming empire.

From the founding of the Bakufu right up to Yoshimitsu's coming to power, the most serious obstacle to Ashikaga sovereignty remained unaltered: how to bind the shugo close enough to the central government to guarantee at the very least their compliance and at best their cooperation, without allowing their very proximity to the centers of power to encroach on the shogun's privileges. The great shugo were nominally appointed by the shogun for the purpose of maintaining order, apprehending criminals, and collecting taxes in their respective provinces, but in fact many of them were already among the most powerful figures in their various regions and the Bakufu appointment was little more than an official recognition of that fact.

Tozama shugo like the Ōuchi, "outer" daimyo who were not related to the Ashikaga by blood or house vassalage, posed a special threat to Bakufu authority. In addition, the schism between the senior and junior imperial lines aggravated the problem of keeping public order, since it provided shugo who wished to resist the shogun with a patriotic justification, that of supporting the "legitimate" rights of Go-Daigo's descendants. One family of this sort, which proved to be a continual thorn in the Bakufu's side long after the defeat of the loyalist heroes Kusunoki Masashige and Kitabatake

Chikafusa, was the Kikuchi. They were not subdued until Imagawa Ryōshun pacified northern Kyushu in the 1370s, and they remained steadfastly loyal to the Southern Court until their fall.[31]

The Ōuchi, the loyalists, the various shugo rivalries such as that between the two Ashikaga collateral houses Hosokawa and Shiba, all contributed to Yoshimitsu's decision to address himself first to the problem of samurai discipline at the highest level. A subtle and persuasive maneuverer, the new shogun alternately coerced and cajoled shugo into serving his government in both military and administrative capacities. In the Meitoku rebellion of 1391, he used the Ōuchi to defeat the Yamana, both of whom were potentially menacing rivals of the Ashikaga as well as of each other, and in 1399 he mobilized other shugo to crush the Ōuchi in turn. Although the Ōuchi later revived to build an even stronger provincial apparatus by the mid-fifteenth century in western Japan (Suō and Nagato provinces), Yoshimitsu's victory gave his government unprecedented elbow room in the crowded and violence-prone political landscape of medieval Japan.

One by one, the *shugo-daimyō* (for such they had become by the 1380s) responded to Yoshimitsu's carrot and stick methods and came to take up permanent residence in Kyoto. While it is true that, from the earliest days of the Bakufu, related vassals and collateral lines of the Ashikaga, like the three *kanrei* families, had been deeply involved in the central government and spent much of their time in the capital, non-related *tozama shugo* displayed a dangerous independence. It was to counter such centrifugal tendencies that Yoshimitsu undertook a series of pilgrimages during the 1380s. These trips were unquestionably motivated more by political instinct than religious piety, and were designed to emphasize the Bakufu's sovereignty to *shugo-daimyō* who might be contemplating rebellion and, like the royal progress of European monarchs, to make the shogun's presence felt by his subjects in areas far from Kyoto.

In 1389 the shogun journeyed to the Itsukushima shrine on the island of Miyajima, west of present day Hiroshima.[32] The island bordered on the territory of the Ōuchi, who controlled the provinces of Suō and Nagato in that region. Yoshimitsu used this trip as a pretext to meet with the incumbent shugo Ōuchi Yoshihiro (1356-1399) on his home territory in order to persuade him to take up residence in Kyoto. Yoshihiro consented to move to the capital, and the shogun's success in uprooting him illustrates the conscious formulation, more than two hundred years before the Tokugawa *sankin kōtai* system, of a policy of semi-compulsory residence in the Muromachi capital.[33] Not only did Yoshimitsu make them settle in Kyoto and participate in Bakufu councils, but he also forced *shugo-daimyō* like the Ōuchi to implement policies that would inevitably strengthen his own hand and correspondingly weaken their own regional autonomy. Yoshihiro's pivotal role in suppressing the Yamana revolt (1391) and in reunifying the senior and junior imperial lines (1392) are two cases in point.[34] In the former instance, Yoshimitsu had exploited the rivalry between these two great shugo of western Honshu to good effect, a tactic his son Ashikaga Yoshinori employed even more systematically. Even at its strongest, the Bakufu needed the support of one or another of the *shugo-daimyō's* vassal bands to mount a victorious military campaign, and in the Meitoku rebellion it was Ōuchi manpower that was decisive. Shortly thereafter, Yoshihiro helped to engineer the rapprochement between the Northern Court, which supported Ashikaga hegemony, and the Southern Court, which had been in exile in Yoshino for seventy years. By accomplishing this reconciliation—on false pretenses, as it turned out—Yoshimitsu was the first shogun who could claim to have received the approbation of both lines of the imperial family.

In 1395 the shogun dismissed Imagawa Ryōshun from the post of Kyushu commissioner. During the quarter-century when Imagawa had loyally served the Bakufu in this capacity, he had managed to make himself virtual dictator of northern Kyushu. Having done this in the shogun's name, he remained an obstacle to the further pacification of the rest of Kyushu and, in the larger sense, he prevented Yoshimitsu from extending his personal authority in the area. The three important shugo houses of the Shōni, the Ōtomo, and the Shimazu, while indicating their willingness to pledge loyalty to the Bakufu, refused to submit to Imagawa, even though he was a regional commissioner delegated by the central government. The pacification of northern Kyushu and the reconciliation of the two imperial lines had, furthermore, fundamentally altered the shogunate's policy in this area. Until then, military requirements dictated that the *Kyūshū tandai* be given broad powers, but with the coming of peace the Bakufu was able to absorb his political functions and the regional system of appointments took care of daily administration. When this position was achieved, the private power base that Imagawa had constructed in the shogun's name became not only superfluous, but a definite obstacle to further Bakufu penetration.[35]

There is more than a little irony in Imagawa's summary dismissal, since it would be hard to find a Bakufu official who did more than he did to develop an ideology of shogunal supremacy, both in his acts and his writings. Even though he conceptualized his relationship to the shogun as founded upon the feudal ties of fealty and homage of a vassal for his lord, the result was the same.[36] One may speculate that it was precisely because he viewed the relationship in terms of a decentralized feudal system that Yoshimitsu wanted to demote him. It is also interesting that Yoshimitsu chose to dismiss Imagawa a year after he himself resigned as shogun to assume the august title of *daijōdaijin,* Chancellor in the old Ritsuryō imperial ranking system, an audacious feat not duplicated until Hideyoshi received the same title almost two centuries later in 1586. Soon after becoming *daijōdaijin,* Yoshimitsu resigned this office as well to enter holy orders. This did not mean a retreat from public life, however, but was a common practice for heads of state who wished to retain the substance of power while relieving themselves of the ceremonial burdens of office. Like the shogun's dismissal of Imagawa, these other actions were steps in a strategy which tried to thrust aside the traditional limitations observed regarding the imperial court and the autonomy of powerful retainers.

As he advanced from shogun to *daijōdaijin,* and then relinquished both titles, Yoshimitsu's authority and stature continued to grow. The ambiguous status of a monk was, in the traditional Japanese polity, ideally suited to his purpose. Both the offices of shogun and Chancellor were associated in the public mind with immutable expectations and limitations, and both were, in the final analysis, emanations of the imperial institution. It would be difficult for a shogun to be more than the protector of that institution under such circumstances; he could never claim a legitimate princely status for himself. When Yoshimitsu became Chancellor, he entered the highest rank of the Kyoto aristocracy. That in itself modified his public image for, although he retained the prerogatives of the shogunal office, those prerogatives were now augmented by an aristocratic component of the highest pedigree. In effect, the evolution toward a synthetic legitimation based on feudal, bureaucratic, and aristocratic elements was achieved when Yoshimitsu took the tonsure in 1395 and finally discarded all of his worldly titles.[37]

In pursuit of his goal of controlling the *shugo-daimyō*, Yoshimitsu in 1399 eliminated the remaining potential obstacle by neutralizing Ōuchi power in the Home Provinces. Ōuchi Yoshihiro, his ally and valuable deputy of only five years before, had been chafing under the shogun's increasingly autocratic rule and, from his provincial seat in western Honshu, he plotted rebellion. According to Satō Shin'ichi, Yoshihiro had three possible reasons for suspecting Yoshimitsu of planning his destruction. When, in response to a shogunal command to punish the Shōni in 1397, Yoshihiro obeyed and fought them as well as two other rebel families in Higo and Hizen provinces, he heard later that Yoshimitsu had also secretly ordered those other shugo families to attack the Ōuchi. In the second place, a rumor began to circulate that Yoshihiro would soon be relieved of his shugoships to Kii and Izumi, two provinces close to Kyoto which he had recently received as rewards for his part in suppressing the Yamana revolt. And third, he was given no reward to compensate for the death of his brother Mitsuhiro during the Shōni campaign. In short, when the shogun summoned him to Kyoto, Yoshihiro feared that it was for the purpose of having him assassinated.[38] Yoshimitsu seized the opportunity presented by Yoshihiro's refusal to comply with his summons to return to the capital and had him declared an enemy of the Bakufu. With the help of the Akamatsu, Kyōgoku, and Hosokawa shugo, he destroyed Yoshihiro's forces in a great battle at the port of Sakai near present-day Osaka, in 1399. Yoshihiro's suspicions were well-founded, as subsequent events would demonstrate. From the time he resigned as chancellor, Yoshimitsu's relations with *tozama shugo* changed as he endeavored to give Ashikaga relatives greater priority. Moreover, he wished to reserve the lucrative trade with China for himself and was loath to share it with powerful *shugo-daimyō* of questionable loyalties.[39]

In less than ten years, the shogun's dissembling had given him a string of uninterrupted political triumphs. The one issue that remained to be resolved was the Bakufu's relationship with its eastern branch in the Kantō, which was headed by a semi-autonomous *Kantō kubō*, an Ashikaga deputy shogun in Kamakura. The post of *Kantō kubō* had been created by Takauji in 1349 when he appointed his nine-year-old son Motouji (1340–1367) as its first occupant. Takauji intended it to be a temporary device for controlling the unruly eastern territories, but instead it became a genuine source of friction after Motouji's son Ujimitsu (1359–1398), who succeeded to the post in 1367, began to vie with the shogun for national supremacy in a way that Takauji had not anticipated. The Kantō remained intractable until the sixth shogun, Ashikaga Yoshinori, was able to bring it temporarily under Kyoto's control, but at no time during the Muromachi period was the Kantō ever fully integrated with the central government except in the most superficial way.

Compounding Yoshimitsu's domestic successes, he undertook the first active foreign policy ever initiated by a shogun and, although his initial motivation in doing so was primarily political, in the long run this aspect of his program was to have disproportionate effects on the Japanese economy. The most immediate results, however, were in the realm of shogunal legitimacy, and notably in the way foreign policy encouraged popular acceptance of his monarchical role. Until his reign, the only conception of a monarch enunciated in Japan was that of the emperor, in whom divine descent and godlike attributes were fundamental for receiving legitimation. The orthodox loyalists who advocated imperial rule, led by their general and ideologue Kitabatake Chikafusa (1292–1354), made much of these as necessary qualifications in their struggle against the Ashikaga.[40] But the success of Yoshimitsu's program made him in effect Japan's king, for he possessed virtually all of the powers that we have come to associate with traditional kingship. His considerable taxing authority with respect to the shugo, the moneylenders, and religious institutions; his right to appoint and dismiss all important officials; his superordinate position vis-à-vis temples and shrines, and especially the Zen sect; his juridical supremacy over the bureaucracy and the courts via his personally signed decree; and his military preeminence all bespeak a nascent Ashikaga monarchy. Given the broad powers the shogun came to exercise, and the synthetic nature of the legitimacy that maintained them, it was quite appropriate for the Chinese emperor to grant Yoshimitsu (and not the Emperor Go-Komatsu then enthroned in Kyoto) the title "King of Japan" (*Nihon kokuō*) when official relations were inaugurated between the two countries.

The start of official Sino-Japanese relations came at a critical juncture in the evolution of Yoshimitsu's government. The piecemeal appropriation of imperial prestige and the remaining vestiges of court authority had been one way to legitimate his autocracy, and when he became Chancellor in 1394 he reached the end of this process. But the more he adopted traditional imperial authority, the less effective was the puppet emperor as guarantor of shogunal legitimacy, until eventually Yoshimitsu found it expedient to seek other sources of legitimation. Foreign relations between the Muromachi Bakufu and the Ming empire should initially be viewed in this domestic context.

In 1401 Yoshimitsu sent the Hakata (Kyushu) merchant Koitsumi and a trusted priest as his ambassadors to the Chinese court to inaugurate formal diplomatic relations. Koitsumi had just returned from China and apparently was influential in convincing

Yoshimitsu of the profitability of Bakufu-sponsored trade with the Asian mainland.[41] The 1401 embassy returned to Japan in the eighth month of the following year, accompanied by a Ming emissary. The Chinese were most concerned about the depredations which were caused by Japanese pirates called *wakō* along their littoral, and Yoshimitsu pleased them by his show of responsiveness when he immediately ordered the Shimazu shugo in Kyushu to suppress *wakō* activities in the region.[42] In the ninth month of 1402 the shogun received his Chinese guest at his Kitayama villa nestled in the hills west of Kyoto, at which time he was given the famous credentials in which he was referred to as the "King of Japan."[43]

In the second month of 1403 Yoshimitsu designated the abbot of the Tenryūji monastery to head a company of three hundred on the second voyage to the Ming court,[44] and six months later a ship sent by the Ming arrived in Hakata.[45] In the fifth month of 1404 the shogun once again received the Ming ambassador,[46] and this time sent the monk Myōshitsu along with him on his return to China two months later. Although this was actually the third Bakufu-sponsored voyage to the mainland, it was the first time that the official tallies issued by the Chinese government were employed. Hence, the voyage of 1404 marked the formal beginning of the Sino-Japanese tally trade (*kangō bōeki*), but at that time contact between the Bakufu and the Ming had already become regularized, with Chinese entering Kyoto in the autumn of 1404 and the flow of ambassadors, traders, and churchmen in both directions increasing steadily thereafter.

In the eleventh month of 1405, on the occasion of the fourth official voyage, Yoshimitsu delivered on his promise to the Chinese emperor to control piracy in the waters between their two countries by turning captured *wakō* over to the Chinese authorities.[47] In 1406 he once again granted the Ming ambassador an audience, and sent Bakufu representatives to both China and Korea. In 1408, the year of Yoshimitsu's death, two more official convoys sailed to China. During the final eight years of his shogunate, therefore, Yoshimitsu was responsible for sending at least seven

regular tribute missions to the court of the Yung-lo Emperor
(r. 1402-1424). That the shogun appointed a merchant as one of
his ambassadors on the very first voyage was indicative of the
commercial importance with which contact with the Ming was
regarded, and of a significant alteration in the Bakufu's and the
samurai's attitude toward commercial enterprise as a source of
income.

The establishment of diplomatic contact with China expanded
the boundaries of shogunal authority both politically and economically. The kingly title that Yoshimitsu accepted enthusiastically
from the Ming emperor symbolized a new sense of Japanese
nationhood with respect to the outside world, with the shogun—
not the emperor—as its primary symbol. Although the relationship
acknowledged by the shogun was a tributary one, the fact that he
accepted the title for himself and not in the name of Emperor
Go-Komatsu, as he should have done according to traditional
Japanese protocol, tells us to what degree political symbols were
being employed in the service of real power, rather than vice
versa. Even though his son and successor Yoshimochi later rejected
the title and temporarily discontinued the tally trade, Yoshimitsu
had demonstrated that the shogun was to be Japan's head of state
and could rule in his own name if he so desired. The tally trade also gave the shogun a lever in the form of official patronage, the
power to decide who might participate in the voyages and share in
the profits.

In addition to the political capital which accrued to the shogun
by initiating the tally trade, these ventures carried out under
Bakufu patronage became a totally new source of government
revenue. The financial importance of the trade increased as the
fifteenth century progressed, but even in its initial voyage the
economic potential of such a Bakufu monopoly could not have
been overlooked. At the very least the political leverage that it
gave the shogun over those who would participate in the venture,
including *shugo-daimyō* and wealthy temples, could ultimately be
converted into an economic asset. The official trade soon became
the foreign component of a domestic economic policy which was

increasingly mercantilist. An incipient mercantilism, to be sure, since the policies pursued by the Muromachi shoguns did not reach their full flower until the Tokugawa period two centuries later. But these policies were, nonetheless, conscious efforts by the Muromachi Bakufu to foster commercial expansion as a means of augmenting its own revenues.

In Muromachi Japan the first indications of such mercantilistic practices were characteristically parasitic on the non-agrarian sector of the economy and entailed taxing the sake breweries (*sakaya*) and moneylenders (*dosō*) which had already become conspicuous elements in urban society. The earliest mention of professional moneylenders dates from 1255, and by 1272 they were being referred to by the name they would retain throughout the Muromachi age—*dosō*, named after the underground storehouses which were the symbols of their profession.[48] Among these *dosō* were many whose business interests included rice-wine breweries, the *sakaya*. The association between *sakaya* and *dosō* was so intimate that they were often treated as a single entity, *sakaya-dosō*. The *sakaya-dosō* had never been very closely associated with the Kamakura Bakufu, and it was Ashikaga Yoshimitsu who first brought them directly within the Muromachi government's jurisdiction. In 1393 he issued a decree which nullified the right of temples, shrines, and *shōen* proprietors to tax *sakaya-dosō* and instead made them subject to Bakufu direct taxation.[49] Exactly how many establishments were affected by this legislation is not clear, but we know that there were at least fifty-two *sakaya* in Kyoto in 1419, and a count of 342 exists for the year 1425,[50] so the total number must have been substantial. Yoshimitsu aroused the resentment of many *jisha honjo* by depriving them of an important traditional source of income, but increased his own revenues handsomely as a result.

Besides foreign trade, with its resultant importation of Chinese metallic currency,[51] and commercial taxes, Yoshimitsu influenced economic growth in a third way, by enforcing compulsory shugo residence in Kyoto. There are no reliable figures for the period, but Kyoto's population must have grown rapidly during his shogunate, for great *shugo-daimyō* like the Ōuchi and the Hoso-kawa brought with them large retinues of housemen (*gokenin*), servants, and relatives and spent the wealth which came from the countryside largely in the capital itself. The appearance of towns-folk at this time as a distinct, identifiable grouping of rich and poor freemen with their own ethos—neither peasant nor samurai nor aristocrat—gives evidence of a change in the composition of the urban population.[52] When Takauji chose Kyoto as his capital he gave the city a new lease on life, but Yoshimitsu helped to transform it into Japan's first early modern city and made it a powerful magnet for all segments of Japanese society.

Cultural life was one area where this influence was particularly evident. Kyoto's traditional preeminence was enhanced by the shogun's unrivaled patronage of the arts, a patronage consciously designed to ornament and impress. Shogunal entertainments served the interests of Yoshimitsu the prince by making his palace a magnet for both warrior and aristocrat and his court a meeting place for all the highborn and powerful in the country. As an urban ruler of refined tastes, Yoshimitsu genuinely enjoyed these aesthetic pursuits, but the political importance of his salon was a prime motivating factor in his enthusiastic sponsorship of them. His salon performed the same function in the cultural sphere that his role as "King of Japan" played in foreign affairs, for it strength-ened the unique basis of his legitimacy and contributed to the centripetal pull his government was able to exert over the *shugo-daimyō*.[53] The Muromachi "Palace of Flowers" in the center of Kyoto, and later his Kitayama villa in the northwestern part of the city, became the settings for lavish banquets and linked-verse parties, flower viewings, and dramatic performances of *sarugaku* plays by the Nō master Zeami and others. Such shogunal enter-tainments drew inspiration from commoners like Zeami who were helping to shape a vigorous new culture in the visual and perform-ing arts, aware of its aristocratic past but also appreciative of its new popular roots. In their irreverence and lighthearted ridi-cule of masters and aristocratic types, the *kyōgen* comedies of the fifteenth century created an aesthetic democracy which aptly portrayed the highly fluid society that had given them life.[54]

All of these elements—political, economic, and cultural—made Yoshimitsu's Bakufu a far cry from either the truncated court of the pre-Muromachi emperors or the self-limited regime of the Hōjō regents. The Ashikaga was the only one of Japan's three shogunal dynasties to choose Kyoto as its seat of government, and its most enduring contributions to the country's development all stem from that choice and its consequences.

YOSHIMOCHI'S SHOGUNATE

When Yoshimitsu resigned as shogun in 1394, although final authority remained in his hands, the title was passed on to his eight-year-old son Yoshimochi. When Yoshimitsu died, Yoshimochi was finally freed from his father's domineering presence and broke with three of Yoshimitsu's favorite policies: he shunned intimate ties with the imperial court; he broadened the authority of the *shugo-daimyō;* and he discontinued the tally trade with China. In diminishing contact with the *kuge,* he was following the advice of his elder counselor (*shukurō*), the former *kanrei,* Shiba Yoshimasa. On Yoshimasa's urging, he refused to accept the posthumous title of "Abdicated Emperor" (*daijō tennō*) for his father, which the court was thinking of bestowing on Yoshimitsu. Previously, this title had never been offered to a shogun, but only by new emperors to their abdicated predecessors. In the second policy shift, Yoshimochi decreed that shugo had the right to decide whether land should be treated as confiscated property (*kesshochi*) or not,[55] a decision which had always been the Bakufu's alone. The third reversal, cancellation of the tally trade, has been attributed more to the fact that the new shogun considered the title and the trade monopoly which accompanied it unnecessary, than to *kuge* opposition to Japan's acceptance of tributary status vis-à-vis China.[56]

Yoshimochi is a complex figure, and difficult to evaluate, because he was for so long overshadowed by his illustrious father that his performance as shogun seems somewhat tarnished by comparison. So many of his official acts appear to be reproaches directed

FIGURE 1　A Contemporary View of Yoshimitsu's Golden
Pavilion (Kinkaku) and Surrounding Gardens

*Painting (album), Japanese, Momoyama
Anonymous
Kyō meisho zuchō (Illustrated book of
famous places in Kyoto)*

*Courtesy of the Fogg Art Museum,
Harvard University*

FIGURE 2   Horse Racing at the Kamo Shrine, a Popular Diversion in Muromachi Kyoto

Painting (album), Japanese, Momoyama
Anonymous
Kyō meisho zuchō (Illustrated book of famous places in Kyoto)

Courtesy of the Fogg Art Museum
Harvard University

at his father's memory, meaningless acts of rebellion which did not help the Bakufu to deal with the problems that beset it. He even moved the shogun's official residence back to the Sanjōbōmon palace and left Yoshimitsu's Kitayama villa to fall into desuetude. However, the de-emphasis put on relations with the imperial court —an element so important in Yoshimitsu's synthesis—was in some respects a simple acknowledgment of samurai supremacy. It is also not hard to figure out why Shiba Yoshimasa advocated the break, since he wished to roll back the shogunal autocracy of Yoshimitsu to a sharing of power between shogun and *shugo-daimyō* more favorable to the latter, whose interests he represented.

It is generally conceded that the most important event of Yoshimochi's reign was the Uesugi Zenshū rebellion (1416-1417), which occurred in the Kantō when the shugo of Musashi province, Uesugi Ujinori (Uesugi Zenshū), revolted against the *Kantō kubō*, Ashikaga Mochiuji (1398-1439). Ujinori had been *Kantō kanrei* (the functional equivalent in the Bakufu's Kamakura branch of the *kanrei* who presided in Kyoto), but he resigned in 1415 after a falling out with the *Kantō kubō*. In 1416/8th month, he tried to install Mochiuji's uncle Ashikaga Mitsutaka as *Kantō kubō* and, in collusion with the shogun's younger brother Yoshitsugu, he revolted against Mochiuji and the incumbent *Kantō kanrei*, Uesugi Norimoto. At this point the Bakufu ordered the shugo of Suruga province, Imagawa Norimasa, the shugo of Echigo, Uesugi Fusakata, and the shugo of Shinano, Ogasawara Masayasu, to help Mochiuji, and by the first month of the following year Uesugi Zenshū had been defeated and took his own life. After hostilities ceased, a "confession," obtained from Ashikaga Yoshitsugu after crossexamination by the shogun's retainer Togashi Mitsumasa, resulted in the investigation of Yoshitsugu's allies among the Shiba, Hosokawa, and Akamatsu families.[57] The Toki also were removed as shugo of Ise province, the Yamana were prohibited from serving in the capital, and the Hatakeyama were subject to shogunal scrutiny.[58]

Practically every important member of the Bakufu cabinet was affected by these events. A similar purge was undertaken with renewed fury by the shogun Yoshinori, but the reshuffling in Yoshimochi's government represented a more precarious balance of power between shogunal right and *shugo-daimyō* autonomy than would Yoshinori's campaign. In the aftershock of the Uesugi revolt, the *kanrei* and shugo cabinet which supported Shiba Yoshimasa's views was opposed by the alliance between Yoshimochi and his retainer Togashi Mitsumasa, who advocated a continuation of shogunal autocracy. In 1418/11th month, however, that alliance suddenly fell apart. While Yoshimochi was in retreat at the Kitano shrine, it was rumored that Mitsumasa had taken advantage of his temporary absence to incite the shogun's younger brother Yoshitsugu against him. Mitsumasa's fall from power as a consequence of this alleged conspiracy was a setback for the Ashikaga, since it temporarily allowed the stronger *shugo-daimyō* to play a more important role in the Bakufu than they had been able to previously.[59] That role continued right up to 1428. Even on his deathbed, Yoshimochi complained that his choice of a successor would not be implemented unless the *kanrei*, who at that time was Hatakeyama Mitsuie, and the other daimyo agreed to it. Thus lamenting, he left the decision up to them.[60]

THE SHOGUN AS AUTOCRAT: ASHIKAGA YOSHINORI

Before Yoshinori was chosen by lot to be the next shogun, it seemed as if Yoshimochi had forfeited for all time decision-making power to the *kanrei* and shugo cabinet. It was they who cast the lots, not he, and it was they who ran the Bakufu during the brief interregnum between his death and his younger brother's election in 1429. Yoshinori had been abbot of the Enryakuji monastery on Mt. Hiei, in a position known as the *Tendai zasu*, and at thirty-five years of age was at the peak of his powers when he assumed the office of shogun. Nevertheless, he was immediately confronted by a *kanrei* and shugo cabinet with which he had never dealt before and whose members had no intention of deferring to this newcomer whom they themselves had elevated to office. He also had to deal with the untrustworthy *Kantō kubō* Mochiuji, who had been nursing his resentment of Kyoto while awaiting an opportunity to seize power for himself. Before that chance came, however, another crisis gave Yoshinori his trial by fire. That was the very large Shōchō rebellion, which broke out in 1428 and is often considered the first great popular uprising of the medieval period. It was actually several separate disturbances which coincided with a year of nationwide famine and epidemic, and in both the major cities of Kyoto and Nara, as well as in the countryside in Iga, Ise, Uda, Yoshino, Kii, Izumi, Kawachi, Sakai, and elsewhere, non-coordinated but violent revolts erupted whose participants demanded debt-cancellation decrees (*tokusei*) to alleviate their burden. In the capital itself, mobs took the law into their own hands by raiding the moneylenders' shops and burning the contracts (*shakusho*) that recorded their outstanding debts. The Bakufu, the *shugo-daimyō,* the great temples like the Kōfukuji in Nara, all issued debt cancellations, and one by one the uprisings subsided, but from that time on debtors' revolts became a periodic contributor to the turbulence of the age.[61]

The shogunal office at the time of Yoshinori's ascension had long been acknowledged to possess exclusive legitimate authority to levy taxes on shugo, grant awards, appoint and dismiss shugo, judge disputes among retainers, and decide the headship (*sōryō-shiki*) of shugo and shogunal army families.[62] Ideally, the scope of his authority had not expanded since Yoshimitsu's day, and in fact Yoshimochi's recessional policies had diminished the prestige of the office somewhat. But, unlike Yoshimochi, the younger brother's rule was neither restrained nor conservative. Yoshimitsu had built the shogun into a figure of monarchical proportions by balancing opposing political forces: competition among shugo, conflict within the imperial court, and conflict between *jisha honjo shōen* proprietors and samurai retainers. Yoshimochi inherited this skillfully constructed stalemate of opposing interests, but he contributed little of his own except to handicap the position of his shogunal successors. Nevertheless, Yoshinori ruled as one whose power rested on firm foundations and, ignoring both his elder brother's retrenchment policies and the peculiar nature of his own rise to the shogunate, he became the most autocratic of all the Ashikaga.

The new shogun's political strategy was governed by a contradiction which bore bitter fruit for his descendants: while he dealt with minor infractions of his will as severely as previous shogun had punished open rebellion, he at the same time plotted with and encouraged vassals to betray their own *shugo-daimyō* overlords. A consequence of this unwise and reckless policy was to de-emphasize the feudal component of his own legitimacy and to erode the synthesis forged by his father. Yoshinori made immoderate demands on the Bakufu system and meddled in provincial and clan matters to a far greater degree than had any previous shogun. He effected such interference by using the shogun's traditional right to designate formal clan heads (*sōryō*). The actual decision in these matters had always been left to a council of clan elders, whose choice would then receive the shogun's formal ratification. Yoshinori, however, took literally his right to choose a *sōryō* from among a clan's eligible candidates and infused that right with the will of an autocrat.[63] He deftly manipulated the latent but pervasive friction that existed between head (*sōryōke*) and branch (*shoke*) families of a clan by replacing established senior lines with lower-ranking members of the clan who, of necessity, would then be more pliant in respecting his wishes. Many of these junior members ended up at least nominal members of Yoshinori's personal army, the *hōkōshū,* symbolically expressing their loyalty to the Ashikaga house.

Yoshinori constantly reshuffled shugo appointments and, when unstable tenures did not accomplish his objectives, murder served him equally well. Cases of shogunal intervention in *sōryō* selection and in the concomitant rotation of shugoships occurred in 1433, when he appointed his personal choice to succeed Imagawa Norimasa of Suruga province. He did the same with the Shiba house when their *sōryō* died and, in 1439 upon the death of Kyōgoku Mochitaka, he ignored Mochitaka's younger brother's primary right of succession and appointed an uncle to the vacant post instead. In 1440, he condemned to death Isshiki Yoshitsura and

Toki Mochiyori, shugo of Wakasa and Ise provinces respectively and then divided up the Isshiki lands. In 1441, he banished the future *kanrei* Hatakeyama Mochikuni and appointed a younger brother Mochinaga in his place. And at the time of his own assassination by Harima shugo Akamatsu Mitsusuke that same year, it was rumored that he was planning to replace Mitsusuke with his own favorite, Akamatsu Sadamura. By the time he was slain during a *sarugaku* performance at Mitsusuke's Kyoto mansion, Yoshinori had exercised his shogunal prerogative to interfere in the internal affairs of all seven major families which were the heart of the Bakufu.[64] These seven included the three *kanrei* clans (Shiba, Hosokawa, Hatakeyama) and four which regularly alternated the post of head of the Board of Retainers (*samuraidokoro shoshi*): the Isshiki, Kyōgoku, Akamatsu, and Toki.

In these machinations, Yoshinori betrayed a desire to replace the limited fealty that was due him as feudal lord *primus inter pares* with the more total obedience reserved for a national sovereign. Although the constant reshuffling of shugo and *sōryō* appointments did contribute to his personal monopoly of power, in the long run such tactics weakened the network of *shugo-daimyō* provincial administrations that extended Bakufu control throughout the country and gave his government credibility outside of the capital. Unstable tenures and the threat of even greater sanctions frustrated the shugo's attempt to maintain order and, by deepening the schism between head and branch lines of the great clans, the shogun weakened their internal cohesion. This accelerated their disintegration when locally based *kokujin* squires entered the breach created by intrafamilial discord and seized greater autonomy for themselves.

A persistent and increasingly ominous theme during the Bakufu's first century was the semiautonomy of the *Kantō kubō*, who held sway over the eastern provinces from his organization in Kamakura, which was a tintype of its larger partner in Kyoto. Aided by his deputy, the *Kantō kanrei*, the *Kantō kubō* was responsible for enforcing Bakufu laws, but at the same time he had enormous latitude in making decisions on local issues. The tension between Kyoto and Kamakura reached a head when Ashikaga Mochiuji became *Kantō kubō*. His incumbency lasted from 1409 to 1439, he was the fourth Ashikaga to hold that office, and he was by far the most amibitious one of them all. In 1428/5th month, less than six months after Yoshimochi's death, he planned to march on Kyoto to proclaim himself shogun, but was dissuaded from doing so by his *Kantō kanrei*, Uesugi Norizane.[65] Equally devious and every bit as politically astute, Yoshinori was well aware of the threat posed by the *Kantō kubō*, and he was determined to subdue the east once and for all. In 1430, he plotted Mochiuji's overthrow, and it was only the strenuous opposition of some *shugo-daimyō* which prevented him from carrying out his plan. In 1432/9th month, he traveled east to view Mr. Fuji against the protests of his advisors, to display his power to Mochiuji much as Yoshimitsu had done with the Ōuchi in western Japan more than forty years before. The shogun finally had his way eight years later, when he used as a pretext Mochiuji's aggression against Uesugi Norizane to launch a Bakufu punitive expedition against Kamakura and ordered all loyal vassals to take part in it. That campaign, the Eikyō disturbance of 1438, was led by Imagawa, Takeda, Ogasawara, and other shugo, and ended with Mochiuji's suicide in Kamakura the following year. Yoshinori had used the old shogunal tactic of exploiting a potential rival, in this case Mochiuji, to pacify (the *Kantō*) shugo, and then pitting that rival against a formidable adversary, in this case the Uesugi. After the *Kantō kubō's* downfall, real authority in the Kantō shifted to the Uesugi who, like the other *shugo-daimyō*, soon had to contend with provincial *kokujin* and indigenous chieftains who were consolidating their own vassal pyramids beneath the shugo.

The *shugo-daimyō* remained the critical link between the eastern provinces and the Bakufu, because, even before the Eikyō rebellion when the *Kantō kubō* had jurisdiction over tax collection in the ten Kantō provinces, the right to appoint and dismiss shugo remained an exclusive shogunal prerogative. After the elimination of the *Kantō kubō*, the shogun was that much more influential if only for the few remaining years of Yoshinori's life. That he had

been at all able to devote so much of his time to Kantō affairs itself indicates the relative stability of his position by the late 1430s.
He was the architect of major reforms in bureaucratic and military
organization, he weakened the *kanrei's* power of legislative review,
and he meted out swift and barbarously severe justice to malcon-
tents. In 1434, the Enryakuji monastery complained that three of
Yoshinori's subordinates were conspiring to damage the interests
of the Mt. Hiei establishments and demanded that the Bakufu
punish them. These three—the moneylender-priest Yūshū, the
Bakufu official in charge of Mt. Hiei affairs (*sanmon bugyō*) Ino
Tametane, and the shogun's retainer and *mōshitsugi* officer
Akamatsu Mitsumasa—were part of a newly formed group of con-
fidants, and Yoshinori interpreted criticism of them as veiled
criticism of himself. His response was to launch a bloody campaign against Enryakuji led by the Ōmi shugos Rokkaku and Kyōgoku, which ended in the mass suicide of the resisting monks.[66]
Merchants suspected of criticizing his action were summarily be-
headed,[67] and his dictatorial stance created tension with the Kyoto aristocracy as well.[68]

Yoshinori refined and expanded economic policies which had
been originated by Yoshimitsu, and some of the economic changes
already in progress during the fifteenth century, such as indigenous product specialization and cash crops, continued largely
unaltered down to modern times.[69] Others, like private monopolies
of production and sale called *za,* similar to the guilds of Europe,
obtained their special privileges from the Bakufu and were an
intermediate stage in the state's growing supervision of commercial
life. The *za* had made its appearance at the end of the Heian period (c. late eleventh century) and underwent a gradual expansion
of both its monopolistic privileges and the geographic scope of its
jurisdiction until the fifteenth century, when the rapid growth in
the number of unattached merchants, especially after the Ōnin
War, began to threaten those privileges. The newer merchants
formed new *za* (*shinza*) to compete with the original ones (*honza*),
and the *honza* sought favorable Bakufu legislation to protect their
closely guarded markets.[70] The Muromachi Bakufu protected

them, as it did the other vested interests with whom it became entangled, but the *sengoku-daimyō* of the sixteenth century did not continue the practice. They instead set up free markets (*raku-ichi*) open to all merchants. Once the Tokugawa were securely in power, however, Japan saw a return to the Ashikaga practice of official protection and licensed monopolies.

In 1426, on the eve of Yoshinori's coming to power, there were 342 *sakaya* in and around Kyoto, most of whom were also *dosō* moneylenders. Their presence in the capital on such a massive scale inevitably influenced Bakufu economic priorities, and they were taxed heavily and repeatedly by Yoshinori. A mounting demand for currency was evident in the economy at this time, as may be deduced from the dramatic increase in amounts of copper cash which were then being imported from China.[71] Like Yoshimitsu, Yoshinori welcomed the tally trade and the title "King of Japan" that came with it. Yoshinori's close advisor Sambōin Mansai considered the title eminently appropriate, given that the shogun was indeed autocrat and supreme ruler of Japan. It is unlikely that he was the only one in official circles who felt that way, and the general feeling that the title was disrespectful to the emperor —or even that this was an important consideration—is probably of more recent vintage.[72]

As the revitalized tally trade with China grew in volume, its political importance to the shogun tended to diminish. The shogun could still manipulate his patronage for political ends but, from the quantities of goods which were being shipped to the Ming and the increasing number of non-Bakufu vessels participating including those financed by the Sōkokuji, Sanjūsangendō, and Daijōin temples, and by the Yamana *shugo-daimyo*, it is clear that the government had become more interested in the profits to be made than in the symbolic advantage to be gained from belonging to the Ming tribute system. Major exports of the China trade included copper, sulfur, swords, and sapanwood, and Yoshinori's shogunate marked the beginning of a century of aggressive Japanese trading which the Ming government first tried to discourage by offering progressively lower prices per unit of merchandise purchased and,

FIGURE 3 Kyoto in the Muromachi Period

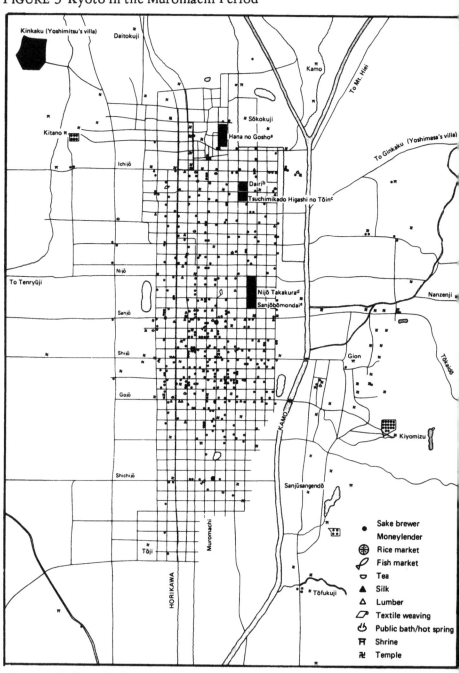

Notes: *a. Yoshimitsu's palace*   *c. Takauji's mansion*   *e. Tadayoshi and*
            b. Imperial palace   *d. Takauji's mansion*   *Yoshiakira's mansion*

(Detail)

when that did not dampen Japanese commercial enthusiasm, they adopted a severely protectionist trade posture. The trend of Japanese exports is clear from the increasing quantities of "supplementary articles," non-tribute cargo carried on official tribute ships. In 1433, for example, the Japanese exported 4,300 catties (1 catty = 1.3 pounds) of copper ore, in 1453, 150,000 catties, and in 1539, 298,500 catties. Similarly with short swords: in 1433, 3,500, in 1453, 9,483, and in 1539, 24,862. Data for sulfur is unavailable for 1539, but the totals of 22,000 catties in 1433 and 364,400 in 1453 indicate a similar trend.[73]

Yoshinori thus presided over a gathering explosion of commercial activity. In the cultural sphere, as in the political and economic, he followed his father's lead. He continued to patronize *sarugaku* Nō, although his personal taste led him to dismiss Zeami, the playwright and actor who dominated artistic life at the shogun's court since Yoshimitsu had discovered him and elevated him to high status. Yoshinori supported different artists as his arbiters of taste and, had he lived longer, he no doubt would have put his personal cultural stamp on an age, as did both his father and Yoshimasa his son. As it turned out, however, he bequeathed the mixed blessing of a growing economy, a tradition of shogunal artistic patronage worthy of a Renaissance prince, and an overwhelming political turmoil which his inexperienced successor was hard put to set to rights.

THE DECLINE OF SHOGUNAL AUTOCRACY: ASHIKAGA YOSHIMASA

Yoshinori's assassination in 1441 dealt a fatal blow to the shogunal monarchy, and the circumstances surrounding his murder were illustrative of the schizoid nature of Ashikaga power and prophetic of the political chaos which was to engulf Japan during the following century. His assassin was Akamatsu Mitsusuke (1381-1441), former head of the Board of Retainers and *shugo-daimyō* of Harima, Bizen, and Mimasaka provinces. Once before this daimyo had come into conflict with a shogun: in 1427/10th month Yoshimochi confiscated Harima, designated it part of his shogunal domain, and promptly awarded it to his own vassal Akamatsu Mochisada. When Mitsusuke asked the shogun to reconsider because of generations of loyal service and was rebuffed, he set fire to his mansion in the capital and removed to Harima. To burn one's Kyoto mansion was a sign of revolt, and only Mochisada's suicide and the support given to Mitsusuke by other shugo enabled him to recover his province.[74] But in 1441/6th month, once again fearing confiscation of his provinces by shogunal fiat, Akamatsu Mitsusuke invited Yoshinori to his Kyoto mansion for a *sarugaku* play and during the performance killed him in full view of everyone. Then he once again put the torch to his residence and escaped to Harima, thus beginning the Kakitsu rebellion. The Hosokawa and Yamana *shugo-daimyō* led the Bakufu punitory expedition into Harima, where Mitsusuke ended his own life rather than risk capture. Yamana Mochitoyo (1404–1473) (also known as Yamana Sōzen), long covetous of Akamatsu territories, received the shugoship to Harima province, and held it until the outbreak of the Ōnin War in 1467. This was the only time throughout the Muromachi period when an Akamatsu was not the shugo of Harima province.

With Yoshinori's sudden fall from power, the attempt to forge a national hegemony was postponed for over a century, although the Muromachi Bakufu itself managed to outlive the monarchical pretensions of its strongest shoguns by almost as long a period. Commenting in his diary the day after the assassination, the emperor's father, Fushiminomiya Sadafusa, wrote that the shogun had brought this dismal fate upon himself and reproachfully added that no shogun in history had died so ignominiously, "like a dog."[75] Other reactions to his death also reflected the general animosity felt toward the shogun. For one thing, the Bakufu punitory force did not leave Kyoto until two weeks after the crime, and the *kanrei* Hosokawa Mochiyuki was rumored to be secretly in collusion with the Akamatsu. The Bakufu liaison to the court (*buke densō*), Madenokōji Tokifusa, visited the shogun's advisor Sambōin Yoshitaka to urge him to think of ways to correct Yoshinori's "mistakes" so that his children would not have to suffer the onus of his rule. *Kuge* who had been punished by Yoshinori for minor offenses were one by one pardoned, including Hino Shigemasa (whose father had been killed by the former shogun), and the Hino family, which provided many a shogun's consort, once more became influential in Kyoto politics.[76]

Warlords who had been removed from clan headships by Yoshinori now scrambled to reestablish themselves. Hatakeyama Mochikuni, shugo of Kawachi, Kii, Etchū, and Noto, marched on the capital from Kawachi a few days after Yoshinori's murder to reclaim the headship from his illegitimate younger brother, Mochinaga. With no shogun at its helm, and many sympathetic shugo in its constituency, the Bakufu had little choice but to recognize his claim.[77] Like Mochikuni, Kaga shugo Togashi Noriie had been removed by the shogun and replaced by his younger brother Yasutaka, and he too retook the headship by main force with the help of the new *kanrei*, who by this time was none other than Mochikuni himself. But Yasutaka secured Hosokawa support for his claim, and finally the Togashi's own *shugo-dai,* named Yamagawa, petitioned the Bakufu to avert further strife by dividing Kaga between the two claimants. The Bakufu eventually did so, making each claimant shugo over half of the province, but the rancor grew ever more violent as each strove for what he considered his legitimate rights. Such bitter intraclan feuding was the lasting effect of Yoshinori's arbitrary interference.[78]

The outbreak of the Kakitsu rebellion, the first major disturbance in thirteen years, the consequent strengthening of the Yamana, and the subsiding of hostilities when the Bakufu issued a debt-cancellation decree, all followed in quick succession.[79] But the Bakufu's problems did not end. Stunned by the premature death of Yoshinori's eight-year-old son and heir, Ashikaga Yoshikatsu, and plagued by the lack of a capable and loyal regent like Hosokawa Yoriyuki to guide the ship of state during Yoshimasa's minority, the dream of a strong central government under Ashikaga guidance languished. Not even the *kanrei* system of rotation among the Shiba, Hosokawa, and Hatakeyama survived this period unscathed, as the three families intensified their competition for political dominance. The Hatakeyama and Hosokawa busied themselves with forming alliances to oppose each other, as they did in the Togashi headship dispute. Hosokawa Katsumoto (1430–1473) was married to Yamana (Sōzen) Mochitoyo's daughter for this reason, and those two families ruined the Hatakeyama for all time by instigating a headship dispute between Hatakeyama Mochikuni's choice, Yoshinari, and his nephew, Masanaga. The Shiba house, closest in pedigree to the Ashikaga main line, suffered from disobedience by their own house vassals the Kai, Oda, and Asakura, and by the 1450s they too were no longer a power to be reckoned with. That left the Hosokawa as the one remaining *kanrei*-class family that was still intact.[80]

Although *shugo-daimyō* continued to reside in Kyoto, they ignored the Bakufu with impunity, headed as it was by a mere child, even as they emulated former Ashikaga policies in strengthening their own provincial domains. The Ōuchi were just beginning at this time to establish rules and laws in imitation of Bakufu ones, such as the regulations concerning compulsory residence by their own retainers in the new provincial capital at Yamaguchi.[81] Even those beneath the shugo, like the Shiba retainer, Asakura Takakage (1428–1481), who would eventually overthrow their masters in the aftermath of the Ōnin War, began at this time to use as their political model organizational principles first utilized by Yoshimitsu and Yoshinori.

As Ashikaga Yoshimasa grew to adulthood and assumed the powers of the shogunate, he tried to reverse the centrifugal tide of events, but he was frustrated by the momentum of *shugo-daimyō* provincial consolidation coupled with the myriad pressures that worked against the shugo system itself. Isolated from his samurai roots, and not fortunate enough to have been groomed for the exercise of power like Yoshimitsu, or to have come into his inheritance during the full flower of maturity like Yoshinori, the eighth shogun assumed the duties of his office under the most inauspicious of circumstances.

Perhaps more than for any previous shogun, Yoshimasa's domestic life intruded on the satisfactory performance of his official

duties. No regime is free of palace intrigue, but his household was
notorious for the plotting and corruption perpetrated by his favorites and, more than any other Ashikaga, he and his government
were dominated by the women in his life. Those women were
three: his mother, Shigeko; his beloved consort, Oimamairi no
Tsubone, who was more than ten years his senior and belonged to
the Odate family, trusted shogunal retainers; and his wife, Hino
Tomiko, of the influential Hino family and a formidable person in
her own right. Yoshimasa married Tomiko in 1455 when he was
twenty years old. A rivalry between Tomiko and the shogun's
mother split his harem into two factions and, after Tomiko's son
died soon after birth in 1459, Oimamairi was accused of putting
a curse on Tomiko and was banished. She committed suicide because of this humiliation, and the loss of his favorite concubine
may have contributed to Yoshimasa's later estrangement from
Tomiko.[82]

In addition to marital difficulties and Tomiko's manipulations,
Yoshimasa also inherited the potentially explosive problem of
debtor-creditor relations which became acute during his reign,
even as the Bakufu was forced to rely more and more on commercial revenues from the *sakaya-dosō* for its income. The onerous
burden of repaying loans from these moneylenders drove debtors—
both rural and urban, commoner and samurai—to revolt, and
among the many such *ikki*, which took place before the Ōnin
War, four were especially serious. In 1447, an *ikki* broke out in
Nara and then in the capital. In 1454, the Tōfukuji temple set up
a toll barrier (*sekisho*) on the Hōshōji Ōji highway to gain revenue
for building a pagoda, but the residents of Daigo and Yamashina
who used the road rose up and not only tore down the barrier but
set fire to Tōfukuji itself. Spurred on by their success, the rebels
raided Kyoto *dosō* of pawned property and carried out private
(that is, illegal) debt cancellations. This caused a drop in the
Bakufu's *dosō* revenues, which prompted the Bakufu to issue a
partial debt cancellation (*bun'ichi tokusei*) whereby debts would
be officially canceled upon payment by the debtor to the Bakufu
of a fixed percentage (in this instance 10 percent) of the amount

owed. In 1457, another *ikki* began as a protest against the erection of new barriers in Kawachi province, probably along the upper reaches of the Yodo River, and then spread to Kyoto. Early in the tenth month, rebels demanding debt cancellation blocked the eastern gateway to the capital. The *dosō* hired their own mercenaries from among the available riffraff in the city, and were joined by the vassals of the Ise family and other warriors as well. While the *dosō* forces stockaded themselves in the center of the capital, the *ikki* occupied the Tōji and Sanjūsangendō temples in the south of the city and, from the west, Nishioka residents attacked Kyoto, led by bands of teamsters (*bashaku*). By the end of the tenth month, the *kanrei's* three hundred mounted samurai, the Isshiki's one hundred, the Toki's two hundred, and the Yamana's two hundred—an army of eight hundred *bushi*—were easily defeated by the rebels, who then proceeded to carry out private debt cancellations. The *dosō* yielded pawned property to the mob, and in the twelfth month the Bakufu issued a partial prohibition on debt cancellation (*bun'ichi tokusei kinzei*) to gain revenue for itself.

The fourth major *ikki* during this antebellum period occurred in 1462, and was led by a masterless samurai of the local squirearchy named Hasuda Hyōe. He led an army into the Sōkokuji and Tōfukuji temples, occupied the sacred woods of the Kamo shrine and the Tōji temple, and burned over thirty *chō* (1 *chō* = 2.45 acres) of land in the city. But this time the *shugo-daimyō* obeyed Yoshimasa's orders, and the Hosokawa in the north, the Yamana, Isshiki, and Toki in the south, and the Kyōgoku and Akamatsu in the east succeeded in defeating the rebels.[83]

The increasing indebtedness of all classes in Muromachi society and the growing propensity of the common people to register their grievances by violent means led Yoshimasa to use debt-cancellation decrees in their various forms as a cornerstone of Bakufu economic policy. As arbiter between peasant and samurai proprietors on the one hand, and the moneylenders on the other, the Bakufu was at the vortex of a dangerous issue, and alternated decrees sanctioning debt cancellation (*tokusei; bun'ichi tokusei*) with those prohibiting it (*tokusei kinzei; bun'ichi tokusei kinzei*) as a way of maintaining order and economic stability, and of minimizing its own financial losses.

In this manner, the half-century of Yoshimasa's reign, which saw a gradual retreat from the zenith of Ashikaga power, also achieved the maturation of an urban government whose dependence on mercantile revenue was directly proportional to the favors it granted to the commercial elite which provided that revenue. The Tokugawa Bakufu achieved a similar modus vivendi with the great merchants of Edo and Osaka during the seventeenth century, but that accommodation was handicapped by ideological tensions caused by the contradiction inherent in the regime's need to employ the services of a merchant class which it officially condemned in Tokugawa Confucian dogma. The Muromachi Bakufu was, from its inception, less concerned about erecting rigid class barriers and was therefore free of the need to justify or camouflage merchant participation in government. On the contrary, Yoshimasa freely made use of the financial talent available in abundance in Kyoto; even the name by which these early financiers were known—*utokunin,* "virtuous men"—has a peculiarly Renaissance ring to it and denoted the value that contemporary Japanese society placed on their services.[84] To the extent that the elite society of Muromachi Kyoto was less rigidly stratified than that of Edo, due to the relative absence of invidiousness between samurai and non-samurai, it was unquestionably a healthier one. Unlike the Tokugawa *chōnin,* who were more important to the society of their own day and certainly as powerful, the Muromachi *utokunin* were not officially spurned by warrior and polite society. Indeed, given the fact that Muromachi merchants were theoretically not deprived of the right to bear arms until Hideyoshi's confiscation of weapons late in the Sengoku age (1588), they could not have been as strictly segregated from the samurai lifestyle as their Tokugawa descendants. The schizophrenic nature of Japanese class conflict was a later development, and one of the unfortunate consequences of the Tokugawa settlement.[85]

Social mobility, itinerance, and political conflict were all climbing simultaneously by the mid-fifteenth century. Under such

circumstances, Yoshimasa tied his government to an urban constituency of great *dosō* and courtiers, with those who were the
adversaries of most of the population that received its income
from the land and were most vulnerable to the moneylenders. In
this respect his reign marked the culmination of the shogun's
evolution from feudal chieftain to urban prince. "The Kamakura
rulers," wrote George Sansom, "have it to their credit that they
perceived in the cultivator the basis of the country's economy, and
saw the importance of justice in their dealings with him as with
others higher in the scale."[86] The Ashikaga shoguns from Yoshimasa on were increasingly indifferent to the Bakufu's agrarian
roots. The Ashikaga had encouraged social mobility and economic
development, as well as a cultural egalitarianism of a sort, and
were the first to give commoners (*bonjin*) specific rights written
into the law,[87] but they failed to institutionalize permanent contact with most of the country outside of the Home Provinces,
which would have protected their national hegemony from rival
claimants.

The decline of the Muromachi shoguns was not simply a function of institutional inadequacy, however. Add to the growing
restlessness of local warlords the chronic extravagance of the prod-
igal Yoshimasa and his indifference to the suffering around him,
and Ashikaga decline becomes even more understandable. In 1458,
Yoshimasa began a large-scale renovation of Yoshimitsu's former
Muromachi palace, which had suffered neglect ever since Yoshinori's
death, when Yoshimasa was living in the mansion of Karasumaru
Suketō. This renovation was begun capriciously immediately
after Yoshimasa had just completed renovating the Karasumaru
mansion to make it more suitable for shogunal habitation, and re-
furbishing work continued even after a great famine broke out in
1460.[88] All of the buildings, the landscaping, and the pond were
not finished until 1464, and in the meantime Yoshimasa began
construction of a villa for his mother, the Takakura gosho, in
1462. Despite the continuing famine in the Home Provinces,
Yoshimasa decided in 1465 to build a bucolic retreat for himself
on the ridge of hills known as Higashiyama, due east of the capital,

in emulation of Yoshimitsu's famous villa northwest of Kyoto. Also in imitation of Yoshimitsu he decided to resign as shogun, pass the title on to his brother Yoshimi (1439–1491), and retire to his new compound to live the life of an abdicated sovereign.[89]

To finance public works on such a lavish scale, given the limited clout that his government could now directly exert outside of the Home Provinces, Yoshimasa resorted to repeated levies of forced labor and draft animals in Yamashiro province, and collected "temporary" taxes from *shugo-daimyō, shōen* proprietors, and mercantile elements in the Kyoto area.[90] That situation might well have continued, with the Bakufu becoming the rapaciously effective government of an extended city-state, and the *shugo-daimyō* considering their tax burden a small price to pay in return for a free rein in their provincial domains. But trauma now intervened in the form of the Ōnin War, which radically accelerated the drift of power away from the central government.

The Ōnin War (1467–1477) disrupted all normal activity in the capital, and the business of government was no exception. Aristocrats and commoners alike fled the ravaged city but, after hostilities had moved on to the provinces, the dispersed residents returned to rebuild Kyoto, and the Bakufu also returned to normalcy of a sort. The war and its aftermath could not be ignored, however. In 1473, while the war still raged, Yoshimasa relinquished the title of shogun as he had intended and passed it on to his young son Yoshihisa. Yoshihisa was born in the interim between the time Yoshimasa had promised the office to his brother Yoshimi and the war, and the shogun's broken promise became one of the primary catalysts leading to the war's outbreak. Feeling betrayed, Yoshimi sought support for his claim from Yamana Mochitoyo. This situation, combined with succession disputes in the Hatakeyama and Shiba clans and the pervasive rivalry between Yamana and Hosokawa, catalyzed the conflict. By its very scale, the Ōnin War demonstrated how much the country had grown during the years of Ashikaga rule, and indicated the direction that political development would take in the century to come.

The results of the eleven-odd-year conflict were inconclusive despite the involvement of over 100,000 fighting men at its height. No single *shugo-daimyō* was able totally to dominate the others. Nevertheless, the socioeconomic conditions that had formerly contributed to the expansion of Bakufu authority—rising productivity, itinerance, the commercialization of agriculture, administrative innovations—now aided the growth of a new group of warlords, known as the *sengoku-daimyō*.[91] As for the *shugo-daimyō*, few of them survived the Ōnin War with their provincial power intact. Succession disputes, disobedient vassals, the weakness of their initial base all took their toll. *Shugo-daimyō* fortunes, more than they had realized, were irrevocably entwined with those of the Bakufu. The revenue that they had received from the countryside and passed on to the central government until about 1486,[92] after that date remained in the provinces, where it was used to consolidate local power. Paradoxically, the rapid decentralization of taxing authority that began after the Ōnin War may have paved the way for greater centralization in the sixteenth century by spreading the benefits of the country's wealth more uniformly everywhere and thereby allowing more backward areas to catch up to the Home Provinces. In any case, the autocratic model that was created and imperfectly implemented by the Muromachi shoguns became the basis for Japan's unification at the end of the sixteenth century by Toyotomi Hideyoshi (1536–1598) and Tokugawa Ieyasu (1542–1616).

Like the Hundred Years' War in France, the Ōnin conflict involved only sporadic fighting across a battle line that bisected Kyoto into two armed camps, that of the western (Yamana) and eastern (Hosokawa) armies. But it required massive mobilization of men and stimulated production (and outright thievery) to meet the needs of such a vast levy of idle troops. It also, as happened in Europe, encouraged fortune hunters and the dissatisfied to grab a spear to try to improve their lot. While Kyoto was devastated by fire and pillage during the early years of fighting, provincial cities benefited by welcoming the merchants, craftsmen, and aristocrats who fled to them in search of a safe haven. The most famous example of the wholesale importation of metropolitan culture into the countryside occurred in Yamaguchi, the provincial seat of the Ōuchi, who created a "little Kyoto" by patronizing an important artist like Sesshū (1420–1506) and absorbing a substantial influx of aristocrats who found life in the capital too hazardous.[93] In its later phases, the war spread to the countryside, while Kyoto itself was rebuilt relatively quickly. Yoshimasa revived his project to build the Higashiyama villa, and as early as 1474 he was already planning to send trading ships to China (in the guise of tribute vessels) to obtain much-needed copper currency. In 1476, a ship finally set sail laden with horses, swords, sulfur, screens, and fans to be exchanged for cash and books. In 1478, the ship returned carrying 50,000 *kanmon* of cash for the shogun's treasury. So successful was the venture that he sent another ship in 1483, on both occasions doing so in his capacity as *Nihon kokuō*, the King of Japan.[94]

In 1483, Yoshimasa finally moved into his new Higashiyama retreat and, to add to the estrangement between him and his wife, Tomiko, his relationship with his son, the new shogun Yoshihisa, now began to deteriorate as well. In 1485, their differences erupted into open confrontation between the *hōkōshū*, the shogunal army which followed Yoshihisa's orders, and the magistrates (*bugyōnin*) who still obeyed Yoshimasa even though he was no longer shogun. The incident led Yoshimasa to take the tonsure but, unlike the case with his ancestor Yoshimitsu, this time the act signified a genuine withdrawal from political life, with Yoshihisa becoming the new focus of loyalty for those who would revive Bakufu power.[95] Unfortunately for the advocates of Bakufu self-strengthening, their cause died with Yoshihisa's death during a punitory campaign into Ōmi province against the *shugo-daimyō* Rokkaku Takayori (1462–1520). He predeceased Yoshimasa by one year.

Six more Ashikaga were to reign as shogun until the last, the fifteenth shogun, Yoshiaki, was finally deposed by Oda Nobunaga (1534–1582), but never again were they to regain control of a substantial part of the country outside of the capital district. Just as the Ashikaga house had exploited the symbolic value of impotent bearers of legitimate authority, so they became valuable as window dressing for Hosokawa *kanrei* who became de facto rulers in Kyoto during the early sixteenth century. Even Hosokawa hegemony lost much of its content, however, during the violent struggle for ascendancy that ensued among the *sengoku-daimyō*. The Ashikaga failure served as a warning to those daimyo, and to the three great unifiers who subdued them, not to sever the ties to the land or to the fictive feudal bonds that existed between themselves and their retainers. In both respects, the Ashikaga experience had an enduring influence on Japanese government.

THREE

Muromachi Economy and Bakufu Income

Because the Muromachi period went through major shifts in the production and distribution of societal wealth, traditional sources of government income became less accessible than they had been earlier, and as a result the Ashikaga were forced to engage in a constant search for additional revenue. Financial solvency was an ever-elusive goal, however, and not because the Bakufu was particularly inefficient or backward, or because its officials were especially venal or corrupt. The cause lay with trying to deal with a society that was undergoing political convulsions at all levels, with "the lower superseding the higher" (*gekokujō*) in a bewildering variety of combinations and circumstances. A riot of social mobility and economic flux placed the Bakufu at the very storm center of opposing groups: the great aristocratic and temple and shrine proprietors (*jisha honjo*) tried to enlist the Bakufu's backing to guarantee their manorial incomes at the same time that the military houses, from mighty *shugo-daimyō* down to steward (*jitō*) and local warlord (*kokujin, jizamurai, zaichi ryōshu*), worked to obtain government non-interference in their expropriation of that very same manorial income. In one context or another, and at one time or another, all of them were Bakufu clients, and sudden shifts in government policy reflected the confused state of affairs. Furthermore, the Bakufu's drive to enlarge its own financial base often put it in direct opposition to both of these pressure groups, for in the land-based economy one party's gain was the other's inevitable loss.

No matter how the Bakufu maneuvered, its land income was never adequate to meet expenses, and so to supplement this deficiency it began to exploit commercial and trade-related wealth as an alternative. The sake brewers and *dosō* moneylenders, silk producers, bean paste (*miso*) factories, and even fish markets became the new targets of shogunal acquisitiveness.[1] The largest of the mercantile establishments served as creditors to the samurai and aristocrats and to almost everyone else as well, including the shogun himself. This complicated the problem of responsible government, since the very warriors who were supposed to suppress debtors' revolts were often themselves in debt and would end up by joining the rebels instead. These *ikki* were only the most violent way to present one's grievances to the Bakufu, but the pressure they put on the government highlights the complicated condition of the Bakufu's financial edifice and the difficulty it had in pursuing a consistent economic policy.

Rising levels of consumption by the shogun and *shugo-daimyō* further aggravated the problem of finding sufficient revenue. Ashikaga extravagance from Yoshimitsu to Yoshimasa is legend. The palaces and villas that they erected for themselves, their largesse in contributing to temples and shrines, and their role as patrons of the arts unquestionably put a strain on finances. *Shugo-daimyō* also suffered from the dual burden of increasing expenditures for themselves and their large Kyoto mansions, and onerous Bakufu taxes throughout the first half of the Muromachi period. There is no doubt that Kyoto was not only the most expensive place to live in fifteenth-century Japan but provided almost unlimited opportunities for conspicuous consumption: in dress, in architecture and interior appointments, and in lavish banquets, entertainments, and other diversions. Whereas the Bakufu recognized the gravity of the problem and periodically issued decrees exhorting the shugo and the Buddhist clergy to thrift and frugality, the shogun himself set a bad example, as his prodigality was apparent to everyone.[2]

Government income was probably rising from the late fourteenth century up to the Ōnin War. Even if one conservatively assumes that the Bakufu was unable to tap a greater percentage of Japan's gross national product than had its Kamakura predecessor, the rising productivity of both agriculture and handicraft industry at least provided a quantitatively larger reservoir to exploit. Although the Ashikaga failed in the end to make the Bakufu the government of a centralized state amenable to their dynastic ambitions, their innovations in revenue-collecting were drawn upon and recast by their provincial contemporaries, the *shugo-* and *sengoku-daimyō,* and even by the succeeding Tokugawa. Given the relative decentralization of all political and economic functions in medieval Japan, there are some striking indications of the influence that the Muromachi Bakufu managed to exert on economic activity. Even as late as 1484, for example, the powerful Ōuchi took the Kyoto exchange rate for gold and silver set by the Bakufu as their own rate in Yamaguchi and strictly enforced it throughout their provincial domain.[3] Just as important as the shogun's real and symbolic transformation into a monarch, therefore, was the process whereby the state "began to acquire that essential element of its supremacy—financial resources incomparably greater than those of any private person or community."[4] To be sure, the Muromachi Bakufu never achieved overwhelming leverage but, as in the realm of administrative technology and military organization, the innovations of the Ashikaga in financial policy were important beginnings of institutions that would reach a mature form in the seventeenth century via the prerogatives of the Tokugawa shogun.[5]

The three primary revenue sources of the Ashikaga were similar to those in all early capitalist-agrarian autocracies: land (income and taxes), taxes and privileges regarding domestic commercial enterprise, and overseas trade. Agricultural changes of an irreversible nature had already begun in Japan when the Ashikaga first came to power, and they grew apace during the next century. These included double- and triple-cropping, the specialization of agricultural production with emphasis on cash crops concentrated in certain regions (such as tea growing in Uji), and the commutation to cash amounts of sums previously paid in kind.[6] These advances were made possible by improvements in irrigation, greater use of livestock and fertilizer, and new varieties of wetland rice.[7] Some of the increases in agricultural and marine production were quite remarkable. During the fourteenth century, for instance, the manor Yugeshima no shō situated on the Inland Sea produced salt from salt ponds on man-made beaches equal to three times the salt produced in early Tokugawa on a comparable natural beach.[8] Such production was highly labor-intensive, and it is not hard to imagine the amount of toil required in such an age to produce even a marginal surplus.

In industrial technology, most of the major breakthroughs did not come until the sixteenth century, such as gold mining, cupellation of silver, smelting copper, and making steel from iron sand. During the fourteenth and fifteenth centuries, progress was made in the use of the clay-slime process for smelting iron, of the felling (or pit) saw in construction, and of the carpenter's plane. But the Muromachi period is known more for the spread of knowledge and use of techniques that had already been discovered than it is for technological innovation per se.[9]

The end result of technological change was the creation of a crop surplus, evidenced in the sale by Muromachi peasants of the right to a fixed amount of income (*shiki*) to be paid out of their harvests, over and above their lands' estimated annual yields. The selling price for this right was based not on land area, but on the amount of harvest yield (*taka*). Four deeds to land sold in Kamikuze no shō in 1376 show that the selling price was approximately seven times the annual income of the *shiki*. During early Muromachi, most sales of this sort were made by peasants, but later on the Kyoto temples and *dosō* moneylenders became more active and land rights were unified under large holders, as occurred in the case of the Tōji temple which unified its control over land rights in Kamikuze and Shimokuze *shōen*.[10] Between the fourteenth and sixteenth century, purchased lands became part of the ubiquitous process of confiscation, forfeiture, regranting, and reconfirmation which gradually took surplus income away from the

FIGURE 4 Carpenter

Painting, Japanese, Muromachi
Anonymous
Fragment of Shokunin zue *(Illustration of various craftsmen)*

Courtesy of the Fogg Art Museum,
Harvard University

peasants and local merchants and resulted in their absorption by daimyo or higher authorities.[11]

What was the subtle relationship between these social and economic changes—the development of a domestic market system and foreign trade, handicraft industries and the commercialization of agriculture, the spread of currency, the use of credit, and the redistribution of newly generated wealth—and Bakufu income? Let us examine the Bakufu's three primary revenue sources and the political ramifications of each.

AGRARIAN REVENUE

The Shogunal Domain (Goryōsho). Until the late fourteenth century, the estates under direct shogunal title scattered throughout Japan provided the shogun's household and his Bakufu with a substantial part of their operating income. During this early phase, the shogunal domain, known as *goryōsho,* consisted of four distinct types of holdings: (1) original Ashikaga family estates (*Ashikaga honryō*) held since the Kamakura period or received from Emperor Go-Daigo during the Kemmu Restoration; (2) lands confiscated by the Bakufu after Go-Daigo's overthrow (*kesshochi*); (3) lands subject to temporary wartime tax levies called half-tax land (*hanzeichi*), although those taxes came to be collected at other times as well; and (4) other lands of miscellaneous origin.[12] Estimates made by Japanese scholars in this century of the total number of shogunal estates have risen steadily. In 1932, Ono Terutsugu put the number of *goryōsho* at sixteen.[13] Greatly expanding on Ono's findings, Okuno Takahiro estimated that there were about 170, and recently Kuwayama Kōnen has enlarged the total still further to identify about two hundred separate estates.[14] The scattered nature of the Ashikaga *goryōsho* has been emphasized by Kuwayama and others, but actually, of the two hundred-odd demesnes, about three-quarters were located either in the Home Provinces or in those due east of them, forming a territorial concentration in the center of Honshū between powerful shugo domains in the west and the semi-autonomous Kantō to the east[15] (see Figure 5).

FIGURE 5 Japan's Provinces During the Muromachi Period

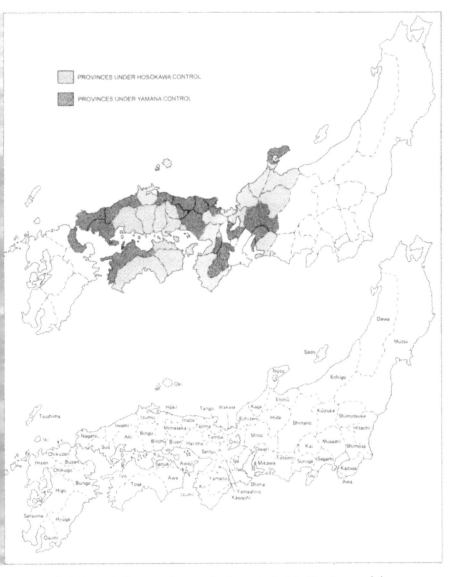

Note: Shaded areas indicate provinces under the control of the Hosokawa and the
Yamana during the Ōnin War (c. 1467–1477).

The income from each *goryōsho* estate was originally specifically earmarked according to the purpose for which it was intended, such as for the Board of Administration (*mandokoro ryōsho*), for clothing (*gofuku ryōsho*), and food (*kugo ryōsho*) for the shogun's household, for repairing palace buildings, and so forth.[16] During the fifteenth century, however, this convention was superseded by the practice of making appropriations as needed on the basis of aggregate revenues, the same way that modern governments do. This alteration in the method of allocating expenditures was one consequence of the spread of the practice of converting tax rice (*nengu*) into monetary equivalents before transfer to the Bakufu.

As to the relative importance of the different types of shogunal estates, the original pre-Muromachi period Ashikaga family holdings may be the least significant both economically and politically. There were very few *goryōsho* in the Kantō, and even Shimotsuke province, the Ashikaga's ancestral home, boasted no more than two of these by the mid-fifteenth century. At the end of the Kamakura period, Ashikaga family holdings were already widely scattered over Hitachi, Kōzuke, Musashi, Kazusa, Awa, Owari, Mikawa, Tamba, Tango, Mimasaka, and other provinces,[17] and such dispersion may have actually facilitated the sudden shift of family activity to the Kinai after 1336. There is evidence that family lands in the original Kantō base functioned as part of the shogunal domain until the early fifteenth century.[18]

In addition to their original hereditary estates, most of the lands the Ashikaga received as a consequence of the Kemmu Restoration also failed to become a permanent part of the *goryōsho*. Emperor Go-Daigo awarded those lands to Takauji primarily from former Hōjō possessions but, of the thirty properties (in seventeen provinces) granted to him, and fifteen properties (in ten provinces) granted to Tadayoshi, most were lost during the war between the courts, or were regranted as gifts to temples, shrines, and retainers.[19] Like Go-Daigo before them, the Ashikaga had obligations to loyal supporters in almost every province, and the simplest way to meet those commitments was to distribute lands confiscated from their enemies as rewards to their followers.[20] It is, nevertheless, highly likely that the Ashikaga kept some of the spoils of victory for themselves.

Hanzei (half-tax) lands originated during the Nambokuchō period when the Bakufu earmarked one-half of the rice harvest of temple, shrine, and *kuge shōen* as emergency "military rations estates" (*hyōrōryōsho*) for its retainers. *Hanzei* began with Takauji's decree of 1352,[21] which made *shōen* in Ōmi, Mino, and Owari provinces subject to *hanzei* for a period of not more than one year, but as warriors grew bolder the meaning of *hanzei* changed. Samurai took advantage of their temporary status as beneficiaries to make their claim to *hanzei* income quasi-permanent, and shugo were especially active in this respect. They and the class of small independent military squires in the Home Provinces carried out their own local *hanzei* policies to the detriment of manorial proprietors. Predictably, Takauji's *hanzei* policy secured the support of these *bushi* for his regime.

The practice of designating *hanzei* lands as part of the shogun's *goryōsho* derived from the strenuous opposition expressed by *jisha honjo* proprietors, who tried to protect their estates from shugo seizure by securing Bakufu guarantees that no more than one-half of their income would be taken because of *hanzei* status. In return for such protection, they agreed to give the Bakufu a percentage of the one-half remaining in their possession as a national tax. Kuwayama has maintained that the *hanzei goryōsho* were established specifically for the purpose of securing additional government revenue from the *jisha honjo* estates.[22] Another Japanese historian, Shimada Jirō, interpreted the *hanzei* system as one way the Bakufu could legally reconcile the contradiction inherent in simultaneously giving guarantees of security to *shōen* proprietors while yielding to the demands of local samurai chiefs.[23] In practice, the actual beneficiary of the system depended on how much authority the Bakufu could bring to bear, and that varied with time and place.

The fourth category of shogunal domain consisted of lands whose proprietors wished to protect their holdings from physical absorption or annexation by *shugo-daimyō* and others, or cases in

which a vassal used it to recapture title to property that he had
been deprived of. By having such lands designated part of the
goryōsho, those proprietors were able to use shogunal influence
as a shield, and the Bakufu, reciprocally, was able to establish
islands of influence in areas far from the Home Provinces.[24]

Bakufu Land Taxes. The second primary source of government
revenue from land was the taxes levied on proprietors, and especially on the shugo. Prominent among these was the *tansen,* a tax
collected on the basis of cultivated area, the amount levied per *tan*
varying with the specific *tansen* levy. (Although the exact size
varied from place to place, in general 1 *tan* = 300 *tsubo* = .245
acres; 10 *tan* = 1 *chō.*) In legal terms, the *tansen* was a temporary
tax levied to pay for extraordinary state expenses, such as imperial
investiture and abdication ceremonies, shogunal banquets and
celebrations, and large-scale construction projects involving palaces, temples, and shrines. *Tansen* decrees varied in their effective
scope, since they could apply to the whole country, or to several
provinces, or even to one local area.

A second type of land tax was the *shugo shussen,* which was
calculated according to the number of provinces a lord held shugoships over, regardless of the size of his personal landholdings or
the yield of his harvests.[25] Like the *tansen, shugo shussen* was also
supposedly a temporary tax but, depending on the needs of shogun and Bakufu at any given time, like *tansen* it could be exacted
at very frequent intervals. It became a persistent drain on the
shugo-daimyō and, during periods of strong shogunal leadership,
the only difference between *shugo shussen* and a permanent tax
was that the amount assessed varied from one levy to the next.

The Bakufu established its exclusive authority to levy *tansen*
about 1380.[26] Until that time, the imperial court was still issuing
tax edicts and exemptions. In the case of *yakubutakumai,* a *tansen*
type of tax whose receipts were usually earmarked for expenses
incurred in repairing, rebuilding, and performing rites at the Ise
shrines, the court retained levy and exemption authority until
about 1390.[27] This ten-year delay in the Bakufu's absorption of
authority reflected the historically intimate ties between the court

and the Ise shrine, and the Bakufu's success in obtaining final taxing power there reflects the unprecedented stature of Yoshimitsu's
government.

The shugo played an important role in collecting the *tansen,*
either directly or through their deputies, the *shugo-dai.* In 1372,
the Bakufu ordered all shugo to submit land registers (*ōtabumi*)
listing all lands subject to national taxes (*kōden* lands) then in the
possession of *jisha honjo* proprietors or of stewards and house
vassals (*jitō gokenin*). It then commanded the shugo to collect
thirty *mon* per each *tan* of taxable land in order to pay for a new
shrine palanquin (*omikoshi*) for the Hie shrine. This law is considered the milestone legislation which established the shugo's authority to collect *tansen* for the Bakufu, and also the law which
determined that the unit of taxation would stay the same as it had
been in the Kamakura period.[28] As shugo extended their personal
control over the countryside, they began to levy their own *tansen*
independently of Bakufu sanction. Such *shugo tansen* were collected in 1401 and 1405 by the Hosokawa in Tamba province, in
1413 by the Ōuchi in Suō, in 1428 by the Akamatsu in Harima,
and in 1430 by the Kyōgoku in Izumo. *Shugo tansen* became gen-
eralized by the mid-fifteenth century.[29]

The Bakufu was not oblivious of the dangers involved in relying
too heavily on the *shugo-daimyō* for collecting its land taxes, nor
was it unaware of the bad influence shugo could exert on tax collection down the line. *Shugo-daimyō* tended to pocket an ever
greater portion of tax receipts for themselves, and indirect tax
collection encouraged the local proprietors to do the same to their
superiors, the shugo, until at all levels tax evasion and misappro-
priation threatened to rob the central government of its revenue.
The Bakufu responded to the problem by organizing two parallel
tax collection hierarchies, one mediated by the shugo and the
other not.[30] Unmediated tax collection focused on the "Kyoto
tax" (*kyōsai*), which was paid directly by the taxpayer to the
Bakufu. Such direct payment was favored by small proprietors,
including the bulk of the samurai in the shogunal army, because it
prevented more onerous demands from being made by the shugo

and his agents and permitted landlords to keep a larger share of their annual harvest for themselves. Starting in Yoshinori's reign when *shugo tansen* became widespread, the Bakufu used the *kyō-sai* system to separate the *hōkōshū* from other retainers, and as an incentive to attract samurai into the shogun's army with the promise of increasing their immunity from shugo extortion.[31] In another sense, *kyōsai* acted as a counterforce to *shugo tansen*, which the Bakufu found it difficult to suppress by more direct methods.

From the shogunal domain and from agrarian taxes the Bakufu amassed one important component of its annual income. It was almost impossible to increase beyond a certain point the amount of revenue that could be squeezed from those traditional sources, and the pressure of rising expenditures encouraged the search for new sources of wealth to buttress a chronically depleted treasury. The Bakufu found those sources in the economy's commercial sector and in the *gozan,* the Rinzai Zen Buddhist monastic community.

COMMERCIAL REVENUE

Whereas periodic markets began to appear as early as the latter half of the thirteenth century,[32] it was under the early Ashikaga shoguns that commercial activity first became politically and financially relevant to the central government. Different from its predecessors, the Muromachi Bakufu came to see in the merchants, moneylenders, *sakaya,* textile and oil manufacturers, and other industries of the Kyoto region a convenient and plentiful tax base, and the policies it pursued in tapping that base influenced both the development of the commercial economy and its own day-to-day operations.

Handicraft industries very early began to form guild-like organizations called *za* at the two central cities of medieval Japan, Kyoto and Nara. Around those cities, villages came to specialize in one or another commodity and often migrated as a unit to the city to continue their manufacturing under more economically advantageous conditions. In 1376, sixty-four persons from the village of

Oyamazaki moved to Kyoto to manufacture and market their oil more profitably.[33] They formed a *za,* as did the malt (*kōji*) producers of Kitano and the lumbermen of Horikawa. These *za* received Bakufu protection, which meant, in effect, that they were able to exercise a de facto monopoly well beyond the geographic limits within which the monopoly rights granted to them by the Bakufu were legally enforceable.[34] Thus, the Horikawa lumber *za* had a monopoly for large sawn planks (*ogaita*) protected by the Bakufu, but that single monopoly gave them the comparative advantage which enabled them to capture half of the lumber sales for the entire capital.[35] The Kitano malt *za* had a monopoly in the vicinity of the Kitano shrine in northwestern Kyoto, but the Bakufu's protection extended to the capital's environs, and all other malt warehouses (*kōjishitsu*) were ordered destroyed. The Oyamazaki oil *za* monopoly extended throughout western Japan (except for Yamato), protected in this case by shugo enforcement of shogunal orders. *Za* were also exempted from paying tolls at barriers (*sekisho*), whether the toll stations were those of the Bakufu or other parties. Indirectly, Bakufu control over Kyoto strengthened the Ashikaga hold over the national economy through the enforcement of these *za* monopoly rights. The government was not so much encouraging economic growth as it was fostering a system of official protection to facilitate its own enrichment. In this way the Bakufu managed to diversify its financial base and took its cut from the Yodo fish market and from a loom tax levied on weavers with equal alacrity.[36]

Kyoto was ringed by the cities of Sakai, Nara, Tennōji, and other towns which defined the market sphere of the Home Provinces and, after the start of the tally trade by Yoshimitsu, that core area exerted an even stronger centripetal pull on the country's economy.[37] Add to the core area the more than thirty ports along the Inland Sea which catered to maritime trade, plus a goodly number of other towns of from one to several thousand households in size (Sakamoto, Otsu, Yodo, Hyōgo, Hakata),[38] and the Muromachi Bakufu may be said to have had a very substantial commercial economy to levy its taxes on.

The Moneylending Establishment. By the fourteenth century, the group in the capital known as *dosō,* whose original function was to store others' valuables in their secure warehouses, had gradually expanded their operations to include lending money at interest. Many of the *dosō* proprietors also owned *sakaya.* Such a preponderance of this particular industry among the money-lenders may be accounted for by the expense required to set up a factory for producing sake, which was a very large initial capital investment by the standards of the time, and also by the hand-some profits it guaranteed the manufacturer. The association be-tween moneylending and sake brewing led them to be treated as a single entity, *sakaya-dosō.* There was another type of money-lender, the *hizeniya,* who specialized in lending money with inter-est computed on a daily basis.

It has already been noted how Yoshimitsu placed the *sakaya-dosō* under his jurisdiction in 1393 when he decreed them subject to Bakufu taxation. Although contact between the central govern-ment and the *dosō* can be traced back to 1347, until 1393 taxing authority was shared with the imperial court.[39] Exactly how many establishments were affected by Yoshimitsu's radical legislation is not clear. It is known that there were at least 52 *sakaya* in Kyoto by 1419, and a count of 342 was already noted for 1425. At the end of the century (c. 1492–1500), after Kyoto's reconstruction following the devastation of the Ōnin War, there were at least 61 *sakaya* in the capital.[40] Such a large and resilient group of money-lenders could not help but exert a powerful influence on the urban economy, the Home Provinces, and the Bakufu.

In terms of both sheer physical size of their factories and the taxes they were required to pay, *sakaya* were the biggest businesses in medieval Kyoto, with the possible exception of the cumulative wealth of the *gozan* temples. A tax register of 1452 listing *jiguchi-zeni* assessments supports such a conclusion. The *jiguchizeni* was the urban equivalent of the *tansen* and was computed on the basis of area occupied by a given commercial establishment. A similar tax called *mabechizeni* was computed according to the street frontage of a factory or business. In the 1452 tax register, most taxpayers, including mat makers (*tatamiya*), oil merchants (*abura-ya*), carpenters (*banshō*), cypress-bark roofers (*hiwadaya*), umbrella makers (*kasaya*), and other small tradesmen had frontages of about three *jō* (1 *jō* = 10 *shaku* = approx. 10 feet) and were taxed from one to two *kan* each; the one *sakaya* listed, however, had a frontage of eight *jō*, and a tax of four *kan* 50 *mon* (1,000 *mon* = 1 *kan*). Again in 1460, whereas the bark roofers, carpenters, coopers (*musubioke*), rice merchants (*komeya*), dyers (*kon'ya*), blacksmiths (*kajiya*), oil merchants, rice-cracker shops (*senbeiya*), comb shops (*kushiya*), tea merchants (*chaya*), and other common businesses in the capital's Gion district were taxed for frontage of one or two *jō*, the one *sakaya* was listed as having a width of six *jō*.[41] Size of course, was not the only indicator of wealth. A more accurate index of the combined profitability of *sakaya-dosō* was the extent to which the Bakufu focused its attention on this sector of commerce more than on any other.

Besides direct taxation, the Bakufu milked revenue from Kyoto's burgeoning plutocracy by using them as licensed tax farmers. It sold the right to collect taxes from designated districts, or from related enterprises within a given area, in return for a fixed price. The purchaser of that right then accepted responsibility for collecting and transferring to the Bakufu an amount contracted for, and kept for himself anything above that amount that could be extorted from the taxpayers as his personal profit. The burghers and priest-moneylenders who contracted to collect Bakufu taxes became an essential part of the government's financial administration and collected taxes from such varied *za* enterprises as cotton, silk, hemp, rice, and salted fish, the loom tax on weavers, and duties on the public baths throughout the capital.[42] The institution of Bakufu debt cancellation in some of its forms was another variant of indirect taxation, specifically the two forms known as partial debt cancellation (*bun'ichi tokusei*) and the negative counterpart prohibiting such partial debt cancellations (*bun'ichi tokusei kinzei*). Both of these amounted to government extortion designed to gain the Bakufu additional income. The partial debt cancellation essentially demanded a bribe from debtors which was a fixed percentage of the outstanding debt (usually 10 percent) in return for Bakufu cancellation of the debtor's obligation to repay the balance of the loan to the creditor, regardless of the stipulations in the original loan contract. Conversely, the corresponding prohibition of this law protected the creditor's right to collect upon payment to the Bakufu of an amount equal to 10 or 20 percent of the amount of the original loan in exchange for government sanction of the moneylender's contract. In the long run, it was more lucrative for the Bakufu to protect the creditor in such disputes. When it issued a debt cancellation, the Bakufu in effect forfeited its tax revenue from the *dosō* but, if it issued a prohibition on debt cancellation, that did not happen. By protecting the moneylender's contract, the government could then tax them again through normal levies, since the *dosō* could not very well justify a claim of bankruptcy or try to evade payment.[43] The Muromachi Bakufu debt-cancellation decrees were quite different from those issued during the Kamakura and Sengoku periods in that they were not limited in their applicability to just one part of the Bakufu's vassal band, nor were they designed to protect a specific class.[44] They were general laws without status exemptions (except for religious organizations), and their primary objective was to gain extra revenue for the central government.

Toll Barriers (Sekisho). A traditional way to make money on transient local traffic was the private toll barrier (*sekisho*), which was set up at fief boundaries, busy river crossings, and important crossroads. Whereas the Bakufu opposed such private *sekisho*, it took advantage of the increasing volume of trade in the Home Provinces by erecting its own toll stations around Kyoto. There were seven of these *sekisho*, and they were a source of constant friction between the Bakufu and the populace. Mass opposition was especially volatile when Yoshimasa and his wife Tomiko used the barriers to create an artificial rice shortage in the city so as to raise the selling price. Such manipulation to aid Tomiko's speculating no doubt contributed to the popular outcry that accompanied every Bakufu attempt to reinstitute the toll stations. A mere two months after they were first officially established in 1459/7th month, Yoshimasa was forced to dismantle them.[45] Revolts demanded their dismantling again in 1478, when the Bakufu used imperial palace repairs as an excuse to exact tolls, and in 1484. On both occasions the government was forced by popular discontent to remove the *sekisho*.[46]

Toll barriers never became a major source of shogunal revenue, but the ones in Kyoto and at important ports like Hyogo and Yodo no doubt supplied badly needed cash to the late fifteenth century Bakufu at times of larger than average deficits. The financial activities of Hino Tomiko and her circle demonstrated, in any event, that the Muromachi government was not spared the universal malady of administrative peculation and corruption in high places, although the actual extent of malfeasance is not clear.

Foreign Trade. The tally trade (*kangō bōeki*) had begun primarily as a political and diplomatic initiative by China to stabilize the international order in East Asia under Ming suzerainty, but the Ashikaga gradually transformed it into a vehicle for the Bakufu's financial gain. When the recently founded Ming empire first made contact with Japan, the country was still in the throes of the civil war between the shogun's supporters and the loyalist followers of Emperor Go-Daigo. By the time Yoshimitsu received the Chinese ambassador in 1402, however, the domestic situation had stabilized sufficiently for the shogun to permit himself to devote some attention to Japan's foreign relations. Unofficial maritime trade with Sung China had been vigorous and frequent, but the Mongol conquest of Southern Sung late in the thirteenth century, followed by the abortive but highly disruptive Mongol invasions of Japan in 1274 and 1281, took their toll, and contact with the mainland declined. When a native Chinese dynasty once more seized the throne of heaven in 1368, a new burst of aggressive diplomatic activity radiated from Nanking. The Japanese responded warmly to Ming overtures, and formal relations were established by Yoshimitsu, soon to be followed by the launching of the first official tally ships between the two countries.

The tally trade began as a polite exchange of tribute articles from the shogun to the Ming emperor, and generous gifts bestowed on the shogun in return. But the Japanese were aggressive traders and expanded the quantities of supplementary non-tribute merchandise to such a degree that the Chinese eventually accused them of dumping goods in excess of allowable quotas. Violent disputes arose when the Japanese traders felt that officially set prices for non-tribute articles were too low.[47]

During the century and a half of its existence, the tally trade underwent several phases. During the first phase, which coincided roughly with Yoshimitsu's reign, the trade was a Bakufu monopoly. After Yoshimochi suspended the trade, a second phase began with Yoshinori's reestablishment of relations with China in 1432 and lasted until shortly after Yoshimasa's death (c. 1493). During the second phase, the tally trade was a joint financial venture of the Bakufu, the great temples (Sōkokuji, Tenryūji) and powerful *shugo-daimyō* (Ōuchi, Yamana, Hosokawa), and the wealthier merchants who often financed the other participants as well. The third phase, which lasted until the middle of the sixteenth century, reflected the central government's bankruptcy both politically and economically. The Bakufu was not even a participant, and the tally trade became largely a monopoly of the Ōuchi and Hosokawa daimyo. Their rivalry, and the nuisance it caused Chinese maritime authorities, finally brought about the cessation of the trade in 1549.[48]

Among the goods imported from China via the trade, copper coins were the commodities that bulked most conspicuously in the requests made by the Ashikaga shoguns. It is still unclear why the Bakufu preferred to import a foreign currency from such a great distance rather than to mint its own. The level of domestic technology was certainly adequate: an economy capable of manufacturing the world's finest swords was also capable of minting its own coins. The answer must rather be sought in non-technological factors. The Bakufu may have reasoned that it could better enhance its own fiscal strength by using a trusted and respected medium of exchange, instead of trying to introduce a domestic coinage which lacked such credibility. When the central government of Sung China first introduced paper money it had great difficulty in getting the population to use it, and the Muromachi government may have wished to save itself the trouble of promoting a domestically produced coinage. The expense required to establish mints may also have been a consideration, for coins very often cost more to cast than their face value gave them in the marketplace.[49] During late Muromachi, locally produced coins began to appear, but those were regarded as inferior by the Bakufu and were ideally not to be used for paying taxes, and if they were used a different rate of exchange was to be applied in calculating their worth.[50] The massive importation of Chinese coins thus provided the Bakufu with a reliable means of exchange and obviated the need for manufacturing its own coins and then trying to impose them on an imperfectly united nation.

Other than the sumptuous gifts and copper coins which the shogun received directly from the Yung-lo and Hsuan-te Emperors, the growth in volume of the tally trade by its other participants also benefited him indirectly via the import tax (*chūbunsen*). This duty equaled one-tenth of the total value of imports and was levied on all vessels returning to Japan as part of the official trade.[51]

THE GOZAN MONASTERIES

As enthusiastic and devout patrons of Zen Buddhism, the Ashikaga shoguns put the power and the treasure of their government at the disposal of the great Kyoto monasteries collectively referred to as the *gozan*, the "Five Mountains." It was a shogun, Yoshimitsu, who first established the *gozan* monastic structure which gave the Zen church enormous prestige in the capital and linked it irrevocably to the Bakufu. But the *gozan* soon gained a reputation for wealth and for capable economic and fiscal management, skills which may have arisen as a consequence of their being a late sect to develop in Japan and one, therefore, less generously endowed with estates than some of their predecessors. They became a lucrative source of funds to their hard-pressed patron and, stated most strongly, it was the *gozan*, not the *sakaya-dosō* or *shugo shussen* levies, which cumulatively were the Bakufu's major financial

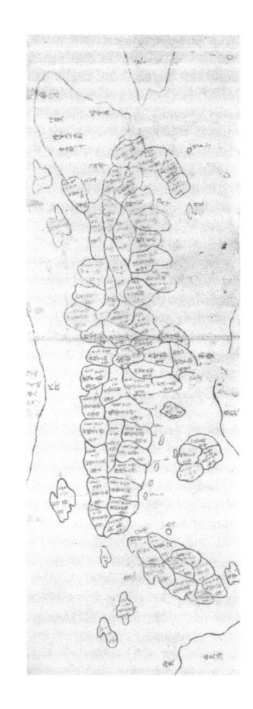

FIGURE 6 A Map of Muromachi Japan from a 1402 Japanese Buddhist Cosmology

Painting, Japanese, Muromachi Ryūi (signed) Nihonkoku narabi ni shumi Shotenkoku zu (Buddhist cosmology compiled from Indian sources), 1402

Courtesy of the Fogg Art Museum, Harvard University

support.[52] Whether or not their contribution was as vast as the proponent of this extreme position maintains, there is no doubt that they were essential to the Bakufu's financial solvency. Their wealth was tapped in several ways: by direct taxation in the form of *tansen* and other temporary levies, by the Bakufu's open sale of priestly offices and titles, and by means of compulsory "gifts" requisitioned by the shogun from time to time. By mid-Muromachi, many *gozan* priests were as active in the secular economy of the capital as they were in the management of their own monasteries, and especially the so-called eastern-rank priests (*tōbanshū*) whose duty it was to oversee the monastic economy. These *tōbanshū* priests were also moneylenders, lending the money they collected for the repose of believers' dead relatives, called *shidōsen,* at relatively low rates of interest to *sakaya-dosō,* who then reloaned it at higher rates. Whereas the Bakufu did not exempt *sakaya-dosō* from debt-cancellation decrees, it always specifically excluded Zen *shidōsen* loans from being subject to their stipulations.[53]

In the category of direct taxation, there are many examples of the Bakufu exacting large amounts from *gozan* temples. In 1435/4th month, the Sōkokuji was taxed 1,000 *kanmon;* in 1459/10th month, the *gozan tōbanshū* were taxed 2,000 *kanmon* to pay for moving the Bakufu to newly constructed quarters; in 1462/11th month, the shogun taxed the Sōkokuji 1,000 *kan;* in 1463/8th month, the *gozan tōbanshū* were assessed 6,000 *kanmon* to pay for Buddhist death anniversary observances for the former shogun Yoshimochi; in 1464/7th month, the Sōkokuji *tōbanshū* had to pay a *tansen* of 400 *kan* for the Emperor Go-Hanazono's abdication ceremony; in 1465/11th month, a *tansen* of 1,700 *kan* was levied on the Sōkokuji *tōbanshū* to pay for Emperor Go-Tsuchimikado's accession; in 1486, the *gozan tōbanshū* were taxed 50,000 *hiki;* and in 1499/9th month, the *gozan* was taxed 1,000 *kanmon.*[54]

Besides direct taxation, the Bakufu's practice of selling licenses of appointment (*kumon*) to newly chosen Zen abbots (*jūji*) was another way in which the *gozan* involuntarily contributed to the government treasury. As the Bakufu became increasingly impecunious, the practice of selling *zakumon* became fashionable. *Zakumon* were appointments to the rank of abbot sold to individuals who did not intend to assume the post but wanted official confirmation of their rank nonetheless. *Zakumon* became common from about the end of Yoshimochi's reign and, despite his personal efforts to contain the abuse, they flourished once more under Yoshinori. During Yoshimasa's reign, the sale of abbacies became a way to defray expenses incurred for palace construction, monastery repairs, and official ceremonies.[55] Starting late in Yoshimochi's reign, the period of service required of a Zen abbot during a single term was shortened from the original three-year-two-summer term, so that by Yoshimasa's time two or three men might have served in the same abbacy in quick succession during the course of a single year. The abuse reached its extreme after the Ōnin War when there were numerous cases of "one-night" or "one-season" abbots. Obviously, the shorter the term of office the greater the turnover, and the greater the turnover, the greater was the Bakufu's income from the sale of *kumon*. It grew to the point where, on a yearly average, this income from *kumonsen* (*kumon* fees) was actually a greater source of government revenue than the Ming trade.[56]

The second method of indirect taxation was the shogun's practice of demanding "gifts" (*kenmotsu*) from the Zen temples. An average annual total from contributions of this sort, used to pay for shogunal pilgrimages and the like, was about 2,000 *kanmon*. On the basis of available information, Imatani Akira has estimated that the combined Bakufu revenue from simony (*kumonsen*) and *kenmotsu* at least equaled the annual 6,000 *kan* that was collected from the *sakaya-dosō*.[57]

Although it is hard to state categorically which source of Bakufu revenue was larger than the others, it is quite evident that the central government was experimenting with a great variety of new moneymaking schemes. To implement those plans it needed a flexible, competent, and reliable administration, and the development of such an apparatus was just as important as the revenues themselves.

FOUR

The Bakufu System: Bureaucracy and Administration

The shogun was indisputably the central symbol of the Muromachi
Bakufu, and as such he personified organizational and ideological
changes in the political life of medieval Japan; but those changes
also found expression in the organs of the Bakufu itself. The
Muromachi government may not have ruled all of Japan's sixty-
six provinces with equal effectiveness, but in Kyoto and the Home
Provinces it provided a forum where the major metropolitan interests could find a hearing for their petitions and, with moderate
success, used that forum to compensate for the weakness of its
national base. The legitimation which only the shogun's imprima-
tur could bestow, and the importance of his bureaucracy in ex-
pediting the implementation of policy, were significant factors
contributing to the support which the Bakufu continued to receive
from *shugo-daimyō* even after the Ōnin War. The Muromachi
bureaucracy was essentially a clearing house for the basic social
and political conflicts in late medieval Japan. In its periodic reor-
ganizations the Bakufu reflected the endless controversies surrounding problems of centralized versus regional authority, land versus
non-agrarian sources of government revenue, and individual versus
collective decision-making power. Even as the Bakufu's authority
declined during the century of struggle following the Ōnin War, it
provided the administrative model imitated everywhere during the
sixteenth century and on the national level in the Tokugawa Bakufu.[1]

What did the Bakufu bureaucracy consist of? The *Busei kihan* was a contemporary handbook of public administration and the legal process allegedly written by the Bakufu magistrate-bureaucrat (*bugyōnin*) Matsuda Sadayasu.[2] In it is one of the most complete descriptions extant of the Muromachi government. The *Busei kihan* treats seriatim the Board of Coadjutors (*hikitsuke-naidan*), the Board of Retainers (*samuraidokoro*), the Board of Inquiry (*monchūjo*), the Office of Urban Property (*jikata bugyō*), and the Board of Administration (*mandokoro*), and explicitly acknowledges as its antecedent the *Sata mirensho,* a handbook of Kamakura legal procedure that was compiled between 1319 and 1322.[3] The responsibilities of each organ are enumerated in some detail. To the *bugyōnin* of the Board of Coadjutors are attributed adjudicative authority in cases involving: illegal land seizure, non-enforcement of shogunal orders, illegal withholding of government taxes, acts of defiance against Bakufu representatives, litigation against one's superior in the hierarchy of land ownership, quarrels over inheritance, violations of Bakufu commands, boundary and water disputes, and female inheritance. Matters involving shogunal confirmation of land-ownership, awards granted for military service, and problems concerning forced labor were, however, reserved for personal review by the shogun.[4] Such personal review was called *gozen gosata* and became a more frequent practice as the shogun's position grew stronger. The Board of Retainers, as the government organ empowered to deal with warrior discipline and police matters, had jurisdiction in situations where criminal violence was an important element: rebellion and treason, night attack, robbery (burglary/larceny), brigandage, piracy, murder, bloodshed, arson, beating, trampling, pillaging, stealing harvests,[5] mugging, prostitution, quarrels stemming from gambling, and cutting the tails of cows and horses! It also performed capital punishments (beheading and hanging), as well as deportation of criminals, imprisonment, torture, and manacling.[6] Since the *samuraidokoro* was involved in criminal rather than civil administration, its workings will be examined along with the Bakufu's military apparatus in Chapter Five. The Office of Urban Property consisted of commissioners responsible for cases involving residential land, homes and other buildings within the capital, as well as cases arising out of disputes over legal title to such property.[7] The original function of the *jikata bugyō*'s precursor, called the *jikata kanrei,* was to find and allocate confiscated land in Kyoto for the military houses. Only after the imperial court's metropolitan police force (*kebiishichō*) declined between 1381 and 1387 did the *jikata* office acquire jurisdiction over all residential land in the capital.[8] The Board of Inquiry was the record office for the samurai houses which kept documents and deeds in its archives for future reference. For that reason it was also responsible for verifying errors and detecting forgeries, as well as for providing copies of lost or destroyed documents. In the early Muromachi period, it also had jurisdiction regarding other matters concerning the shogunal house but lost these to the Board of Administration during the latter half of the fourteenth century.[9]

The Board of Administration's jurisdiction grew faster than that of the other organs. Its sphere of operations included a wide spectrum of economic matters involving interest, *suiko* loans (made to purchase seed which were to be repaid after harvest),[10] exchange rates for converting rice to money equivalents, terminable property (*nenkichi*), repurchase of land entrusted to a creditor as collateral for a loan (*honmotsu kaeshi*),[11] pawned land and other pawned property, non-interest bearing loans (*karimono*), forfeiture of rights to reclaim pawned property, and the sale of land.[12] During the Kamakura period, such mixed property matters had been the joint responsibility of the Board of Inquiry and the *mandokoro,* but in the first century of Ashikaga rule these problems, along with those involving income from the shogunal domain and *sakaya-dosō* commercial revenues, became the *mandokoro's* exclusive preserve. The expansion of the Board of Administration and other changes in the Bakufu's internal dynamics were designed to free the Ashikaga from a confining feudal heritage and provide them with a bureaucracy capable of enforcing shogunal commands.

EARLY ORGANIZATION

The Bakufu absorbed almost intact the hereditary bureaucrats who had belonged to the Hōjō government in Kamakura. Far from being excluded because of their previous political affiliation, these legal scholars and administrative specialists were welcomed into the new government. As previously mentioned, they were even commissioned to draft the Kemmu Formulary, the document Takauji claimed as his fundamental law and manifesto.[13] These patrimonial bureaucrats were joined by members of Ashikaga related or vassal families. In spite of their diverse political ancestry, by the early fifteenth century these groups were integrated into a corps which aptly fit Marc Bloch's description of those who "well in advance of the bourgeoisie came to form the general staff of the revived monarchies . . . Their emergence was the premonitory sign that there was arising a new power . . . the bureaucracy."[14]

The early Bakufu consisted of a Council of State (*hyōjōshū*) and the aforementioned Boards of Inquiry, Retainers, and Administration. The Council of State was a general legislative and deliberative body of about forty high-level officers who were drawn from two different groups. About ten of them were Ashikaga relatives or vassals, and seven of these ten headed the lower courts and adjunct bodies associated with the Council, the primary adjunct body being the Board of Coadjutors. The remaining thirty-odd members came from families who had worked in the former Kamakura Bakufu.[15] From the very beginning, Takauji's brother Tadayoshi supervised the Bakufu bureaucrats and used the less prestigious, more malleable Board of Coadjutors as his base. All *hikitsuke* decisions made between 1338 and 1349 bore Tadayoshi's signature rather than the shogun's.[16] The upheaval caused by the Ashikaga usurpation, and the subsequent conflicting claims made by *shōen* proprietors versus samurai, caused a shift in the basis of decisions made by these Coadjutors. The basic principle observed by Tadayoshi's *hikitsuke* remained respect for the lineage of inheritance, and it was still difficult for a warrior to win a case against a temple, shrine, or other original (*honjo*) proprietor. But in actual fact, the Ashikaga Bakufu exceeded the bounds of the Hōjō principles which they claimed as their guidelines and bent those principles to accommodate samurai demands for compensation which they could only with difficulty ignore.[17]

Almost as a reflex, when the Bakufu was put on the defensive concerning expropriation of *jisha honjo* property, it became less respectful toward the imperial court. In cases where the court's judicial organs (the *fudono* and *kirokusho*) had been relatively autonomous in the past, such as disputes between two *honjo* proprietors, the court now began to feel pressure from the Bakufu. Matters that would have been treated internally by the court in the Kamakura period now followed a more complicated route. Under the new regime, an imperial authorization to hear a case was followed by a Bakufu trial, after which the Bakufu transmitted its opinion (*buke shissō*) back to the imperial court. Only then could the emperor or cloistered emperor issue a final decision (*rinji* and *inzen,* respectively) based on the Bakufu's recommendations.[18] In general, if one of the parties to a case brought before a *kuge* court was dissatisfied with the verdict and appealed to the Bakufu, it would oblige by offering its opinion.[19] Clearly the Ashikaga lost little time in eroding the imperial institution's remaining judicial authority, and the *kuge* were accomplices in their own disenfranchisement by always bringing their petitions to the Bakufu whenever their own courts did not grant them favorable decisions. The upshot was a gradual unification of jurisdictions at the hands of Bakufu courts which were open to both *kuge* and samurai plaintiffs.

In 1358, Takauji died and his son Yoshiakira became shogun. The heir to twenty years of Bakufu aggrandizement, Yoshiakira's administration reflected his uncle Tadayoshi's concern to maintain the inherited bureaucracy intact, and his father's interest in rewarding his retainers and allies. Takauji had been served by the Kō family as house steward (*shitsuji*), but his son felt the need for a deputy of more exalted status who could integrate the shogun's private and public interests. He therefore created the office of chief minister (*kanrei*) in 1362. For the next seventy years—until

Yoshinori's shogunate began in 1429—all shogunal decisions were made with at least the tacit approval of the *kanrei* and the council (*yoriai*) of shugo over which he presided as chief minister. The first occupant of the *kanrei* office was Shiba Yoshimasa (1350–1410), an Ashikaga relative of high lineage and heir apparent to the Shiba house. The new *kanrei* was still only thirteen years old, and real authority rested with his father, Shiba Takatsune (1305–1367), who allegedly found it personally demeaning to accept a position as the shogun's deputy for himself.[20] In spite of their great power, or perhaps because of it, both father and son were forced to flee Kyoto in 1366 when Yoshiakira turned against the Shiba and ordered them to return to Echizen province or be executed. One interpretation says that the shogun was incited against the Shiba by a rival shugo, Sasaki (Kyōgoku) Dōyo,[21] but this alone does not seem a persuasive argument. The fact that the head of the Board of Retainers at this time was Shiba Yoshitane and the head of a section of the Board of Coadjutors was Shiba Yoshitaka meant that three of the most important Bakufu offices were occupied by pawns of Shiba Takatsune. Yoshiakira found it convenient to make a clean sweep by declaring Takatsune a traitor and ordering the Yamana, Sasaki, Toki, and Yoshimi shugo to attack him in Echizen.[22] The Shiba shugoships were reassigned to other clans, thereby dealing a permanent blow to Shiba power. At the end of 1367 Yoshiakira chose Hosokawa Yoriyuki (1329–1392) as his new *kanrei,* and at the same time named him guardian of his ten-year-old son and heir apparent, Yoshimitsu. Yoshiakira died a month later, and Yoriyuki used the combined powers of shogunal regent and *kanrei* to make himself a formidable figure within the Bakufu. During Yoriyuki's term in office, the chief minister emerged as the most influential man in government except for the shogun. With no one to challenge him, Yoriyuki took the reins firmly in his own hands and became an exponent of frugality, a zealous administrator, and an advocate of shogunal supremacy.[23]

In 1368, the young shogun's coming-of-age (*genpuku*) ceremony was celebrated with much fanfare, the festivities lasting for three days. Gifts were exchanged, and the tie between Yoshimitsu and his bureaucracy was expressed when the shogun gave swords to his *bugyōnin* officials, and they reciprocated by giving him horses, swords, and other valuable gifts.[24] Soon thereafter, the *kanrei* had Yoshimitsu preside over the first meeting of the Council of State for the new year (the *hyōjōhajime* ceremony).[25] That was the young shogun's first official act, although he did not formally receive his title of *seiitaishōgun* until the end of the year. It is of symbolic importance because it involved him with the Bakufu's highest-ranking bureaucratic organ, and not with an assembly of warlords per se, thus anticipating the direction in which the shogun's sovereignty would evolve in subsequent decades.

In 1372, the fifteen-year-old shogun signed his first decree (the *gohan hajime* ceremony), a document that concerned a land grant (*kishinjō*) to the Iwashimizu Hachiman shrine.[26] Also during the early 1370s, Bakufu supervision of the *gozan* monasteries was tightened by setting minimum tenures for abbots and chief priests, limiting the size of monastic communities, and prohibiting extravagance and favoritism.[27] Before Yoriyuki resigned as *kanrei,* Yoshimitsu was already ensconced in his newly constructed Muromachi palace, which he moved to in the third month of 1378. The stage was set for the Bakufu's most important changes since 1336, and Hosokawa Yoriyuki's dismissal as *kanrei* in 1379 signaled their beginning.

BUREAUCRATIC EXPANSION UNDER YOSHIMITSU

Chapter Two described how Yoshimitsu's foreign and domestic policies made him Japan's strongest ruler in over a century. One of the vehicles that proved most important in building his autocracy was the bureaucracy, and especially the Board of Administration—the *mandokoro*—the very heart of his Bakufu. Although the *mandokoro* did not achieve its greatest power until Yoshinori's reign, even under Yoshimitsu it played a critical role in refocusing the locus of Bakufu decision-making so that the shogun could counteract feudal privilege. The first *mandokoro* steward (*shitsuji*) was of the Nikaidō family. The office had been held by members of this Kamakura bureaucratic family continuously since 1224, and they were among the many Kamakura officials who had been absorbed into Tadayoshi's corps. In 1379, however, the Nikaidō were replaced by the Ise, a family which had not been part of the Kamakura regime and which rose to prominence because of its special hereditary relationship to the Ashikaga. That relationship was founded upon three services the Ise performed for the shogunal house: they had been Ashikaga vassals since the Kamakura period and even served as *shugo-dai;* they were responsible for the care and education of the shogun's children;[28] and during Yoshiakira's reign they were intermediaries between the shugo and the shogun and were considered experts on protocol.[29] The Ise's appointment to the *mandokoro* may have been influenced by the power struggle between Hosokawa Yoriyuki and his rival Shiba Yoshimasa, and Yoriyuki's replacement as *kanrei* by the now adult Yoshimasa in 1379. Whether or not was the case, the Ise's appointment coincided with a period when the shogun's growing confidence was beginning to be felt in Kyoto. Around 1380 the Bakufu finally succeeded in establishing its exclusive authority to levy *tansen* land taxes.[30] Ten years later, it also relieved the imperial court of authority to collect the *yakubutakumai* national tax used for periodic rebuilding of the Grand Shrine at Ise;[31] likewise for *zōdairiyaku,* taxes levied for repair and maintenance of the emperor's palace. By the turn of the century, the authority to erect and grant permission to erect toll barriers had also passed from the emperor to the shogun.[32] In taking over *yakubutakumai* collection, the shogun had assumed responsibility for maintaining a shrine so sacred that no previous warrior clan had ever dared to violate the court's right to that source of income. As if that were not enough of a precedent, the shogun then gave his own bureaucrats in the Bakufu carte blanche to collect and allocate revenue for the shrine as they thought fit. Also at about this time, court officials called *kuge densō,* who were associated with temples and shrines, were absorbed into the Bakufu structure. There they became a means for the shogun to exercise greater control over the religious institutions with which they were affiliated.[33]

After the shogun rapidly eliminated the imperial court's remaining administrative rights, he was then ready to turn his attention toward expanding the Bakufu's economic sphere of influence. The Board of Administration was the means he used to accomplish this. The critical turning point took place in 1393, when he issued the historic decree placing *sakaya* and *dosō* under the tax collecting mandate of the *mandokoro*.[34] The commercial enterprises not only provided a new wellspring of revenue, but a new reservoir of literate and numerate government employees as well. Merchants and priest-entrepreneurs with names like Shōjitsu, Gyokusen, Jōsen, Jōkō, and Zenjubō were encouraged to join in the work of collecting and recording taxes for the Bakufu, and the result was a division of labor within the *mandokoro* which accurately reflected the diversity of sources from which the Bakufu had come to receive its sustenance. There were officials who were responsible only for land taxes like the *tansen;* others who occupied themselves with the shogunal *goryōsho* domain. Officials called *kurabugyō* supervised the collection of the *munebechisen* household tax and of commercial taxes from *sakaya-dosō*, bean-paste manufacturers, and *hizeniya* moneylenders.[35] The actual collection of commercial revenues involved still other officers called *nōsenkata*, who were men of merchant and priestly callings who engaged in tax farming for the Bakufu. They were selected from among officially designated shogunal moneylenders known as *kubō okura*.[36] Some *sakaya* did not fall under *nōsenkata* jurisdiction but paid their taxes directly to the Bakufu.[37] Such direct payment was, nevertheless, made to *mandokoro* bureaucrats who were part of the *nōsenkata* organization, although they were not *kubō okura* official moneylenders.[38] The *nōsenkata* may not have enjoyed the same status as regular Bakufu magistrates but they had their own office there, and their actual contribution to financial administration was neither denied nor camouflaged.[39]

The *mandokoro* was supervised by two officials: the steward (*shitsuji*) and his vice-minister, the *shitsuji-dai*. As already noted, the *shitsuji* office was a monopoly of the Ise family from 1379 on and, because of their hereditary link to the Ashikaga, the

mandokoro steward greatly resembled a chamberlain with paramount responsibility to maintain the economic well-being of the
shogun's household. As formal chief of the Board of Administration, he was also its representative in negotiating with the imperial
court. The vice-minister, on the other hand, was in charge of the
"public" sector of the board's work, and therefore supervised
most of its financial business.[40] He was chosen from among the
Bakufu's *bugyōnin* families, such as the Sei, Jibu, Fuse, Suwa,
Saitō, and Matsuda, and the post was not the hereditary preserve
of any one of them. Vassals of the Ise, the Ninagawa, occupied a
special position known as *mandokoro-dai* and assisted the Ise in
handling the financial needs of the shogun and his court.[41] There
were thus actually two parallel but overlapping hierarchies within
the *mandokoro,* a dualism that clearly reflected its transformation
from a warlord's household secretariat to a unified national treasury
with jurisdiction extending to all government revenues and embracing *kuge,* samurai, mercantile, and clerical officials in its organization.

By Yoshimitsu's death in 1408, the Bakufu had acquired three
cardinal political levers that its Kamakura predecessor had never
claimed or possessed. The three were: a system of compulsory
shugo-daimyō residence in the capital, a political monopoly to
license foreign trade with China, and extensive rights of tax collection and regulation of the growing commerce in the Home
Provinces. With this firm foundation, Yoshinori was in a position
to take the next step: the diminution of *kanrei* influence over the
bureaucracy.

BUREAUCRATIC SUPREMACY UNDER YOSHINORI

The 1360s had been a dividing line between unstable and stable
shugo tenures. After that decade, most of the shugoships became
the hereditary property of certain families, providing a stability
which permitted them to strengthen their provincial organizations
and to cement the ties of fealty between themselves and the stewards (*jitō*) and housemen (*gokenin*) under them. Those shugo

deputies, in turn, gradually took over as *shōen* officers (*daikan*), squeezing out the *jisha honjo's* former bailiffs in the countryside.[42] The new-found security felt by *shugo-daimyō* in their provincial domains may have contributed to the relative ease with which Yoshimitsu made them take up residence in Kyoto. The *shugo-daimyō* cabinet headed by the *kanrei* reached the peak of its influence after Yoshimitsu's death, and for most of Yoshimochi's reign they were the real focus of decision-making. As we have seen, even the choice of a shogunal successor was left to them to decide. They no doubt anticipated a continuation of Yoshimochi's relative passivity when they selected his younger brother by lot to succeed as shogun in 1428, but they were wrong.

The combination of a growing Board of Administration and a long but uninspired reign by Yoshimochi left the Bakufu at a crossroads. The Council of State—Board of Coadjutors (*hyōjōshū-hikitsuke*) machinery had stagnated since Yoshimitsu's day and was no longer an effective decision-making structure. In 1428, the high-ranking Shingon Buddhist prelate and shogunal advisor, Sambōin Mansai (1378–1435), called for its revival,[43] and Yoshinori did take some initial steps in that direction, but he eventually replaced the Board of Coadjutors' jurisdiction with a simpler "opinion" (*iken*) procedure. Unlike the coadjutors, who were subordinated to the Council of State, the newer formula involved low-level judicial bureaucrats called *yūhitsukata* who were inferior to the coadjutors in rank but free of hierarchical connections with other Bakufu organs. Therein lay their advantage: they were directly answerable to the shogun alone. Despite their humble position in the official hierarchy, their functional prominence bespoke the rising status of such low-level officials during the mid-Muromachi period.[44]

In short, Yoshinori's reforms did for the Bakufu's adjudicative function what Yoshimitsu's had done for its economic administration. Both were developing the administrative technology of early modern Japan and, in other areas as well, similarities between these two Ashikaga autocrats were not lost on their contemporaries.[45] The core of Yoshinori's reorganization required a change

in the mode of transmission for shogunal decrees. All important
decrees had previously been countersigned by the *kanrei,* a symbolic statement of the mixed nature of Ashikaga sovereignty during its first century. Whatever gains the shogun made in expanding
the powers of his office was done with at least the tacit approval
of the *kanrei* and shugo cabinet. Ashikaga Yoshimitsu had forced
the *shugo-daimyō* to live in Kyoto so that he could observe their
activities, but he was not prepared openly to antagonize their
collective authority. Yoshinori, on the other hand, soon made it
clear that he would not respect feudal precedent. Until the third
month of 1429 all the documents he signed were "private" ones
called *gonaisho,*[46] enforcement of which was via the *kanrei's*
signed order (*kanrei shohan gechijō*).[47] But in the fourth month
of 1429 Yoshinori promulgated the first of his personally signed
"public" decrees, called *gohan (no) mikyōjo.*[48] The importance
of these decrees was that they were not countersigned by the
kanrei. The shogun instead had them countersigned by one or
more of his own magistrates.[49] This countersigned document,
called the "jointly signed *bugyōnin* order" (*bugyōnin rensho hōsho*), became the hallmark of Yoshinori's autocracy, and survived
his downfall to become the procedural mainstay of Bakufu authority during the latter half of the fifteenth century.

By-passing the *kanrei* enabled Yoshinori to establish an unmediated chain of command between himself and his bureaucrats. Between the seventh month of 1429 and the end of 1430, he reformed
the Council of State and Board of Coadjutors, and then with the
aid of one of his *bugyōnin,* Inō Tameshige, set up the *gozen rakkyo* system.[50] This was a litigation procedure appropriately named
"judgment in the shogun's presence" (*gozen gosata*), since it required the shogun's personal involvement in hearing the cases
brought to trial. The first judgment of this sort was handed down
in 1430/9th month.[51] At the same time, the shogun issued explicit
instructions concerning *bugyōnin* duties, including an important
stipulation of the new litigation system that prohibited the presence of anyone besides the shogun and the bailiff (*kubariwake
bugyō*) when a defendant appeared before the Bakufu tribunal.[52]

During Yoshimitsu's shogunate, the bailiff had been under the *kanrei's* jurisdiction, thus preventing effective personal supervision by the shogun, but for a brief decade Yoshinori succeeded in establishing one-man rule, and bureaucratic practice reflected that fact.

Yoshinori took the most radical step of any shogun in rejecting the collective decision-making principle in favor of a personal dictatorship buttressed by the bureaucracy. By the same token his reign also marked the zenith of the Board of Administration's position within the Bakufu, since it was the organ most closely allied with shogunal initiatives taken by earlier Ashikaga rulers. Whereas a strong shogun could wrest power away from the quarrelsome shugo, however, his centralization could not eliminate the destabilizing consequences of political assassination and popular rebellion which engulfed Japan in 1441. Yoshinori was murdered by a disgruntled *shugo-daimyō* and that ended shogunal autocracy, but it did not destroy the bureaucratic apparatus which had been an instrument of that autocracy.

THE ENDURANCE OF
BAKUFU BUREAUCRATIC INSTITUTIONS

The *shugo-daimyō* met with little opposition in taking over the government during the interregnum following 1441. Until Yoshimasa came of age in 1456, his Bakufu was in effect run by three successive *kanrei*: Hosokawa Mochiyuki, Hatakeyama Mochikuni, and Hosokawa Katsumoto. While the young shogun was still in no position to defend his own prerogatives, let alone those of his officials, they were to some extent protected by his *mandokoro* steward, Ise Sadachika (1417–1473), and the Bakufu's *gozan* commissioner (*inryōkenshu*), Kikei Shinzui.[53] And although the loss of shogunal power was irretrievable after 1441, the Bakufu's bureaucracy remained intact, as did the system of direct transmission of orders between shogun and *bugyōnin,* illustrated by the close ties that prevailed between Yoshimasa and Ise Sadachika in the *mandokoro.* Whatever one might say of Sadachika's character

—and his venality and greed were notorious—he was without question the shogun's man.

Despite the obstacles that confronted him, the shogun Yoshimasa's policies before the Ōnin War revealed historic Ashikaga tendencies toward strengthening the shogun's personal role in government. Until 1456, for example, Yoshimasa relied on the precedents set by Yoshimitsu's court for his own ceremonial usage but, in 1458 at a state banquet called the *naidaijindaikyō*, he switched to Yoshinori's usage instead. In that same year he also revived the *inryōken* (the Bakufu Zen temple office) which had lapsed since his father's murder, and reappointed Yoshinori's *inryōkenshū*, Kikei Shinzui, to head the office, ordering that "all matters concerning the priesthood must be reported as in the past." Other incidents indicate that Yoshimasa was actually able to assert himself over *kanrei* and shugo on numerous occasions. In 1455, Hatakeyama Yoshinari and Yasaburō became embroiled in a family headship struggle. The Yamato Kōfukuji temple's warrior-priest (*shuto*), Tsutsui, and provincials, Hashio and Kataoka, supported Yasaburō's claim but lost, and in 1457 the lands of all three were declared shogunal domain with Yoshinari appointed overseer (*daikan*) over them. The Kōfukuji campaigned to regain its lands, and finally Yoshimasa agreed to donate them to the temple, but not before he and his deputies had exacted their price. While they received monetary compensation, however, the *kanrei* Hosokawa Katsumoto was given nothing. Again, in 1457 Hatakeyama Mochikuni sent his vassals Konda and Yusa to Yamato province, mendaciously claiming that it had been ordered by the shogun. Because Mochikuni had repeatedly acted on false pretenses in this way, Yoshimasa confiscated one of his estates and gave it to his own trusted retainer Ise Sadakatsu. In 1459/3rd month, Yoshimasa awarded land to Isshiki Chifukumaru in a *gohan (no) mikyōjo* decree which was implemented by Omi shugo Sasaki Shirō upon receipt of a *bugyōnin* order dated 1459/4th month/10. The fact that a *bugyōnin* order and not a *kanrei* order was used to transmit the shogun's will indicated that the *kanrei*'s power had been checked and temporarily by-passed during this time.[54]

The phenomenon of a Bakufu responding to shogunal desires or to those of his favorites like Ise Sadachika, and at the same time exhibiting the influence of its urban setting is illustrated in the functioning of the Office of Urban Property (*jikata bugyō*) during Yoshimasa's reign. Originally staffed by members of Council of State families Nikaidō, Nakahara, Settsu, and Hatano, from about 1396—almost contemporaneously with the stabilization of shugo tenures and of the Ise as *mandokoro shitsuji*—it became the hereditary post of the Settsu.[55] By mid-Muromachi, the *jikata* commissioner had extensive authority in the transfer and disposal of urban real estate, but what is most important is that in its daily operations his office represented the principle of bureaucratic superiority within the Bakufu at a time when samurai were not wont to observe the government's admonitions. The *jikata bugyō* was superior to the head of the Board of Retainers in the chain of command that descended from the shogun. That meant that a shogunal order would first be received by the Office of Urban Property, which would transmit it to the *samuraidokoro*. From the *samuraidokoro* a command would then be issued to put the order into effect.[56]

Besides the superiority of civil to military authority within the Bakufu, a second principle of bureaucratic organization was also observed in the priority given to official government bureaucratic office over aristocratic *kuge* rank. An incident took place in 1442 over an argument between two members of the *hyōjōshū* over which of them would sit in the higher position when they took their places during council sessions. Inō Hizen nyūdō Eishō claimed that his higher (*kuge*) aristocratic rank entitled him to the superior seat, but Hatano Izumi no kami was chairman (*tōnin*) and as such thought himself entitled to it. The upshot was that Hatano's *kuge* rank was raised slightly to give him an edge over Inō and permit him to take the higher seat.[57] The principle of bureaucratic superiority to aristocratic rank was thus upheld.

The Ōnin War was especially destructive of administrative machinery. Beyond the extreme venality which the war encouraged among some high-ranking members of the shogun's entourage,[58] the aftermath of the war determined that the Bakufu would never again be a viable national government. As the government of an extended city-state focused on Kyoto and the Home Provinces, however, certain features of the prewar Bakufu were adapted to the new political situation and proved to be highly resilient, given the turmoil of the times. One of those features was the "jointly signed *bugyōnin* order" (*bugyōnin rensho hōsho*), Yoshinori's innovation, which continued to be issued until the very end of the Muromachi period. In the end, the Bakufu *bugyōnin* accepted jobs with new strongmen, just as their Kamakura ancestors had done when the Ashikaga seized power two hundred years before. Some of them, like Matsuda Hideo, became *bugyōnin* in Nobunaga's service; others were even registered as members of Nobunaga's vassal band.[59] While the jointly signed *bugyōnin* order survived until this ultimate dispersion of Bakufu personnel took place, however, the decree identified with the *kanrei's* authority—the *Muromachi bakufu mikyōjo/gechijō*, also known as *Muromachi shogunke (no) mikyōjo*—ceased being issued during the Ōnin War. Specifically, the last such decree was promulgated by the *kanrei* Hosokawa Katsumoto in 1471.[60]

A new system for transmitting Bakufu orders was in the formative stage, reflecting the shogun's loss of independence and his great need for the Hosokawa *kanrei's* support. The concrete demonstration of that dependence was the appearance of a new type of document, the "*kanrei-dai* order" (*kanrei-dai hōsho*) in 1471. Because the Bakufu had difficulty in enforcing its own jointly signed *bugyōnin* orders in Yamashiro after the war, it was compelled to rely on the Hosokawa, who became the catalytic agents which doomed the old structure of authority. The Bakufu's chain of implementation had always been from shogunal decree (*gohan no mikyōjo*) to *kanrei* transmission of that decree (*Muromachi bakufu mikyōjo*) to shugo enforcement order (*shugo jungyōjo*). The new system started with a jointly signed *bugyōnin* order but then, instead of the *kanrei's* transmission, the next order was issued by the *kanrei's* own deputy the *kanrei-dai* (*kanrei-dai hōsho/soejō*). Upon receipt of this order, deputy shugo then issued their enforcement order *(shugo-dai jungyōjō).*[61] Under the new system, therefore, Bakufu decisions were enforced via the deputy *kanrei,* who formed a bureaucratic organization which was separate from the Board of Administration and was staffed by members of the Hosokawa's lower-ranked vassal families, such as the Yasutomi, Uehara, Kasai, and Teramachi.[62]

The erosion of Bakufu authority was gradual. The *kanrei's* organization penetrated by degrees to the lowest level of administration, by-passing even the *shugo-dai, shōen daikan,* and *kokujin* squires (c. 1491), and absorbed the Office of Urban Property's jurisdiction (c. 1508). From the time Hosokawa Takakuni became *kanrei* (c. 1508), the *kanrei-dai* order was used in Yamashiro, Settsu, Tamba, parts of Izumi and Kawachi, and as far from Kyoto as Bizen and Etchū—as far, in fact, as Bakufu authority still extended.[63] It should be kept in mind, however, that it took the *kanrei-dai* at least twenty years to make significant inroads into Bakufu prerogatives, and it was not until the sixteenth century that this parallel bureaucracy actually replaced the Bakufu's orders with its own. On the contrary, during the immediate postwar period, Yoshimasa's *bugyōnin* enjoyed a revival of prestige such as they had not experienced since the days of Yoshinori's reforms. Group consciousness and morale within the Bakufu were high even as late as 1485, and persistent attempts by petitioners to curry favor with them clearly showed that they still retained a good deal of influence.[64] In sheer physical numbers, this period witnessed a growth in the size of the shogun's bureaucratic corps with estimates ranging from forty to about sixty *bugyōnin* for the year 1485.[65]

The decades following the Ōnin War saw the culmination of a process initiated almost a century before, during which time the Ashikaga became progressively more dependent on the revenues that could be found in and around Kyoto as their land-based income declined. Their dependence subtly altered the imperatives of bureaucratic control in the Home Provinces, so that, even after the devastation left by a decade of warfare, when one might have expected to find an enervated government apparatus in Kyoto, the exhaustion of the great *shugo-daimyō* and the war of all against all then raging in almost every province of the country left a power vacuum which the shogun's magistrates readily filled. Although vigorous rule by the shogun was no longer a real possibility, the Bakufu continued to provide a competent administration until the Hosokawa recovered from the war sufficiently to begin their usurpation. Characteristically, the *kanrei-dai* had been originally appointed to facilitate the implementation of Bakufu orders but, as happened all over Japan during the sixteenth century, they began to use their own military power to interfere with judgments handed down from above. By the middle of the century, the *kanrei-dai* were even issuing their own orders concerning debt cancellation and counterfeit coinage (*erizeni*) which the *mandokoro* had always handled exclusively.[66]

It is doubtful whether the Muromachi bureaucracy ever numbered more than one hundred *bugyōnin* at its height, and the largest count extant is of no more than seventy. What is important is not the scale of this government, however, for it was very small not only by present-day but even certain premodern standards. Rather it is notable for what it attempted: the reintegration of an administrative structure which had become very fragmented, and the recruitment of new social elements into the Bakufu whose skills and talents answered the needs of a government trying to manage a society in flux and a developing economy. The encrusted layers of privilege which had resulted in separate jurisdictions for samurai, imperial aristocrats, and temples and shrines were gradually eliminated as the Ashikaga tried to consolidate administration and reduce autonomous jurisdictions. They succeeded in establishing a mini-autocracy in the Home Provinces on the basis of this unification. Their Bakufu expressed in institutional terms the mentality of a capitalist-agrarian state willing to employ mercantile wealth and expertise to establish a feudal dynasty's sovereign power. The dynasty failed, but the mentality took root.

FIVE

The Bakufu System: Military Organization

Although it originated as a military government, the Muromachi Bakufu lost touch with both its agrarian roots and its martial origins. The popular cliché that the Ashikaga shoguns lacked the military resources to exert effective coercive sanctions against their enemies is not without its element of truth. Yet they did try to organize a coalition of forces while presiding over a society beset by constant internal war in which severe socioeconomic dislocations made it extremely difficult to sustain long-range military effectiveness.

Briefly stated, the shogun adapted to the changing political climate of the late fourteenth and fifteenth centuries by shifting his dependence from the *shugo-daimyōs'* retainers (*hikan*) to his own personal army. The shogunal army was a reliable nucleus of professional mounted warriors who were pledged to defend the Bakufu against traitors, popular uprisings, and other crises. Just as the transformation of the Board of Administration into a shogunal exchequer secured the economic livelihood of the Bakufu and the political reliability of the central bureaucracy, the formation of a shogunal army gave the Ashikaga independence of military response until late in the fifteenth century. These were the two bulwarks of Ashikaga hegemony: the hereditary bureaucrats in the *mandokoro* who protected the shogun's economic privileges and his administrative prerogatives, and the shogun's army, known as the *hōkōshū,* which protected him physically. Around those two foci clustered those who for one reason or another sought to identify themselves with the central government. Under the *mandokoro's* aegis, the great merchant-moneylenders of Kyoto—both lay and clerical—became a privileged elite of tax farmers and non-hereditary bureaucrats. Similarly, local samurai proprietors—*kokujin, jizamurai, gokenin*—could gain privileged status and lessen their vulnerability to *shugo-daimyō* coercion by linking themselves to the shogun via the *hōkōshū.* Neither the Bakufu bureaucracy nor the shogun's army was numerically impressive, but their strategic position at the fulcrum of power gave them a disproportionate influence over the successful execution of Bakufu policy and a critical role in the preservation of the medieval shogunal monarchy.

The army that accompanied Takauji in his coup d'état of 1336 was a mounted force composed largely of Ashikaga house vassals and collateral vassals (*fudai*) of varying degrees of reliability. This was a feudal army par excellence: hard to mobilize and hard to keep mobilized for extended periods of time, it was notoriously unreliable in the fray, as Takauji's own betrayal of Emperor Go-Daigo's cause amply illustrates. The Ashikaga collateral houses who fought on Takauji's side included the Shiba, Hosokawa, Hatakeyama, Imagawa, and Isshiki, all of whom became prominent *shugo-daimyō.* Besides being military governors and generals, they served the shogun as head of the Board of Retainers (*samurai-dokoro tōnin/shoshi*) and as *kanrei,* performing the diffuse functions demanded of them in a feudal system. That very multiplicity of duties, however, coupled with their own personal ambitions, created conflicts of interest between self and shogun which curtailed their military usefulness to the Bakufu.

Yoshimitsu was the first shogun to try a new arrangement in order to strengthen his military forces. Partly as a consequence of the civil war which found recurrent justification in the schism between the two imperial lines, and partly because he wished to have at his disposal a more accountable armed force, Yoshimitsu established a personal bodyguard called the *gobanshū.*[1] During

the Meitoku (Yamana) rebellion of 1391, the great *kanrei*-class
shugo contributed on the average no more than two to three hundred mounted samurai each toward the Bakufu's punitory force.
The shogun's own *gobanshū,* on the other hand, was some three
thousand strong.[2] There is no denying that the shugo armies were
collectively more numerous than the shogun's, but they could not
always be depended upon to donate their services to the utmost.
In the Kakitsu rebellion of 1441, the shugo Yamana Mochitoyo
contributed the largest fighting force,[3] but he was motivated by a
desire to crush his rival Akamatsu Mitsusuke in order to become
the new shugo of Harima province. There was little concern for
avenging the shogun's murder or upholding the Bakufu's authority. The response of the other *shugo-daimyō* after the assassination
was slow and lackluster and emphasized the need for an independent shogunal army divorced from the feudal pyramid of lord and
vassal.

SHUGO AND SAMURAIDOKORO

Four *shugo-daimyō* families, the Yamana, Akamatsu, Isshiki, and
Kyōgoku, with few interruptions after 1400, alternated the headship of the Board of Retainers among themselves. Other shugo
houses which also held the office of *samuraidokoro shoshi* more
than once included the Sasaki, Toki, and Imagawa. Originally empowered to preserve order in Kyoto and enforce vassal discipline,
from the time of Yoshiakira's shogunate the *samuraidokoro* lost
general jurisdiction over retainers and was only able to exercise
such control over those in Yamashiro province since the *samuraidokoro shoshi* was ex officio shugo of that province.[4] The Board
of Retainers lost its general authority over vassals as a result of
the founding of the *kanrei* system, but at the same time its police
powers over the capital city and criminal cases there was broadened.[5] The regularity with which the post of *samuraidokoro shoshi*
was rotated among the families was in sharp contrast to succession
in other Bakufu organs, such as in the *mandokoro. Samuraidokoro
shoshi* rarely held office for more than two or three years at a

time, and this no doubt contributed to its capacity to act as an effective, impartial arbiter of samurai disputes and disorderly acts in Kyoto. Outside of the capital, the shugo's justice took precedence, enforced through the *shugo-dai* and other vassals of the shugo houses. But after 1441, the *shugo-daimyō* blatantly went their separate ways militarily, forcing the shogun to rely on his several thousand *hōkōshū* samurai as his only dependable armed force.

THE SHOGUN'S NEW ARMY

The shogunal army saw its beginnings during the Kamakura period, when a group of bodyguards known as the *kinjū* was first organized to protect the shogun and to perform ceremonial functions.[6] The term itself originally referred to the Heian period emperor's bodyguard, and the shift to its use for the shogun's own bodyguard reveals how the political center of gravity had shifted quite early in the medieval period. During the early years of the Ashikaga regime, the custom was established of keeping a body of warriors available to accompany the shogun on pilgrimages and visits to the imperial court and also to represent him on such formal occasions as he was unable to officiate in person. During the late fourteenth century this group grew in size and importance. Yoshimitsu organized them into the *gobanshū*, which was divided into five banners (*ban*), and from then on the military significance of the corps began to overshadow its ceremonial function. In addition to their role in the Yamana rebellion (1391), in 1415/6th month they were part of a punitory force ordered by the Bakufu to pacify the soldier-monks of the Enryakuji monastery, who had brought the shrine palanquin of the Hie shrine into the city to coerce the Bakufu to meet their demands. In 1428, some of the *gobanshū* samurai accompanied shugo Yamana Mochitoyo's expeditionary force to suppress a rebellion in Ise province.[7] Through Yoshinori's efforts, the *gobanshū* was once more reorganized, this time to emerge as the *hōkōshū*. Like its predecessor, the *hōkōshū* was divided into five banners, but it was larger, more heavily

Ashikaga in its manpower, and unwaveringly loyal to the Bakufu. This army remained more or less intact until 1491, surviving even the centrifugal pressures of the Ōnin War. During the last sixty years of the *hōkōshū's* existence, the family constituency of each banner remained almost unchanged, and each retained a strong sense of solidarity.[8]

Hōkōshū samurai came from three manpower pools: (1) Ashi-kaga-related (*ichimon*) families and junior lines and vassals of *shugo-daimyō* houses; (2) Ashikaga family original vassals (*kihon hikan*) and house officials (*karyō bugyōnin*); and (3) powerful provincial *kokujin* squires.[9] Among the Ashikaga-related families were the Hosokawa, Hatakeyama, Isshiki, Imagawa, Ueno, Mo-monoi, Niki, and Arakawa, and from other *shugo-daimyō* families were the Sasaki, Toki, and Ogasawara. Shugo families of especially high lineage, such as the Shiba and Shibukawa, Kira and Ishibashi, were absent from the *hōkōshū* lists.[10] As for Ashikaga family original vassals dating from the Kamakura period, there were the Ise and the Kō. The house officials who were represented included the Yokose, Kuriihara, Teraoka, Hikobe, Ebina, Murakami, Shi-dara, and Kojima. These were the *hōkōshū* men who became over-seers (*kanrinin*) of the shogun's *goryōsho* estates and were paid out of the revenue from those lands. The *mandokoro* bureaucrats Ise and Ninagawa, as well as the Ōdate, Asahi, Saitō, Andō, Hiki-da, Yamato and other *bugyōnin* were also of this second type, although their relationship to the Ashikaga may not have extended as far back as the Kamakura period.[11] The third component group in the *hōkōshū* included *kokujin* proprietors like the Kobayakawa of Aki province, whose lands differed from those of the Ashikaga house officials in that they were usually concentrated in one province. As *hōkōshū* warriors, the estates of these *kokujin* were protected by Bakufu decree from entry by a shugo's officers (*shugo-shi funyū*), and they had the right to pay *tansen* land taxes directly to the Bakufu without the intermediate step of collection by the shugo and his agents. This method of direct payment was the previously mentioned *kyōsai* and was a prime incentive for *ko-kujin* to want to join the shogun's army.[12] Not only with respect to taxation, but in cases of capital crimes committed by *hōkōshū* warriors, even if a shugo was the victim he was forbidden by the Bakufu to take the law into his own hands. In all such instances the shugo had to refer the case to the central government for review.[13] The privileges accorded to *hōkōshū* samurai set the third category of members, the *kokujin* proprietors, against the *shugo-daimyō* under whose nominal authority they existed, and severely restricted shugo activities in their territories. The growth of this third group more than that of the other two reflected the political maturation of the shogunal monarchy.

During the early days of the shogunate, there were relatively few Ashikaga relatives in the *gobanshū* and numerous members from *shugo-daimyō* branch families. After the formation of the *hōkōshū*, and largely as a result of Yoshinori's efforts, however, many relatives were added to the rolls and from that time on they consistently held the headships (*bantō*) to all five banners. The *bantō* families were: (1) Hosokawa Awaji, (2) Momonoi, (3) Hatakeyama Harima/Ueno, (4) Hatakeyama Mochizumi/Nakatsukasa, and (5) Ōdachi.[14] Whereas the *gobanshū* up to Yoshinori's time retained its effectiveness because of the active participation of shugo in the *kanrei-shugo* cabinet system, the descendent *hōkōshū* derived its driving force from being directly subservient to the shogun alone.[15] It is no accident that the expansion of the shogun's army and the swelling of its Ashikaga majority coincided with the zenith of shogunal autocracy under Yoshinori, for that was also the period of most aggressive interference by the shogun in the shugo clans' internal affairs. Yoshinori used the *hōkōshū* to undermine shugo kinship solidarity and authority by helping those who joined his army acquire lands that belonged to the main house (*ichizoku*) of their respective clans.[16] He thus hurt the *shugo-daimyō* in two critical areas of their jurisdiction. First, by negating the shugo's right to collect taxes from members of the shogun's army he deprived the shugo of an opportunity to seize additional revenue, and then in the matter of internal clan discipline by interposing himself between the shugo main house and branch families (*shoke*) of a clan he eroded the foundation of the shugo's strength.

With respect to tax collection, however, the countervailing limitation was applied to one of the shugo's more recently acquired prerogatives. During the late fourteenth century, an expanded shugo authority came to include: *karita rōzeki*, the apprehension of suspects accused of stealing harvests, *shisetsu jungyō*, the implementation of Bakufu orders, and tax collecting via the shugo's agents (*shugo-shi*) and *shugo-dai*. Exclusion of shugo from *hōkōshū* lands meant, therefore, not only with respect to their traditional criminal jurisdiction, but also prohibited them from collecting the *tansen* which they had only recently been empowered to do.[17]

Shogunal interference in what once had been internal clan matters was in part the result of the separation of the title of clan head, *sōryō* (the rights accompanying the title were called *sōryō-shiki*), from the land which formerly had been an integral part of the title. With the symbolization of the post of *sōryō* during the fourteenth century, outside interference increased—first from Emperor Go-Daigo and then from the Bakufu. Until 1441, shogunal meddling in clan matters was not limited to the shugo, however, but extended equally to stewards and house vassals (*jitō gokenin*) throughout the country.[18] Although Yoshinori's assassination ended the period of unrestricted tampering of this sort, the desire of *hōkōshū* warriors themselves to remain under Bakufu protection and patronage gave impetus to the policy and enabled Yoshimasa to preserve the interests of many who had first been recruited by Yoshinori. The forging of a direct link between those samurai and the shogun may even have been the catalyst that sparked open opposition between them and their original shugo overlords. Such confrontations took place between the Toki and their Mino *shugo-dai* Saitō, between the Shiba and their Echizen *shugo-dai* Asakura, between the Owari shugo and their *shugo-dai* Oda, and between the Akamatsu shugo and their vassals the Urakami.[19] These internecine struggles were the harbingers of the Sengoku period.

A majority of *hōkōshū* samurai resided in Kyoto where they could defend the Bakufu most effectively. Remaining in Kyoto did not totally isolate them from their lands, however, since the estates of roughly 40 percent of the total number for which information exists were located in the four provinces of Omi, Mikawa, Owari, and Mino, all of which lay in a bloc due east of the capital.[20] The shogun had more trouble in granting lands to his *hōkōshū* on a large scale to the west of Kyoto, since in that direction he faced blocs of provinces under the Hosokawa, Yamana, and Akamatsu, all strong *shugo-daimyō*.

Despite the concentration of *Hōkōshū* warriors in Kyoto, others remained in the countryside where they performed an intelligence-gathering function for the Bakufu. As noted already, they were also employed as intendants (*daikan*) of the Board of Administration to inspect and oversee the shogun's *goryōsho* estates, although many tended to stay in Kyoto and delegate such duties to their own subordinates.[21] The existence of a *hōkōshū* presence both in Kyoto and in the provinces and their contribution to the Bakufu's longevity made the shogunal army one of the most notable accomplishments of the Muromachi synthesis. Their triple function of peacetime guard, wartime army, and corps of *goryōsho* overseers greatly enhanced the resilience of the Ashikaga regime in the face of setbacks which came in the mid-fifteenth century. Perhaps more important, they proved to be the forerunner of military organization under their successors, the *sengoku-daimyō* and the Tokugawa.

SIX

The Muromachi Bakufu in Comparative Perspective

The Muromachi Bakufu presided over a synthesis of political, social, and economic changes which began the shift away from autarkic-agrarian feudal structures in Japan during the fourteenth and fifteenth centuries. In the political arena, this Muromachi synthesis included the following features:

(1) The creation of a new type of shogun who commanded the status and authority that no single Japanese ruler had possessed since the Heian period. This new kinglike ruler resulted from the fusion of bureaucratic, feudal, and aristocratic components of political authority in the person of one man, the Ashikaga shogun, and gave Japan a model of leadership comparable to the European Renaissance prince. The political traditions of the Heian bureaucratic state, the feudal command structure of the Kamakura Bakufu, and the underlying tension between these two patterns contributed to the new shape of political leadership under the early and middle Ashikaga dynasty.

(2) The evolution of an administrative corps which owed absolute and exclusive loyalty to the shogun. This was to some extent a revival and adaptation of the earlier Heian bureaucratic tradition which demanded that officials serve the emperor exclusively. The establishment of the Ashikaga Bakufu in Kyoto—the very heart of this tradition—no doubt gave further impetus to the stress on loyalty to the ruler. Strong shoguns like Yoshimitsu and

Yoshinori devised policies that were destructive of dual loyalties and therefore destructive of feudal government in general.

(3) The parallel emergence of a professional armed force which acted with undivided loyalty in the shogun's interests. The desired goal was a small army which the shogun could rely on when all else failed. This is the same objective desired and striven for by Renaissance monarchs in the West. Although the immediate need was for an army which could give the shogun undivided loyalty, in effect this requirement dictated that such a force be organized differently from traditional feudal levies and led to the beginnings of a fulltime, non-mercenary force.

(4) The general refinement of administrative technology in all areas of government, including taxation and finance, litigation, and the utilization of talented individuals not of samurai or aristocratic origin. The Muromachi Bakufu employed moneylenders and clerics as tax collectors and financial officials, and several times reformed the process of litigation to strengthen the authority of the central government.

The social and economic environments in which these political changes took place also constitute important elements of the Muromachi synthesis, including:

(1) The development of a commercial agrarian economy in the Home Provinces around Kyoto. This involved an increase in the production of cash crops and a surge in the demand for money, and this economy served as a model for the gradual expansion of handicraft manufacturing and a market economy on a national scale. Such a shift away from autarkic agriculture also led to greater social fluidity and itinerance in response to the pull of regional markets.

(2) The transformation of Kyoto into Japan's paradigmatic early modern city, possessing a large and influential mercantile population and a cultural life which rivaled that of European Renaissance capitals in the character, variety, and energy of its art, drama, literature, and crafts. Unlike Heian-kyo, Muromachi Kyoto throbbed to the rhythm of life determined by its nouveaux riches samurai overlords, and that vitality has endured to become one of the hallmarks of Japan's urban landscape.

(3) The creation of a general atmosphere receptive to change and innovation, an important component of which was the high degree of geographic and social mobility, and an important consequence of which was a greater than average propensity to rebellion and violence. The fourteenth and fifteenth centuries in Japan spawned extraordinary experimentation, a willingness to try new methods born of the absence of a strong unifying political and economic order such as the Tokugawa enjoyed. Like the European Renaissance, Muromachi Japan was rocked by internecine struggles and destabilizing social change but also expressed a spontaneity and a freedom in its various institutions that its successors seem to lack.

These qualities and institutions, which were the components of the Muromachi synthesis, did not all develop to the same degree or at the same rate, and some were even interrupted or terminated during the turbulence of the sixteenth century and the subsequent repression of early Tokugawa. Nevertheless, the apparent chaos of the Sengoku period and the temporary decentralization of important governmental functions during that time should not mislead us into thinking that the Muromachi contribution was negated or substantially reversed. The sixteenth century may be viewed as a time of gestation and adaptation, during which the rest of the country absorbed and applied innovations that had first appeared in the Ashikaga Bakufu and its urban milieu. As the new administrative and commercial technology filtered down to what had once been *shugo-daimyō* domains, the new upstart *gekokujō* daimyo put them into operation in almost every corner of the empire. Although these efforts were on a limited scale at first, the rapidity with which power was consolidated during the latter half of the sixteenth century speaks for the effectiveness of the new methods of control and economy. When Hideyoshi and his Tokugawa successors came to power, it was then a relatively simple task to enforce uniformity throughout the country. While no one would deny that chaos was a genuine and important part of the sixteenth century restructuring of Japan's political order, the Sengoku period was also a time in which provincial Japan assimilated and diffused patterns of government and economy that in the fifteenth century could only have been found in the Kyoto region. The groundwork having been laid, the stage was then set for the burst of growth that early Tokugawa Japan is justly famous for.

In reflecting upon the institutions of the Muromachi Bakufu which have been examined in the foregoing chapters, one is struck by their similarities to Western European states of the fourteenth and fifteenth centuries. In both Europe and Japan, expansion of the monarch's power required considerable reorganization of financial, military, and administrative/judicial organs of the central government; in both, the attempt was made to centralize along two dimensions which were fundamentally interdependent, although they may be separated analytically. The two dimensions were, first, the struggle between monarchy and polyarchy, and second, the expansion of the monarch's personal authority within the central government itself. The second aspect of centralization involved the gradual transfer of de facto authority from collective bodies of seigneurial or feudal origin, to a small but expanding bureaucracy which was the personal apparatus of the king. The first aspect of centralization entailed the ability of that royal bureaucracy to enforce nationwide the authority the ruler had succeeded in acquiring in the capital itself. These two changes occurred simultaneously, although it may be argued that without the second aspect of centralization, the first one would be unattainable.

The history of the Muromachi shoguns during their first century (c. 1336-1441) is one of an erratic but unmistakable drive to establish a monarchy which possessed the two aspects of centralized power. Ashikaga Yoshimitsu may be compared to Louis XI (1423-1483) of France in the degree to which he succeeded in undercutting the feudal nobility by identifying his position with that of the nation as a whole. During this period, traditional checks on the ruler's arbitrary will were truncated, eliminated, or absorbed into his personal political apparatus. In England, the decline of Parliament during the reign of Edward IV (1442-1483) and the simultaneous rise of the Star Chamber is one example of this trend.[1] Yoshinori's bureaucratic reorganization and *gozen gosata* court is another. As in Europe, the Muromachi rulers used the administration of justice to assert their authority, and the rising number of cases that were brought before their courts became an indicator of their legitimacy.

The instability endemic to early capitalist-agrarian societies enabled kings in France and England toward the end of the Hundred Years' War, in Muromachi Japan, in Southern Sung China, and elsewhere, to temporarily outmaneuver vested interests who defended the status quo. They created models of autocracy which they could not sustain for long, but the creation of such models was nevertheless a feat in its own right. These rulers were the first to use revenue-earning schemes which anticipated the mercantilist doctrines of the mature preindustrial autocracies.[2] The formation of foreign trading monopolies like the English Staple,[3] the encouragement of domestic manufacturing and commercial enterprise and (more significantly) redoubled efforts to tax those enterprises, and the accumulation of precious metals and metallic currencies were all components of this premercantilism. Louis XI applied political pressure, for example, to destroy Geneva's thriving commerce and relocate to Lyons the activity for which Geneva's fairs had been famous.[4] He also tried to substitute domestic manufactures for imported luxuries by establishing the French silk industry by edict in 1466, a document which explicitly related the outflow of French gold to the import of silk hosiery from the south.[5] In England, the policies of Edward III (1312–1377) and Richard II (1367–1400) moved beyond the export of English wool staple and pressed instead for the marketing of manufactured cloth to compete with that of Flanders. During the second half of the fourteenth century, this resulted in the halving of England's wool exports, while her more profitable cloth exports rose more than sevenfold.[6] There are many examples of this sort for Renaissance Europe, and the Sung dynasty provides comparable illustrations. The Kao-tsung Emperor (r. 1127–1162), first emperor of the Southern Sung, bestowed the highest sanction on an aggressive foreign trade policy in his edict of 1137, and the importance with which the customs offices (*shih-po-ssu*) were regarded by the dynasty are indicative of premercantilism in China.[7] In Muromachi Japan, the shogun's exclusive franchise to license participation in the lucrative China trade, his Bakufu's deep involvement with Kyoto moneylenders and purveyors of credit, and his eagerness to secure ever greater amounts of semiprecious metallic currency were symptomatic of the same kind of early mercantilist program. In all of the societies mentioned, the ruler exploited new economic forces for political purposes, or encouraged them as a way of augmenting his treasury.

The growth of the ruler's interest in fostering and milking profitable enterprises progressed symbiotically with his innovations in public administration. These included: a perceptible broadening of the pool from which bureaucratic talent was recruited; a reorientation of the loyalties of hereditary bureaucrats away from the feudal tie between lord and retainer toward a statist tie between the monarch and the servants of the state; and the utilization of the king's courts to enforce laws more uniformly to his advantage. Broadening the base of recruitment allowed those of mercantile and non-noble origins an opportunity for the first time to participate in implementing and even formulating policy. In particular, as financial management grew more complex, merchants serving as tax farmers, treasury officials, and royal moneylenders helped to expedite the flow of revenues to the center. In this capacity they came to occupy positions which had previously been restricted to hereditary elites or vassal families of the prince. In Sung China, for example, merchants came to mingle freely in the elite circles of the imperial family and the bureaucracy.[8] In France, the notorious Jacques Coeur, *argentier* to Charles VII (1403–1461), demonstrated how high a commoner of sharp financial instincts could rise in the king's government.[9] They also provided the king with a political counterweight to the traditional agrarian and feudal aristocracies which limited his freedom of action. In Japan, as in China and Europe, the newly enfranchised individuals often owed the security of their commercial operations to official protection, and that mutuality of dependence resulted in a relatively stable alliance between merchant and monarch.

Whereas the newly risen mercantile elements were a useful addition to the autocrat's government, still during this period the hereditary bureaucratic families who originally received their offices as *beneficia* were more fundamental to his regime than the newcomers. They were his reliable nucleus of trained literate personnel who staffed most government offices, and who were prime movers in the political transition from feudal suzerainty to modern sovereignty.[10] Marc Bloch saw the origins of modern bureaucracy in the ruler's co-optation of low-ranking knightly families who traded the sword for the pen and the government office.[11] Low-ranking samurai families evolved into Bakufu bureaucrats of proven loyalty to the Ashikaga shoguns in just this way. Perhaps more than any other feature, it was the attempt to replace divided or multiple loyalties with a sense of exclusive allegiance to the shogun and his government which distinguished the hereditary bureaucrat of the Muromachi Bakufu and other early autocratic states from their feudal agrarian predecessors.

To protect the untested political edifice which the monarchs of these societies had constructed, a military force was needed that was less autonomous and more dependent on the king personally than the traditional feudal band whose military function was more a matter of private right than public duty. The ruler therefore sought alternative types of military organization, designed not to eliminate the traditional knight but to supplement him at the center with a body of professional soldiers who could be counted upon to give the monarch and his regime uncompromised support. Mercenaries were one solution, but their very name suggests why they were unable to provide for a government's long-term security. A more satisfactory, though by no means ideal, solution was an army organized on the basis of both mercenary and aristocratic principles. Such professional armies were quite small in the beginning, rarely exceeding several thousand mounted men, but that was usually enough to tip the balance of military power in favor of the central government. It was a rare wartime situation to find all the traditional feudal barons in a country

arrayed unanimously against the central government, and therefore the core force could easily be augmented from among their
numbers, such as the shogun's use of *shugo-daimyō* armies to keep
their rivals under control. The foremost example of the new type
of army was the *compagnies d'ordonnance* in France, founded by
Charles VII in 1439 and staffed by nobles who served in the capacity not of vassals performing traditional military aid owed their
lord, but as paid regulars in the permanent service of the monarchy.[12] In Japan, the *hōkōshū* was an army of organized banners of
low- and middle-ranked samurai who received remuneration directly from the shogun's own estates, and who were specifically set
apart from other house vassals (*gokenin*) by the permanence of
their military function. In Sung China, a functional equivalent
took the form of central government measures taken against "war-
lordism" by severely dividing and circumscribing the military.[13]
The term itself denoted private appropriation of the right to wage
war, and the Sung tried to redress this historic imbalance between
private violence and the government's espoused right to monopolize legitimate coercion. For a long time, though, these new pocket
armies of the king continued to be augmented by both mercenary
foot soldiers (in Japan called *ashigaru*) and traditional feudal levies,
until changes in the art of warfare rendered the latter obsolete.

SHOGUN, BAKUFU, AND SHUGO: THE SHIFTING BALANCE

This book has traced the evolution of the Muromachi shogun from
a feudal ruler, whose authority was founded on ties of obligation
and reward between lord and vassal, to an autocratic urban prince,
whose authority became increasingly detached from feudal re-
straints—and feudal supports. The Ashikaga shogun's transformation most graphically symbolized in Japan the creative instability
which was also the hallmark of such early autocracies as the Valois
in France and the York-Lancaster in England. It was especially
difficult for those dynasties to exalt their kingly office and change
its traditional content, because there were as yet no doctrines to
explain or justify the enormous increase in the prince's power over

his aristocratic grandees. Yet in all three countries, apologists tried: Commynes in France and Fortescue in England were not unlike Yoshimitsu's apologist Imagawa Ryōshun in several important respects. They all were men of affairs; their comments on government were the "garnered observations and reflections" of those who knew politics and had a practical interest in daily administration; and they all viewed effective government as an end in itself.[14] Dynasties like the Ashikaga were often forced to become their own apologists or lose their legitimacy. In England, the absence of an adequate ideology of autocratic kingship was evident when subjects addressed Edward IV as "Your Grace," an honorific that he had to share with dukes and archbishops. Not until the Tudor monarchs did the king become exclusively "Your Majesty."[15] In this context, the Ashikaga shoguns' campaign to get themselves entitled "King of Japan" and "Chancellor" (*daijōdaijin*) becomes more comprehensible as part of their program to upgrade the uniqueness of their position.

On the subject of self-strengthening mechanisms used by the Ashikaga, because the shogun had been little more than a figurehead for much of the Kamakura period,[16] Takauji's plan to restore the office to its pre-Hōjō stature was his way of strengthening it. Even though Tadayoshi's attempt to enlarge the bureaucracy's influence was in the short run reminiscent of the Hōjō regents using their bureaucracy to isolate the shogunal office from real power, shogun and bureaucracy were joined in a common enterprise during Yoshiakira's reign which led to the first flowering of a shogunal monarchy under Yoshimitsu.

The Japanese feudal ideal of a shogun relying on his shugo for collective support and advice was revised twice during the Muromachi period: first, when the *kanrei* was established to preside over the daimyo in Kyoto and implement shogunal commands; and second, when the *kanrei* was temporarily by-passed and the shogun asserted his personal control over the Bakufu bureaucracy, thereby elevating its status within the government relative to the *kanrei-shugo* cabinet structure. Whereas Yoshinori had the most success in circumventing the *kanrei* and the collective decision-making power of the shugo, even Yoshimasa did so with some effect in the decade before the Ōnin War. These two revisions in the structure of power roughly correspond to the two dimensions of political centralization specified at the beginning of this chapter: broadening the central government's authority at the expense of provincial autonomy by means of collective bodies that draw the barons out of the countryside and into the capital city; and strengthening the position of low-ranking officials over the magnates within the government itself.

The administration of justice became the monarch's trump card in his struggle with the great feudatories. In France, Beaumanoir's dictum that "all lay jurisdiction is held as a fief of the king" was realized in the Crown's dual prerogative to hear suits concerning any "breaking of the peace" and to hear appeals.[17] This was not unlike the Bakufu's privilege of adjudicating property and civil suits, and the tendency for shogun and *bugyōnin* to overrule the "overmighty" *shugo-daimyō* as a consequence of the direct petition procedure established by Yoshinori in the *gozen rakkyo* system. The great thirteenth-century vassals who had been the king's "natural" advisors in both England and France resented their exclusion when those kings began to rely on less exalted deputies. The new officials were chosen for their training and expertise in managing finance or domestic intelligence and, above all, for their skill in managing men.[18] In the France of Philip IV (r. 1285–1314), men trained in the law were employed as ministers and officials. Some, such as Guillaume Nogaret, were of nonnoble birth, while others were noble, and many were clerics.[19] In the England of Edward IV (r. 1461–1470; 1471–1483), a commoner like John Elrington was clerk of the household in the chancery, constable of Windsor Castle, and treasurer of war for the French campaign of 1475 before he was ever knighted.[20] The Ashikaga shogun's employment of Buddhist priests as officials and advisors, and of moneylenders as financial agents, parallels the European developments. Another similarity was that the Muromachi *bugyōnin* and the French and English councilors were all able to survive sudden changes of regime. In Japan, magistrates from the Hōjō government formed part of the original corps of the Ashikaga Bakufu's bureaucracy, and after the fall of the Ashikaga some *bugyōnin* ended up by serving Oda Nobunaga in their original professional capacities. In England, twenty members of the council of Richard III (r. 1483-1485) survived the upheaval after Bosworth and continued to serve the Tudor successor, Henry VII (r. 1485-1509).[21]

Even as kings wished to stabilize their own administrations in order to assure their successors of royal authority, conversely, they pursued policies which were intended to weaken the provincial power of their magnates. In Japan, Yoshinori encouraged retainers to reject the bond of fealty that kept them loyal to their shugo overlords and amenable to clan discipline. We have examined how the shogun negotiated and conspired with them to upset the stability of *shugo-daimyō* domains. In France, Louis XI (r. 1461-1483) behaved in a similar manner when confronted by over-mighty lords like Charles the Bold of Burgundy. He feared Charles, so he fomented a revolt at the duke's city of Liége and also shattered a league called the Allied Nobles of the Public Weal which had led an insurrection against him.[22]

Almost as much of an obstacle as the nobility to the growth of the new monarchies was an articulated peasantry. Like the Bakufu and Crown governments themselves, the independent farmers also reflected an increasing political sophistication and a heightened awareness of political alternatives. The upshot was that every single Ashikaga shogun whom we have examined was plagued by at least one major rebellion, either shugo or peasant inspired.[23] The debtors' revolts and other uprisings (*ikki*) in Japan shared many common characteristics with agrarian risings in Western Europe during the period under consideration. All of them represented a new consciousness of social differences and originated mainly in the more prosperous agricultural areas. Their leaders were well-off and, by the nature of their socioeconomic position, were more likely to chafe under perceived inequities than were poorer elements in the peasantry. They often represented an anti-clerical sentiment. Most of the larger upheavals were associated with a great urban center, such as in Flanders, the Jacquerie around Paris, the Peasants' Revolt which centered on London, and the many debtors' revolts in Japan's Home Provinces centering on Kyoto. This configuration almost always assured the peasants of urban allies in their revolts.[24] It is also likely that the proximity of those peasants to the great metropolitan centers meant that they were the most strongly influenced by the ideas and realities found only in the larger cities.

One further aspect of the problem of establishing strong monarchies in the face of still vigorous feudal elites hinged on smooth succession in the ruling dynasty. When so much depended on leaving an adult heir to inherit royal authority, the tide of autocracy could always be stemmed by murdering its chief exponent, the monarch himself, before a successor was ready to assume the responsibility of office. Yoshinori's death postponed the growth of absolutism in Japan for almost a century because of this, while an unusually long uninterrupted series of adult kings in the Valois line meant that the French monarchy never suffered from such a hiatus, and the English did not experience any such major setback until the end of the Tudors.

ECONOMIC POLICY, REVENUE, AND SHOGUNAL POWER

The key to exploiting the wealth of the capital region depended upon the creation of efficient procedures and reliable officials at the center. While the economic growth of this core region was perhaps more crucial in determining the Muromachi Bakufu's fate than that of either France or England, in all three countries the search for new sources of revenue became imperative to fortify the Crown and, in all three, this capital district became the pilot for the more comprehensive schemes of later periods.

Political centralization required revenue to pay for wars and royal extravagance. The traditional source was, of course, land, but the rising costs of government and more particularly the rising costs of war made it necessary to reduce dependence on land-owning as a financial base and switch to taxation.[25] Even in France, where income from the royal *domaine* was quite sizable, the king's "ordinary" expenses could no longer be met out of his ordinary income.[26] Nevertheless, while they experimented with other methods, governments continued to try to expand the Crown lands. The French monarchy was the most successful in acquiring estates, although even there land came under effective royal control very slowly. Purchase was one method the Valois used to add to their domains but, in areas like the wealthy towns of Lyons and Montpellier, they gained control by a process of attrition which eroded the jurisdiction of previous lords. The total effect of their acquisitions was that, by 1328, the royal domain was about three times the area of the great appanages and fiefs.[27] In England, Edward IV started a royal trend by his efforts to increase feudal revenues, and he appointed commissions of inquiry to investigate evasion of royal dues. Henry VII (r. 1485-1509) continued that policy and took advantage of infringements on his rights as another way of securing income. Landowners were fined heavily for what were often technical offenses, and in 1503 an office was created called "the surveyor of the King's prerogative." This official came to be known as master of the king's wards and was responsible for the management and sale of wardships. By the end of the fifteenth century, the legal procedures which had to be followed when an heir in the king's wardship came of age had become so complicated as to face him with considerable risks. Any slip—however technical—could result in the king's officials reseizing the land, thus forcing the tenant to begin proceedings all over again and lose his land income in the meantime.[28] The Muromachi shoguns tried to add to their *goryōsho*, but purchase on a scale like that practiced by the French monarchy was never undertaken, and the methods employed were closer in tone to those pursued by the English kings. Confiscated shugo lands often found their way into the shogunal domain in one form or another, and the voluntary commendation of lands to the shogun by those who joined the *hōkōshū* and other samurai also augmented the Ashikaga domain. Warriors gladly had their lands declared part of the *goryōsho* to spare them from *shugo-daimyō* extortion, and their taxes were thus co-opted by the Bakufu rather than passing through other rapacious hands first. Nevertheless, the total income from this source was inadequate to meet expenses, and, in Japan, as in Renaissance France and England, an important part of the government's revenue came from previously untapped sources.

It is clear that Yoshimitsu and his successors, like Louis XI and Edward IV, were alive to their "bourgeois allies."[29] Louis XI in particular displayed an acute concern for financial productivity and experimented with almost every possible form of economic *étatisme*. He fostered French fairs like the ones at Lyons. He backed a series of (admittedly unsuccessful) monopolistic ventures in state galleys based on the Languedoc ports and, after its acquisition in 1482, on Marseilles. In an area of economic policy closely linked to military policy, he set up small state arsenals and cannon foundries in various towns.[30] In England, the tax on raw wool exports, so popular in the fourteenth century, gave way in the fifteenth to the taxing of ever-rising cloth exports as one of the king's largest sources of revenue.[31] Edward IV was actually described by some as "a full-fledged wool merchant."[32] Although the Bakufu exacted its commercial revenues in a slightly different manner, the end result was the same. Rather than taxing exports per se, the shogun taxed the right to participate in an officially sanctioned trade by exacting a percentage of the total value of imports (which brought the traders a handsome profit in Japan). Rather than establishing government-run monopolies, he granted his permission to specific domestic manufacturers in a *za* patronage system. But, like the English and French kings, such methods gained for him and his Bakufu the greatest possible comparative advantage in acquiring revenue from the society's free-floating resources.[33]

The same drive that led them to expropriate commercial profits also motivated these governments to tap the wealth of the clergy. An early example of this was Philip IV, who triumphed over papal opposition in his dealings with the Church in France and taxed it heavily in twenty-four of the thirty years of his reign.[34] Since the *gozan* was a creation of the Muromachi Bakufu, shogunal exploitation of clerical wealth did not take the same form as in France and England, where it was a clear-cut adversary relationship. Nevertheless, the principle involved was the same, that of subjecting church-owned property to government taxation.

A paramount dogma of late medieval government had been that the king should "live of his own," that all of his income should come from the royal estates, the customs, and a few other minor items of revenue. He was entitled to demand direct taxation only for abnormal expenditures, such as for war.[35] While this distinction between ordinary revenue and "extraordinary" taxes remained, the fourteeth-century monarchs resorted to the latter with growing frequency. From about the middle of the century, taxes that the French were required to pay their king included direct hearth taxes (*fouages*) which resembled *munebechisen,* indirect taxes on commercial transactions (*aides*), and the salt tax (*gabelle*).[36] Like Japanese *tansen,* French "extraordinary" taxes were always treated as temporary levies, although in both countries they became a permanent feature of economic policy. Under Charles V (r. 1364–1380) *tailles* replaced *fouages,*[37] and those three tax categories then formed the financial basis not only of fifteenth-century French government, but of the *ancien régime* itself. The king originally levied the *taille* with retrospective assembly approval, but from 1451 he levied *taille* and *aide* on his sole authority. That gave the French government a source of revenue much greater than its contemporary English counterpart and played a role in accounting for the later emergence of absolute monarchy in France and a more limited monarchy in England.[38]

Of our three examples, the French government had by far the most highly developed revenue-collecting apparatus, but like the Bakufu it often depended on the practice of farming its revenue by selling the right to collect taxes to the highest bidder.[39] Also like the Muromachi system, the French financial administration did not preclude inequitable geographic distribution of the tax burden. On one occasion, therefore, Paris paid only 7 percent, while on another it paid 40 percent of the *taille* in its *généralité.*[40] The Home Provinces in Japan were perhaps more uniformly heavily taxed over time than the Ile de France, but that probably did not occur at times of disorder, such as during and immediately following the Ōnin War.

In all three countries, the reverse of the power to tax, the power to exempt from taxation, became an equally important weapon in the king's administrative arsenal, for "taxes made a king rich, but he could also buy loyalty and service by waiving his rights."[41] This was precisely how the Ashikaga obtained the unwavering support of the *gozan* and the approbation of aristocratic and monastic Kyoto proprietors, without which their influence in the capital would have been greatly lessened. The power to excuse payment, or to lessen its burden, was also used by the Bakufu to gain extra revenue from the conflict between debtors and creditors, as evidenced by the many decrees issued dealing with debt cancellations and prohibitions on such moratoria that required payment of fees before an individual could benefit from them. The most instructive example of the application of this prerogative by the shogun to gain loyal supporters is seen in the treatment of samurai who joined the *hōkōshū*, and in the privileges they were granted by shogunal fiat.

THE SHOGUNAL ARMY

In both England and France, the Hundred Years' War stimulated changes in the organization and recruitment of fighting men. On the English side the wars were fought by men who were retained in the service of the king, and thus the "indentured retainer" or contract soldier came into being. In 1475, Edward IV invaded France with such a force. Lords and captains of the armada contracted with the king to furnish so many troops at so much per head, and in peacetime they assumed the burden of maintaining those troops. At no cost to the Crown, the king under this arrangement had the nucleus of a permanent English army available when needed.[42] In Muromachi Japan the shogun assumed the burden of full support and maintenance of his *hōkōshū*, and unlike the English king he did his best to sever the ties these soldiers had with their former liege lords. By far the most radical change in military organization occurred in France, where the first sustained acceptance of an army of paid professionals appeared in the *ordonnance* of 1439. The *ordonnance* of 1445 elaborated on the idea; it established an army of fifteen cavalry companies, each composed of 100 lances. (A lance was a battle unit of six men.) In 1446 the system was expanded to 2,000 lances or 12,000 mounted men, and Louis XI raised this total to 2,636 lances (15,816 men) to form the *gens d'ordonnance*, "the first standing army in western Europe."[43] It is true that the companies of the Valois were larger than the Ashikaga *hōkōshū*, but they represented the same assertion of royal control by monarchs bent upon maximizing their authority by applying administrative technology. A professional army loyal to the central government became essential during the Hundred Years' War and the Ōnin War, when both countries experienced an increasing capacity to mobilize men in very large numbers without a corresponding rise in the ability to control the actions of those soldiers. Fifteenth-century Japan and Valois France both suffered as much from the destruction and pillage left in the wake of traveling armies as they did from the actual clash of those armies, and understandably the so-called "tyranny of armies" at this time was seen to be in their disorder as much as in their expense.[44]

For all their disadvantages, the new armies and restructured bureaucracies of the central governments made a strong impression on the provincial magnates and grandees, who widely imitated the Crown's distinctive institutions in their own domains. The Ōuchi in Japan are a prime example of such conscious modeling. In Valois France, the great holders of appanages deliberately copied in their territories the king's administrative machinery, and in England the great men likewise followed the pattern set by the royal government.[45] The rise of the "gentleman bureaucrat" provided estate owners with skilled professionals. Like the hereditary *bugyōnin* families of the Ashikaga and of the *shugo-daimyō*, in England particular families specialized in performing managerial tasks generation after generation for the same liege lords.[46]

THE ASHIKAGA LEGACY:
SUCCESS WITHIN FAILURE

The first Ashikaga shogun and his brother were fundamentally conservative in their political preferences. Takauji tried to reestablish a warrior government like that of the early Kamakura Bakufu, a system which countenanced little shogunal interference in local and familial affairs, but the eternal problem of too little land for too many claimants forced him to modify the model he emulated, and to resort to "temporary" expedients like *hanzei* which further destabilized land tenure and proprietors' security. His brother Tadayoshi had a different ideal in mind, the Hōjō regency which had declared its jurisdiction limited to samurai estates. Unfortunately, pressure from Bakufu vassals and allies, and from Takauji himself, rendered adherence to this self-imposed constraint equally unworkable.

Unable to apply a suitable model from the past, the Ashikaga were forced back on their own resources. The objective conditions presented by limited land acquisition opportunities on the one hand and a taxable commercial economy on the other led them to experiment with a metropolitan shogunal dictatorship. While it is true that the patterns of political authority that emerged in the Muromachi Bakufu had their origins in previous regimes, in the degree of power ideally and actually given the shoguns and in the means employed to protect and expand that power the Muromachi government was very new indeed.

In their attempt to mold a successful political synthesis, Ashikaga shogunal authority clearly reflected the Weberian distinction between "class" (ownership of property) and "status" (social honor or prestige) as determinants of political power.[47] Despite his lack of disposable lands, the shogun was able to convert his status role into a far more effective instrument than could have been assumed on the basis of his strength as a feudal chieftain. In order to accomplish this, the Ashikaga had to free themselves from the stigma of being a usurper regime, a factor which exerted a powerful influence on both foreign and domestic policy. They

FIGURE 7 Horseman Wearing Typical Costume
of Muromachi Rulers

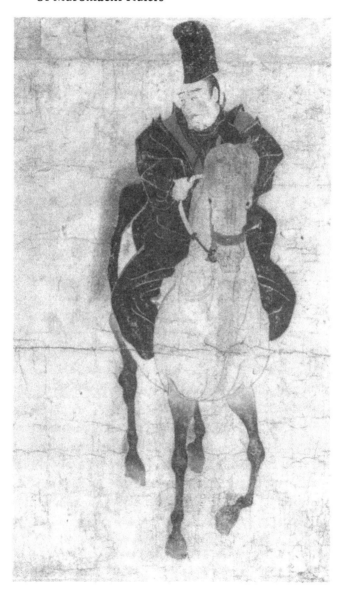

Painting, Japanese, Muromachi   *Courtesy of the Fogg Art Museum,*
Tosa School   *Harvard University*
Horseman in Black

were especially hard-pressed to establish their legitimacy in the face of the prolonged civil war that kept alive the cause of Go-Daigo's junior (Daikakuji) imperial line. This situation prevented the Bakufu from claiming its conformity with the traditional legitimate basis of warrior government—as protector of the imperial court—even after Takauji installed Emperor Kōmyō of the senior (Jimyō'in) line as his protégé and received from him the shogunal appointment. By the end of the fourteenth century, Yoshimitsu acquired the symbolically important three imperial regalia for the senior line and by doing so brought the ideal basis of legitimacy for Ashikaga rule into closer correspondence with actual power. The elimination of the Southern Court, seizure of the Kyoto imperial court's few remaining areas of autonomous jurisdiction, stabilization of shugo tenures, and economic policy designed to increase Bakufu revenue all greatly enhanced the shogun's authority.

More than any other shogun, Yoshinori centralized decision-making within the Bakufu. The type of change which he instituted was part of the coherent development that takes place when kings no longer govern within the restrictive confines of a strictly feudal-agrarian economic and social system, but when newer free-floating resources available to them are not yet sufficient to ensure the permanence of their autocratic reforms. *Shugo-daimyō* opposition to a strong shogunate forced the Ashikaga to depend on segments of Japanese society which were not strong enough by themselves to guarantee a stable government. Those segments included junior branches of shugo houses, independent *kokujin* proprietors, moneylenders and merchants, and the Zen institution. The lack of consistent support from the *shugo-daimyō* explained the alternating phases of expansion and contraction in shogunal authority, with the peaks occurring during Yoshimitsu's and Yoshinori's reigns. Yoshimasa's death marked the end of the Muromachi Bakufu's role as Japan's real central government, and the subsequent century saw the Ashikaga shoguns become the protégés of the Hosokawa and Ōuchi *shugo-daimyō*.

The Ashikaga legacy from the century and a half of real power, however, contributed in no small way to the country's political traditions as each shogun's performance was posthumously converted into a potential component of his successor's legitimate authority. The cumulative effect of such precedents was to make it impossible for the Tokugawa Bakufu to be a feudal regime, despite its rhetoric, but rather a mature capitalist-agrarian autocracy with feudal overlays. Yoshinori's assassination may be understood as more than a simple isolated act of murder, because of the broad chasm he opened between accepted views of legitimate shogunal authority up to his time and the tyrannical way in which he actually exercised the powers of the shogunate. His one-man rule capsized more of Japan's accepted patterns of exercising political authority than did any ruler until Nobunaga and Hideyoshi more than a century later, and the sheer size of the gap between the accepted ideal and the way he implemented it made a strong reaction unavoidable. Still, the very incongruence which the *shugo-daimyō* tried to lessen in the central government became their nemesis in their own provincial domains as well. Like the shogun, they too lacked adequate military power to enforce all of the decision-making authority which they claimed as legitimately theirs, and this became more obvious as their house discipline was undermined by shogunal manipulation of the *sōryō* appointment system. The gap between their ideal and actual authority encouraged disobedience and rebellion by the *kokujin,* their own *shugo-dai,* and other samurai proprietors. The parallel situation in both Kyoto and the provinces, the social flux and lack of military superiority by any one force, led directly to the war of all against all—in Europe the Hundred Years' War and in Japan the Ōnin War and the Sengoku age which followed.

Although the Ashikaga came to power possessing woefully inadequate land wealth, and without the overwhelming military superiority needed to enforce coercive sanctions against all political rivals, their metropolitan base in Kyoto greatly compensated for the regime's military and proprietary deficiencies, for it gave them control over Japan's most important political and economic throttle. Throughout the fifteenth century, Kyoto remained the financial cushion that allowed the Bakufu to undertake its administrative reforms, although it also engendered Ashikaga delusions of grandeur. Control over a major source of easy revenue, the city's commerce, destined the Bakufu to be the vehicle for integrating economic policy and civil suit procedure under the shogun's personal supervision. The expansion of shogunal power at the expense of the collective demands of the *kanrei* and shugo cabinet fostered an ideal of shogunal authority which no fifteenth-century daimyo, not even the Ashikaga, had the real strength to sustain. One is tempted to conclude that the Ashikaga enacted the changes that they did because they had little choice but to experiment, given the fragile, hybrid foundation of their political edifice. In a different sense, though, the very flux of Muromachi society gave them more options than any of Japan's other premodern governments, because stasis was not—could not be—their objective. Survival, and once that was assured, expansion, were the imperatives of the Ashikaga. Only the mature capitalist-agrarian autocracies of the seventeenth and eighteenth centuries, in which actual authority had been brought into closer correspondence with the new autocratic ideal, could afford to make stability one of their primary goals. Indeed, unlike the capacity for adaptation of early autocracies like the Muromachi Bakufu and the Valois monarchy, in mature autocracies like that of the Tokugawa Bakufu and the Bourbon kings, a rigidly enforced stability became the categorical imperative of good government. The successors of the Ashikaga in Japan learned many lessons from their predecessors, but not necessarily the best ones and not necessarily the ones that would have contributed to political experimentation and national enlightenment.

A Concluding Note
on Feudalism and Decentralization

There are those who may feel that this book presents a controversial thesis and then compounds that controversiality by comparing Muromachi Japan to European Renaissance states. The thesis, which asserts that Japan began to turn away from feudalism in the course of what I call the Muromachi synthesis, does place the breakup of a pure feudal system a full century or two earlier than traditional interpretations have placed it. Ideas are, like habits, not easily changed, but I suspect that much of the lingering doubt which may exist about accepting the Muromachi synthesis as a situation similar to European Renaissance monarchy derives from two sources. The first of these is the traditional, yet ironically quite radical, interpretation which maintains that Japan modernized rapidly and threw off its "feudal" yoke very late in its history. Possible transition points cited include the early or mid-nineteenth century, the eighteenth century, and the turn of the seventeenth century, but all of these turning points or great divides are based on one firm assumption: that Japan developed more rapidly than most other nations and, in any event, is somehow "different" from the West. In this assertion, such theories argue back from the present to hypothetical points of departure for the country's modernization, and these points of origin are often also equated with the beginning of political centralization. Related to this is another idea, that Japan actually may have "refeudalized" itself in the course of the sixteenth and seventeenth centuries, reviving a system of political and military power that died an earlier, presumably more natural, death in the West. The bias for many of these interpretations derives from the perspective that both Western and Japanese scholars have adopted over the last century, each for different reasons. That view accepts Japanese backwardness as a given and is therefore compelled to emphasize the radical and rapid nature of patterns of modernization in Japan during the nineteenth and twentieth centuries in order to explain that country's present parity with the West.

There is a second source for the reluctance of many to accept a comparison between the Muromachi Bakufu and French and English Renaissance monarchy. There seems to be far more willingness to separate the issue of governmental decentralization from that of feudalism in general in the European case than in the Japanese instance. In the vocabulary of historians, the Valois and York-Lancaster need not be described as primarily feudal despite the patently decentralized nature of political authority in both kingdoms. Yet any evidence of decentralization for the Ashikaga shoguns is automatically equated with feudalism. There seems to be a cultural polarity at work here, and Japanese historians are as prone to using it as their Western colleagues. Admittedly, if the French kings of the fifteenth century are at the most developed end of a continuum designating the early monarchies, then the Ashikaga would be at the extreme other end, with the English kings lying somewhere between the two. This book makes no assertion that the Ashikaga's real power in any way approached that of the French monarchy, but then neither did the power of any other European monarchy come close to the French for at least a century. As the preceding chapter has shown, the Ashikaga can quite easily, and without verbal gymnastics, be compared to the Europeans and therefore should be placed on the same continuum used to compare certain facets of European institutional development.

The interpretation in this book, while unconventional, is actually a more conservative and believable view of Japanese development than many of those which have preceded it, since it posits an earlier and more gradual evolution away from feudalism in Japan. The implications of the Muromachi synthesis are powerful, since they point toward acceptance of Japan as being less retarded, and henceforth less telescoped in its development, than hitherto thought possible. Feudal institutions, to the extent that they exist in Muromachi Japan, can be acknowledged in the same way that they are recognized in the European cases, without conveying the image of backwardness or the status of latecomer that traditional scholarship has laid on Japan.

The question of centralization is to some degree itself a misleading issue. A monarchy can exist in a non-feudal context without necessarily centralizing all government functions. Indeed, such semi-centralization was the norm throughout Europe until the eighteenth century, when the most successful modernizer and centralizer, France, was still unquestionably the exception rather than the rule. Even a superficial examination of the Tokugawa Bakufu will reveal political and economic resources of a type and magnitude that would have been the envy of most of its contemporary European monarchies.

There is no question that Japan remains unique in many facets of its history and institutional development, and the Muromachi synthesis in no way detracts from that singularity. But the evidence also makes it amply apparent that the feudal model no longer adequately explains what occurred there during the fourteenth and fifteenth centuries. The Japanese were neither so feudal nor so backward then as conventional wisdom once thought. The implications of Japan's Renaissance for modern Japan are also important. The split personality caused by a radical shift from the violent, yet unrepressive, fifteenth century to a peaceful, but repressive, seventeenth century may indeed be as important a determinant of Japanese culture as the dualism represented by the chrysanthemum and the sword. Every historical era contributes something to our deeper understanding of the present, and the Muromachi age does this with the liberality and flamboyance befitting a Renaissance.

Appendixes

Notes

Bibliography

Glossary

Index

Appendix A
ASHIKAGA SHOGUNS

Order	Name	Birth	Became Shogun	Resigned	Death
1	Takauji	1308	1338	1358	1358
2	Yoshiakira	1330	1358	1367	1367
3	Yoshimitsu	1358	1368	1394	1408
4	Yoshimochi	1386	1394	1423	1428
5	Yoshikazu	1407	1423	1425	1425
6	Yoshinori	1394	1429	1441	1441
7	Yoshikatsu	1434	1442	1443	1443
8	Yoshimasa	1436	1449	1473	1490
9	Yoshihisa	1465	1473	1489	1489
10	Yoshitane	1466	1490	1521	1523
11	Yoshizumi	1480	1494	1508	1511
12	Yoshiharu	1511	1521	1546	1550
13	Yoshiteru	1536	1546	1565	1565
14	Yoshihide	1540	1568	1568	1568
15	Yoshiaki	1537	1568	1573	1597

Appendix B: ORGANIZATION CHART OF THE MUROMACHI BAKUFU

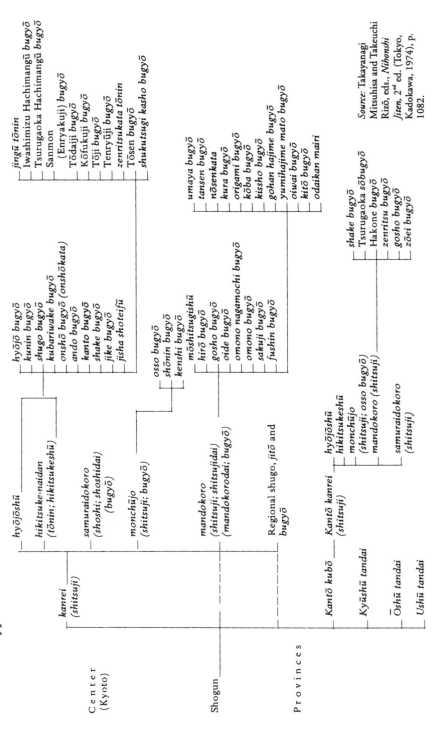

Source: Takayanagi Mitsuhisa and Takeuchi Rizō, eds., *Nihonshi Jiten*, 2nd ed. (Tokyo, Kadokawa, 1974), p. 1082.

Appendix C: THE ASHIKAGA FAMILY AND COLLATERAL HOUSES

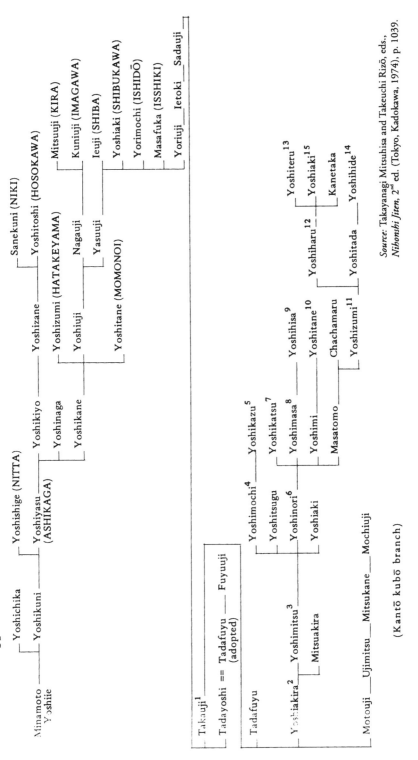

Source: Takayanagi Mitsuhisa and Takeuchi Rizō, eds., *Nihonshi Jiten,* 2nd ed. (Tokyo, Kadokawa, 1974), p. 1039.

Appendix D
SHUGO PROVINCIAL DOMAINS

The following table identifies provinces where the office of shugo was held on a hereditary or quasi-hereditary basis by certain families. The dates indicate the general period during which the families that are named held that office. The dates are only approximate. In certain cases unnamed families occupied the office of shugo for brief periods within the span of years noted, and in others, the families named continued to serve as shugo beyond the final date indicated. For these reasons, the table should be used only as a general guide to a very complex subject.

Province	Shugo	Years in Office
Yamashiro[a]		
Yamato	Kōfukuji	
Kawachi	Hatakeyama	1382–1562
Izumi	Hosokawa	1408–1554
Settsu	Hosokawa	1374–1522
Owari	Shiba	1400–1537
Tōtōmi	Imagawa/Shiba	
Suruga	Imagawa	1337–1560
Kai	Takeda	1336–1573
Izu	Uesugi	1364–1439
Sagami	Miura/Uesugi	
Musashi	Uesugi	1368–1466
Shimōsa	Chiba	1341–1447
Hitachi	Satake	1335–1425
Ōmi	Rokkaku/Kyōgoku	
Mino	Toki	1339–1542
Hida	Kyōgoku	1359–1508
Shinano	Ogasawara	1418–1515

Province	Shugo	Years in Office
Kōzuke	Uesugi	1336–1418
Mutsu	Date	1552–?
Dewa	(no shugo)	
Wakasa	Isshiki/Takeda	1336–1440/
		1441–1551
Echizen	Shiba/Asakura	1381–1471/
		1471–1571
Kaga	Togashi	1336–1505
		(with some in-
		terruptions)
Noto	Hatakeyama	1391–1573
Etchū	Hatakeyama	1380–1487
Echigo	Uesugi	1362–1550
Sado	(unknown)	
Tamba	Hosokawa	1392–1545
Tango	Isshiki	1392–1517
Tajima	Yamana	1372–1536
Inaba	Yamana	1363–1547
Hōki	Yamana	1337–1502
Izumo	Kyōgoku	1392–1508
Iwami	Yamana/Ōuchi	
Oki	Kyōgoku	1392–1508
Harima	Akamatsu/Yamana	1336–1550/
		1441–1467
Mimasaka	Yamana/Akamatsu	
Bizen	Akamatsu/Yamana	1336–1521/
		1441–1467
Bitchū	Hosokawa	1392–1518
Bingo	Yamana/Hosokawa	1379–1497/
		1390–1400
Aki	Yamana/Takeda/Ōuchi	
Suō	Ōuchi	1336–1551
Nagato	Ōuchi	1358–1551
Kii	Hatakeyama	1400–1515
Awaji	Hosokawa	
Awa	Hosokawa	1337–1514
Sanuki	Hosokawa	1337–1511
Iyo	Kawano	1394–1550
Tosa	Hosokawa	1337–1473
Chikuzen	Shoni/Ōuchi	1336–1408/
		1441–1451

Province	Shugo	Years in Office
Chikugo	Ōtomo	1399–1516
Buzen	Ōuchi/Ōtomo	
Bungo	Ōtomo	1336–1550
Hizen	Imagawa/Shibukawa/Shoni	
Higo	Imagawa/Kikuchi	1380–1399/
		1410–1513
Hyūga	Shimazu	1391–1566
Ōsumi	Shimazu	1336–1566
Satsuma	Shimazu	1336–1566
Tsushima	Sō	1378–1560

Source: Takayanagi Mitsuhisa and Takeuchi Rizō, eds., *Nihonshi Jiten,* 2nd ed. (Tokyo, Kadokawa, 1974), pp. 1103–1118.

Note: [a]The *samuraidokoro shoshi* usually served ex officio as shugo of Yamashiro.

Abbreviations Used in the Notes

CHS I   *Chūsei hōsei shiryōshū 1—Kamakura bakufu hō,* eds., Satō Shin'ichi and Ikeuchi Yoshisuke (Tokyo, Iwanami Shoten, 1970).

CHS II   *Chūsei hōsei shiryōshū 2—Muromachi bakufu hō,* eds., Satō Shin'ichi and Ikeuchi Yoshisuke (Tokyo, Iwanami Shoten, 1969).

CHS III   *Chūsei hōsei shiryōshū 3—buke kahō 1,* eds., Satō Shin'ichi, Ikeuchi Yoshisuke, and Momose Kesao (Tokyo, Iwanami Shoten, 1969).

DNS   *Dai Nihon shiryō*

"Tsuikahō"   "Muromachi bakufu tsuikahō"

Notes

1. THE MUROMACHI PERIOD IN JAPANESE HISTORY

1. When feudalism is referred to in this book, I have in mind a general sociopolitical system that possesses the following characteristics:

   (1) The ruling class consists of warriors of differing ranks who are held together in groups by means of comprehensive, personal bonds of loyalty and mutual service between the superiors and subordinates (i.e., lords and vassals) among them.

   (2) Political authority is treated as a private possession by these warriors, and the ruler's political authority is reduced to the likelihood that vassals will voluntarily adhere to their oaths of fealty.

   (3) The society's goods and services, especially land ownership and control, are distributed primarily on the basis of rank distinctions between these warriors in the political power hierarchy. Personal vassalage is rewarded by enfoeffment, that is, land or the rights to its income is the reward for political and military subordinated service.

   (4) These private tenures of land in turn condition the exercise of public rights and duties.

   This working definition has been influenced by the views of Coulborn and Strayer, Weber, Asakawa, and Levy, which are summarized in John W. Hall, "Feudalism in Japan—A Reassessment," in John W. Hall and Marius B. Jansen, eds., *Studies in the Institutional History of Early Modern Japan* (Princeton, 1968), pp. 15-51.

2. The above discussion was abstracted from the works of the authors mentioned which are cited in the Bibliography at the end of this book, and from Tōyama Shigeki & Satō Shin'ichi, eds., *Nihonshi kenkyū nyūmon* vol. 1 (Tokyo, Tōkyō Daigaku Shuppankai, 1954) and vol. 2 (1962), and Inoue Mitsusada & Nagahara Keiji, eds., *Nihonshi kenkyū nyūmon* vol. 3 (Tokyo, Tōkyō Daigaku Shuppankai, 1969).

2. THE ASHIKAGA SHOGUN IN MUROMACHI JAPAN

1. Jacob Burckhardt, *The Civilization of the Renaissance in Italy,* vol. 1 (New York, 1958), p. 107.
2. *Kemmu shikimoku* (Kemmu Formulary) in *CHS II,* p. 3.
3. Capitalist agriculture and its role in the development of the world colonial economy in the sixteenth century is treated in great detail in Immanuel Wallerstein, *The Modern World-System* (New York, Academic Press, 1974).
4. Whereas one local market in 1438 offered only 600 *mon* per *koku* of rice, the Kyoto rice market was buying it for 1 *kan* 429 *mon* per *koku.* Sasaki Gin'ya, *Shōen no shōgyō* (Tokyo, 1964), pp. 230–231.
5. Ishii Susumi, *Kamakura bakufu* (Tokyo, 1971), pp. 398–399.
6. Satō Shin'ichi, *CHS II,* pp. 3–4.
7. The high incidence of continuity in Bakufu personnel and organization from late Kamakura to early Ashikaga is decribed in Satō Shin'ichi, "Muromachi bakufu kaisōki no kansei taikei," *Chūsei no hō to kokka* (Tokyo, 1971), pp. 485, 487–488.
8. Reliable figures are notoriously absent for this period, but one authority estimated that, from c. 930 to the beginning of the fourteenth century, the total area under cultivation grew from about 862,000 *chō* to about 946,000 *chō.* If that is true, then whatever increase there was in agricultural production came not so much from expanding the area under cultivation as from technological improvement, specifically the intensive use of fertilizer and multiple cropping. Since the first mention of double-cropping in Japan dates from 1264, it is likely that the benefits of these innovations in terms of surplus production began to be enjoyed only in the second half of the thirteenth century. See Furushima Toshio, *Nihon nōgyō shi* (Tokyo, 1956), pp. 102–103, 107.
9. Yoshiakira was conferred the rank of *sadaijin jūichii,* but posthumously. He died on 1367/12th month/7 and received the title on the 30th. *Gukanki* in *DNS* 6, vol. 28, pp. 710–711.
10. Yoshimitsu's accession to this rank is recorded in the *Kugyō bunin,* in *DNS* 7, vol. 1 (1394/12th month/25), p. 764.
11. Go-Daigo's Kemmu Restoration of 1333–1335 was an attempt to use the military power of the samurai clans to reestablish the political supremacy of the imperial house. The fatal flaw in this plan was its ultimate reliance on the support of those very military families whose power it intended to supplant. George Sansom, *A History of Japan 1334–1615* (Stanford, 1961), describes in some detail the restoration and its immediate aftermath, as does H. Paul Varley, *Imperial Restoration in Medieval Japan* (New York, Columbia University Press, 1971).

12. James Murdoch, *A History of Japan*, vol. 1 (London, 1925), p. 580.
13. Kō no Moronao was Takauji's steward (*shitsuji*) and Kō no Moroyasu was head of the Board of Retainers (*samuraidokoro shoshi*).
14. Satō Shin'ichi, *CHS II*, p. 409.
15. *Kemmu shikimoku*, art. 7, 1336/11th month/7, Ibid., p. 5.
16. "Tsuikahō," art. 2, 1338/2nd 7th month/29, *CHS II*, pp. 11–12.
17. Satō Shin'ichi, *Chūsei no hō to kokka*, p. 482.
18. Satō Shin'ichi, *Nambokuchō no dōran* (Tokyo, 1971), pp. 208–211.
19. Uwayokote Masataka, "Jōkyū no ran," *Nihon rekishi 5 chūsei 1* (Tokyo, Iwanami Shoten, 1962), pp. 177–178, and Uwayokote Masataka, *Hōjō Yasutoki* (Tokyo, 1958), pp. 51, 54–55.
20. *Shitsuji bunin shidai*, in *DNS* 6, vol. 24, pp. 346–348.
21. Satō Shin'ichi, *Nambokuchō*, pp. 327–328.
22. Ibid., pp. 328–329. The decrees referred to are "Tsuikahō," art. 78, 1355/8th month/22, and art. 79, 1357/9th month/10, *CHS II*, pp. 37–38.
23. Satō Shin'ichi, *Nambokuchō*, pp. 343–344.
24. Ibid., pp. 345–349.
25. "Tsuikahō," arts. 89–90, 1367/12th month/29, *CHS II*, p. 41.
26. Ogawa Makoto, *Hosokawa Yoriyuki* (Tokyo, 1972), p. 109. Yoshimitsu became *jushiinoge*, then *sangiken sachūjō* in 1373, *jusanmi* in 1375, and in 1378 rose quickly from *gon dainagon* in the third month to *ukonoenodaishō* in the eighth month and *jūnii* in the twelfth.
27. Ibid., p. 119.
28. "Tsuikahō," arts. 96–97, 1368/6th month/17, *CHS II*, pp. 42–43.
29. *Kaei sandaiki*, 1370/10th month/2, in *DNS* 6, vol. 32, p. 305.
30. *Kaei sandaiki*, 1379/2nd 4th month/14, in *Shinkō gunshoruijū* vol. 20, p. 209. Biographical information about Yoshimitsu may be found in Usui Nobuyoshi, *Ashikaga Yoshimitsu* (Tokyo, 1960).
31. Sugimoto Hisao, *Kikuchishi sandai* (Tokyo, 1966).
32. Yoshimitsu's pilgrimage to the Miyajima shrine is recorded in detail in *Rokuon'in dono Itsukushima mōdeki*, in *Shinkō gunshoruijū* vol. 15, pp. 111–116.
33. Even in the Tokugawa Bakufu it was not until 1635 that the *sankin kōtai* system became part of written law under the third shogun, Iemitsu. Tsuji Tatsuya, *Edo kaifu* (Tokyo, Chūō Kōronsha, 1971), p. 314. See also Toshio G. Tsukahira, *Feudal Control in Tokugawa Japan: The Sankin Kōtai System* (Cambridge, Mass., Harvard University Press, 1966), p. 36 and passim.
34. Yoshihiro's role in these two important events is described fully in Matsuoka Hisato, *Ōuchi Yoshihiro* (Tokyo, 1966), pp. 122–145.
35. Ibid., pp. 151–152. Two other possible explanations have been offered to

account for Imagawa Ryōshun's dismissal. Yoshihiro may have been trying to form a league with the Ōtomo of Kyushu and Imagawa in order to check Yoshimitsu's growing power, but Ryōshun out of loyalty to the shogun rejected the offer. Yoshihiro slandered Ryōshun in retaliation and informed Yoshimitsu that he was plotting against the Bakufu, when Yoshihiro himself was the real conspirator. Alternatively, the new *kanrei*, Shiba Yoshimasa (his second time in that office), may have wanted to make a member of his ally, the Shibukawa family, the new Kyushu *tandai*. These two possible interpretations were offered by Satō Shin'ichi, *Nambokuchō*, p. 456.

36. A pertinent example of Imagawa's views about shogunal supremacy and his own place in the structure of government is the key sentence, "Wareware koto wa shōgun no onmi o wakerarete kudasare mōshisōrō no aida, tarebito mo iyashimare sōrawaji to zonjisōrō,"—"Since I have been made a division of the shogun's body, I will be disgraced by no one." "Imagawa Ryōshun shojo an," in *Nejime monjo*, Kawazoe Shōji, ed., 3.519: 5–6.

    Imagawa's political thought is analyzed in Kawazoe Shōji, "Muromachi bakufu seiritsuki ni okeru seiji shisō—Imagawa Ryōshun no baai," *Shigaku zasshi* 68.12:37–66; a translation of one of Ryōshun's political writings, which took the form of a series of moral instructions, is found in Carl Steenstrup, "The Imagawa Letter," *Monumenta Nipponica* 28.3: 295–316 (1973). See also Kawazoe Shōji, *Imagawa Ryōshun* (Tokyo, 1969), for biographical material on Ryōshun's life.

37. A contemporary observer, the Cloistered Emperor Go-Komatsu, commented to the effect that "governing is being carried on as before without any change" (oyoso seido ika no koto kaku no gotoki no aida sata mōsubeshi) emphasizing the continuing of shogunal power after Yoshimitsu became a monk. *Aragoyomi*, 1395/6th month/20, in *DNS* 7, vol. 2, p. 58.

38. Satō Shin'ichi, *Nambokuchō*, pp. 463–464.

39. Matsuoka Hisato, *Ōuchi Yoshihiro*, pp. 179–184.

40. The loyalist ideology enunciated by Kitabatake is analyzed in Ishii Shirō, "Chūsei no tennōsei ni kansuru oboegaki—gukanshō to jinnō shōtōki o tegakari to shite," in *Nihon kokuseishi kenkyū* 1 (Tokyo, 1966), pp. 233–276.

41. Tanaka Takeo, *Wakō to kangō bōeki* (Tokyo, 1961), p. 51.

42. *Sappan kyūki*, 1402/8th month/16, in *DNS* 7, vol. 5, p. 634.

43. The title and its significance in the development of the idea of the shogun as feudal monarch is discussed in Itō Tasaburō, "Shōgun, Nihon kokuō to shōsu—sono shiteki igi," *Nihon rekishi* 60:2–6 (May 1953).

44. *Yoshida ke hinamiki*, 1403/2nd month/19, in *DNS* 7, vol. 6, pp. 47–48.

45. *Kana nendaiki,* in ibid., 1403/8th month/3, p. 270.

46. *Kanenobu kōki,* in ibid., 1404/5th month/16, p. 700. Thirty years later, on the occasion of the reopening of the *kangō bōeki* tally trade by the shogun Yoshinori, Sambōin Mansai recalled the earlier visit by a Ming ambassador to the capital. See *Mansai jungo nikki* in *Zoku gunshoruijū,* vol. 870, part 2, 1434/5th month/28.

47. Ryusaku Tsunoda and L. Carrington Goodrich, eds., *Japan in the Chinese Dynastic Histories* (South Pasadena, P. D. & Ione Perkins, 1951), p. 114.

48. Okuno Takahiro, "Muromachi jidai ni okeru dosō no kenkyū," *Shigaku zasshi* 44.8:45 (1933).

49. "Tsuikahō," arts. 146–150, 1393/11th month/26, *CHS II,* pp. 59–60. The first instance of Bakufu involvement with the *sakaya* actually dates back to 1347, when a collection was made for building the new Hiyoshi shrine, but at that time not only did the Bakufu share such taxing authority with the imperial court, but even the order itself was issued by the emperor. See Kuwayama Kōnen, "Muromachi bakufu keizai kikō no ichi kōsatsu–nōsenkata kubo okura no kinō to seiritsu," *Shigaku zasshi* 73.9:10 (September 1964).

50. Ono Terutsugu, "Muromachi bakufu no sakaya tōsei," *Shigaku zasshi* 43.7:32–33 (July 1932).

51. There is some dispute among Japanese scholars as to which currencies were being imported from China at this time. Kobata Atsushi takes issue with Okuno Takahiro and others who maintain that Ming copper coins of Eiraku (Yung-lo), Kōbu (Hung-wu), and Sentoku (Hsüan-te) mintings were in plentiful supply in Japan. Instead he asserts that earlier currencies less desirable to the Chinese of the period made up the bulk of specie imports into Japan via the tally trade. See Kobata Atsushi, *Nihon kahei ryūtsū shi* (Tokyo, 1930 & 1943), pp. 532–535 and passim.

The precedent for a shogun requesting copper cash from the Chinese dates back at least to 1261, when the regent Hōjō Tokimune did so (in the shogun's name). Delmer Brown, *Money Economy in Medieval Japan: A Study in the Use of Coins* (New Haven, 1951), p. 11.

52. Hayashiya Tatsusaburō, in *Chūsei bunka no kichō* (Tokyo, 1953), pp. 187–250, and in *Machishū* (Tokyo, 1964), describes the townsmen as a distinctive new social grouping pivotal in the development of medieval Kyoto.

53. This relationship between warrior society and the so-called Kitayama culture of Yoshimitsu's court is discussed by Kawai Masaharu, *Chūsei buke shakai no kenkyū* (Tokyo, 1973), Ch. 5, especially pp. 227–232.

54. Jacob Raz, "The Actor and His Audience: Zeami's Views on the Audience of the Noh," *Monumenta Nipponica* 31.3:272 (Autumn 1976), writes:

The samurai class of the Edo period destroyed the concept of aesthetic democracy and brought the Noh to what it was in the Meiji period, aloof and aristocratic, the ceremonial theatre of the elite. However, it is worth noting that it was obviously no aspiration for democracy that encouraged in Kan'ami and Zeami the ideal of "an actor for all audiences," but rather a down-to-earth experience, sensitivity, and concern for the well-being of the troupe.

55. "Tsuikahō," art. 152, 1408/11th month/3, *CHS II*, pp. 61–62.
56. Tanuma Mutsumi, "Muromachi bakufu—shugo—kokujin," *Nihon rekishi* 7 *chūsei 3* (Tokyo, Iwanami Shoten, 1976), pp. 5–6.
57. *Kanmon gyoki*, 1416/11th month/25, cited in ibid., p. 7.
58. Ibid., 1418/6th month/6.
59. Ibid., p. 7.
60. *Kennaiki*, 1428/1st month/18, cited by ibid., p. 8.
61. Nakamura Kichiji, *Tokusei to tsuchi'ikki* (Tokyo, 1970), pp. 41–47.
62. Nagahara Keiji, *Gekokujō no jidai* (Tokyo, 1971), p. 58.
63. During the Kamakura period, the Bakufu could interfere in succession disputes only under special circumstances, such as when a father had disowned a filial son. Ishii Susumu, *Kamakura bakufu*, pp. 410–411.
64. Momose Kesao, "Tansen kō," in *Nihon shakai keizaishi kenkyū—Chūsei hen*, Hōgetsu Keigo Sensei Kanrekikinenkai, ed. (Tokyo, Yoshikawa Kobunkan, 1967), pp. 33–34.
65. *Kennaiki*, 1428/5th month/25, cited by Tanuma Mutsumi, "Muromachi bakufu," p. 8.
66. Sasaki Gin'ya, *Muromachi bakufu* (Tokyo, 1975), pp. 77–78.
67. Nagahara Keiji, *Gekokujō*, p. 53.
68. Itō Kunio maintains that this tension can be detected in the writings of Fushiminomiya Sadafusa (1372–1456), father of the Emperor Go-Hanazono and author of the *Kanmon gyoki*. See Itō Kunio, "Fushiminomiya Sadafusa tai Ashikaga Yoshinori—'Kanmon nikki' e no bungakuteki apurōchi," *Hiroshima daigaku bungakubu kiyō* 32.1:86–103 (January 1973).
69. A comprehensive cataloguing of regional product specialization in medieval Japan may be found in Toyoda Takeshi, *Zōtei chūsei Nihon shōgyōshi no kenkyū* (Tokyo, 1970), Ch. 1. See also Sasaki Gin'ya, *Chūsei shōhin ryūtsūshi no kenkyū* (Tokyo, 1972).
70. Toyoda Takeshi, "Za to dosō," *Nihon rekishi 6 chūsei 2* (Tokyo, 1963), pp. 169–170.
71. During Yoshimitsu's reign, the Yung-lo Emperor gave the following amounts of money as gifts to the shogun:

Year	Amount
1403	1500 *kan* (1 *kan* = 1,000 coins approx.)

Year	Amount
1407	15000 *kan*
1408	5000 "

By Yoshinori's time, during the reign of the Hsüan-te Emperor in 1434, 300,000 *kan* were brought into Japan as gifts, and the cash resulting from the trade in supplementary (non-tribute) articles amounted to at least 75,000 *kan* in 1433 and 100,000 *kan* in 1453. Wang Yi-t'ung, *Official Relations Between China and Japan 1368–1549* (Cambridge, Mass., Harvard University Press, 1953), pp. 102–104.

72. Sasaki Gin'ya, *Muromachi bakufu*, p. 53.
73. Wang Yi-t'ung, *Official Relations*, p. 91.
74. Tanuma Mutsumi, "Muromachi bakufu," p. 13.
75. *Kanmon gyoki*, 1441/6th month/25.
76. Kawai Masaharu, *Ashikaga Yoshimasa* (Tokyo, 1972), pp. 22–24.
77. Ibid., p. 24.
78. Ibid., p. 27.
79. "Tsuikahō," arts. 213–221, 1441/2nd 9th month/10, *CHS II*, pp. 78–79.
80. Kawai Masaharu, *Ashikaga Yoshimasa*, pp. 32–34.
81. "Ōuchi-shi okitegaki," in *CHS III*, pp. 35ff.
82. Kawai Masahara, *Ashikaga Yoshimasa*, pp. 35–37.
83. These four revolts have been summarized from material contained in ibid., pp. 57–59, and in Nakamura Kichiji, *Tokusei*, pp. 78–91. The Bakufu laws referred to include "Tsuikahō," arts. 237 & 238, 1454/9th month/29 & 1454/10th month/29, *CHS II*, pp. 83–84; and arts. 257–259, 1457/12th month/5, *CHS II*, p. 89.
84. In France, the upper bourgeoisie were accorded the similarly respectful title of *honnêtes hommes*. R. R. Palmer, *A History of the Modern World* (New York, Alfred A. Knopf, 1963), p. 100.
85. The difference between Muromachi and Tokugawa merchants parallels the difference between early and late medieval European merchants, between a sword-wielding traveling occupation and a sedentary one. During the fourteenth and fifteenth centuries, the use of arms was fairly widespread in England, for example, among both London merchants and provincial ones. See Slyvia L. Thrupp, *The Merchant Class of Medieval London* (Ann Arbor, 1968), pp. 250–251 and passim.
86. George Sansom, *Japan: A Short Cultural History* (New York, Appleton-Century-Crofts, 1962), p. 303.
87. "Tsuikahō," art. 104, 1369/10th month/2, *CHS II*, p. 45.
88. Kawai Masahara, *Ashikaga Yoshimasa*, p. 48.
89. Ibid., pp. 47–50.

90. Ibid., p. 147.
91. See John W. Hall's typology of Japanese daimyo in, "Foundations of the Modern Japanese Daimyō," in *Studies in the Institutional History of Early Modern Japan,* eds. Hall and Jansen (Princeton, 1968), pp. 65–77.
92. This is the year given by Kawai Masaharu, *Ashikaga Yoshimasa,* p. 148.
93. Fukuo Takeichirō, *Ōuchi Yoshitaka* (Tokyo, 1969), p. 140; Yonehara Masayoshi, *Ōuchi Yoshitaka* (Tokyo, 1967), p.. 78 and passim.
94. Kawai Masaharu, *Ashikaga Yoshimasa,* pp. 132–135. The two voyages to the Ming are described in detail by Kobata Atsushi, *Chūsei Nisshi tsūkō bōekishi no kenkyū* (Tokyo, 1969), pp. 80–90.
95. Kawai Masaharu, *Ashikaga Yoshimasa,* pp. 140–141.

3. MUROMACHI ECONOMY AND BAKUFU INCOME

1. During the early Eikyō period (c. 1429–1440), the Bakufu designated one part of the Yodo fish market as shogunal *goryōsho* and collected taxes from it. It also dispatched a *nōsenkata* official (see Chapter Four) as the Bakufu's agent at the Hyogo toll barrier. Toyoda Takeshi, "Suiriku kōtsū no shinten," in *Taikei Nihonshi sōsho 24 kōtsūshi,* eds., Toyoda Takeshi and Kodama Kōta (Tokyo, Yamakawa Shuppansha, 1970), p. 79.
2. Examples of Bakufu sumptuary legislation calling for frugality, the avoidance of ostentation in dress and lifestyle, and abstention from frivolous pursuits like gambling, may be found in "Tsuikahō," arts. 86–90, 1367/12th month/29, *CHS II,* p. 41; arts. 102–103, 1369/2nd month/27, ibid., p. 45; arts. 164–167, 1419/10th month/9, ibid., p. 63; art. 186, 1428/10th month/23, ibid., p. 68; arts. 278–281, 1480/4th month/28, ibid., p. 96.
3. "Ōuchi-shi okitegaki," art. 60, 1484/5th month, *CHS III,* p. 57. Much later, the Tokugawa Bakufu took the lead from its predecessor and made a concerted effort to control commerce on a national scale, while subordinate *han* governments came to employ merchants as economic administrators and tax collectors exactly as the Ashikaga had first used them. See Harold Bolitho, *Treasures Among Men: The Fudai Daimyo in Tokugawa Japan* (New Haven, Yale University Press, 1974), pp. 15, 68, and passim.
4. Marc Bloch, *Feudal Society,* vol. 2 (Chicago, 1964), p. 422.
5. Early Tokugawa shogunal prerogatives are outlined in Bolitho, *Treasures Among Men,* Ch. 1.
6. The researches of Tamaizumi Dairyō, which involved analyzing 1,581 deeds of sale from the medieval period, provide an incomplete but graphic illustration of the increasing monetization of the Muromachi economy by comparing the incidence of payment in kind versus cash:

REGION	PERIOD						TOTAL
	1334–1392		1393–1473		1474–1573		
	Rice	Coin	Rice	Coin	Rice	Coin	
Kinai	18	220	6	262	19	311	836
Tōkaidō		36	1	145	2	138	322
Tōsandō	2	5	15	26	19	60	127
Hokurikudō		3		1	1	13	18
Nankaidō	2	34		75	4	33	148
San'yōdō		1		15	1	24	41
San'indō		9		7	4	13	33
Saikaidō	1	5					6
TOTALS	23	313	23	531	50	642	1,581

Source: Kobata Atsushi, *Nihon kahei ryūtsū-shi,* Tokyo, 1969. Orig. publ. 1930, rev. 1943, pp. 43–44.

The trend toward commutation was not uniform, but resulted from different pressures and local conditions. In Senbu-no-shō, for example, a manor which belonged to the Tōdaiji temple in Mino province, the commutation of tax rice (*nengu*) into commodities like cotton and silk became difficult in 1278 because of the sudden rise in the price of silk. Stewards (*jitō*) and peasants both opposed it, and the upshot was the commutation of silk into cash equivalents and the use of cotton for commodity payment (*genbutsu nō*). In 1297, both silk and cotton were commuted into cash amounts, and thereafter the peasants of Senbu-no-shō were permitted to convert the most convenient and profitable produce into cash with which the pay the rice tax. (Sasaki Gin'ya, *Chūsei no shōgyō* [Tokyo, Shibundō, 1961], p. 23.) The general problem of the transition to payment of taxes in currency rather than in crops is treated by Sasaki Gin'ya, "Shōen ni okeru daisen nōsei no seiritsu to tenkai," in *Chūsei no shakai to keizai,* eds., Inagaki and Nagahara (Tokyo, Tōkyō Daigaku Shuppankai, 1969), pp. 381–495.

The important point to remember in considering the significance of the trend toward commutation has been stated by M. M. Postan as involving payments that were "fixed and firm. At the time when they were established they denoted not so much a choice between produce and money as a choice between fluctuating income and fixed income." M. M. Postan, "The rise of a money economy," *Essays on Medieval Agriculture and General Problems of the Medieval Economy* (Cambridge, England, 1973), p. 39.

7. Wakita Haruko, "Muromachiki no keizai hatten," *Nihon rekishi 7 chūsei 3* (Tokyo, Iwanami Shoten, 1976), p. 56.
8. Ibid., p. 56.
9. Ibid., p. 55.
10. Ibid., pp. 59-60.
11. Ibid., p. 61.
12. Kuwayama Kōnen, "Muromachi bakufu keizai no kōzō," in *Nihon keizaishi taikei 2 chūsei,* ed., Nagahara Keiji (Tokyo, Tōkyō Daigaku Shuppankai, 1969), p. 198.
13. Ono Terutsugu, "Muromachi bakufu no sakaya tōsei," p. 37.
14. Kuwayama Kōnen, "Keizai no kōzō," p. 198.
15. Ibid., pp. 225-233 provides the following provincial breakdown for totals of shogunal estates:

Province	Number of Goryōsho Estates
Yamashiro	17
Kawachi	4
Izumi	2
Settsu	4
Ise	6
Owari	8
Mikawa	8
Tōtōmi	3
Suruga	1
Izu	1
Musashi	1
Kazusa	1
Hitachi	1
Ōmi	24
Mino	9
Hida	6
Kōzuke	1
Shimotsuke	2
Wakasa	10
Echizen	8
Kaga	21
Noto	1
Etchū	8
Echigo	1
Tamba	6
Tango	3
Tajima	1

Province	Number of Goryōsho Estates
Hōki	1
Izumo	4
Harima	6
Mimasaka	4
Bizen	2
Bitchū	2
Bingo	1
Aki	2
Suō	1
Kii	2
Chikuzen	3

16. Ichikura Kiyoshi, "Chūsei kōki no kinai no jōsei—Muromachi bakufu no zaisei," *Rekishi kyōiku* 7.8:40–41 (August 1959). In Renaissance France, a similar situation existed, with specific revenues being tied to specific expenditures:

> Tailles were supposed to pay the *compagnies d'ordonnance*; aides were set aside for other military expenses; the *taillon* was supposed to pay for soldiers' rations and quarters; parlement salaries were expected to come from gabelles, and so on. Salaries for the flood of venal offices later in the Renaissance were often linked to specific revenues as well. Expenses of the royal household were supposed to come from the domaines, continuing the medieval notion that "the king should live of his own." Royal charities (*fiefs et aumônes*) were supposed to come from bailiwick chancery fees (*greffes et sceaux*). After Francis I created the office of Parties casuelles to handle the sale of venal offices, receipts from this source were earmarked for the royal household.

Martin Wolfe, *The Fiscal System of Renaissance France* (New Haven, 1972), pp. 283–284. For additional comparisons of this sort with Western Europe, see Chapter Four of this volume.

17. Kuwayama Kōnen, "Keizai no kōzō," p. 198.
18. In an entry in his diary dated 1431/3rd month/20, Sambōin Mansai, Yoshinori's priest-advisor, stated that all of the Ashikaga *goryōsho* in the Kantō had been usurped. Cited in ibid.
19. Kuwayama Kōnen, "Muromachi bakufu no sōsōki ni okeru shoryō ni tsuite," *Chūsei no mado* 12:21–22 (April 1963). The provincial breakdown for these award lands is as follows (Source: Ibid., p. 18.):

Province	Takauji	Tadayoshi
Ise	1	
Owari	1	
Tōtōmi	1	3

Province	Takauji	Tadayoshi
Suruga	2	
Izu	2	1
Sagami	3	2
Musashi	3	1
Mikawa	3	
Hitachi	2	1
Ōmi	2	1
Shinano	1	
Mutsu	3	
Sado	1	2
Chikuzen	1	
Buzen	1	
Higo	1	
Hyūga	2	
Iyo		1
Bingo		2
Harima		1
TOTALS	30	15

20. Kasamatsu Hiroshi, "Chūsei kesshochi kyūyo ni kansuru ichi kōsatsu," in *Chūsei no hō to kokka*, eds., Ishimoda Shō & Satō Shin'ichi (Tokyo, Tōkyō Daigaku Shuppankai, 1960), pp. 430–431 and passim, maintains that Takauji had very little choice but to return confiscated Hōjō lands to those who had prior claim to them.
21. "Tsuikahō," art. 56, 1352/7th month/24, *CHS II*, p. 29.
22. Kuwayama Kōnen, "Keizai no kōzō," p. 201.
23. Shimada Jirō, "Hanzei seido no seiritsu—Muromachi seiken seiritsushi no kenkyū," *Shichō* 58:24 and passim (1956).
24. Besides the obvious one of excluding the shugo and his agents, advantages to be derived from being designated shogunal *goryōsho* included exemption from *munebechisen* levies and priority in using disputed water resources. Ichikura Kiyoshi, "Chūsei kōki no kinki no jōsei," p. 44. Even some *gozan* (Zen monastic) estates were converted into Bakufu *goryōsho*. Fujioka Daisetsu, "Zen'in nai ni okeru tōbanshū ni tsuite— toku ni Muromachi bakufu no zaisei to kanren shite." *Nihon rekishi* 145:28 (July 1960).
25. Kuwayama Kōnen, "Keizai no kōzō," p. 214.
26. Momose Kesao, "Tansen kō," pp. 9–10.
27. Ibid., p. 14.
28. Tanuma Mutsumi, "Muromachi bakufu," p. 24. Tanuma cites Ishihara Yōko, "Muromachi jidai no tansen ni tsuite (1) (2)," *Reikishigaku ken-*

kyū nos. 404–405 (January–February 1974). The *kōden* field totals did not reflect their actual extent, because the *ōtabumi* totals had remained unchanged since the early days of *shōen* development, whereas there had been considerable expansion of cultivated area since that time. Until Hideyoshi's general cadastral survey (*taikaku kenchi*), proprietors successfully resisted the central government's efforts to draw up accurate and up-to-date estimates. (Tanuma Mutsumi, p. 24.)

29. Ibid., p. 36.
30. Kishida Hiroshi, "Shugo shihai no tenkai to chigyōsei no henshitsu," *Shigaku zasshi* 82.11:26 and passim (November 1973).
31. Momose Kesao, "Tansen kō," p. 25.
32. Sasaki Gin'ya, *Chūsei no shōgyō,* p. 59 and passim.
33. Wakita Haruko, "Muromachi ki no keizai hatten," p. 71.
34. Ibid., p. 77.
35. Ibid., p. 78.
36. Ibid., p. 89.
37. Ibid., p. 82. Sasaki Gin'ya, "Kaigai bōeki to kokunai keizai," *Kōza Nihonshi 3 hōken shakai no tenkai* (Tokyo, Tōkyō Daigaku Shuppankai, 1970), p. 178 and passim.
38. Wakita Haruko, "Keizai hatten," p. 70. The port towns were listed in a 1445 ledger called the *Hyōgo kita no seki nyūsen nōchō.*
39. Kuwayama Kōnen, "Muromachi bakufu keizai kikō no ichi kōsatsu," *Shiagaku zasshi* 73.9:10 (1964).
40. Okuno Takahiro, *Ashikaga Yoshiaki* (Tokyo, 1968), p. 62.
41. Ono Terutsugu, "Muromachi bakufu no sakaya tōsei," p. 36.
42. Okuno Takahiro, *Ashikaga Yoshiaki,* p. 62.
43. Kuwayama Kōnen, "Muromachi jidai no tokusei—tokuseirei to bakufu zaisei," in *Chūsei no shakai to keizai,* eds., Inagaki Yasuhiko & Nagahara Keiji (Tokyo, Tōkyō Daigaku Shuppankai, 1962), p. 511.
44. Wakita Haruko, "Muromachi ki no keizai hatten," p. 91.
45. "Sankō shiryō," art. 183, 1459/9th month/7, *CHS II,* p. 230.
46. Nakamura Kichiji, *Tokusei to tsuchiikki,* pp. 108–109.
47. Wang Yi-t'ung, *Official Relations,* pp. 65–67 and passim.
48. Alternative periodizations for analyzing the tally trade are discussed by Tanaka Takeo, "Chūsei kaigai bōeki no seikaku," in *Nihon keizai-shi taikei 2—Chūsei,* ed., Nagahara Keiji (Tokyo, Tōkyō Daigaku Shuppankai, 1965), pp. 302–308.
49. The high cost of minting coins in T'ang China, for example, is mentioned by D. C. Twitchett, *Financial Administration Under the T'ang Dynasty* (Cambridge, Cambridge University Press, 1970), pp. 69–70.
50. The Bakufu issued decrees concerning rates of exchange and permissible coinages in 1505, 1506, 1508–1510, 1512, and 1542, "Tsuikahō," arts.

334–336, 344–348, 360–362, 372–374, 385–389, 486–489, and 490, *CHS II*, pp. 109–114, 117–120, 123–124, 141–142. Concerning the profits which merchants acquired through sharp practices in moneychanging, see Kobata Atsushi, *Nihon kahei ryūtsūshi*, pp. 134–135.

51. Okuno Takahiro, *Ashikaga Yoshiaki*, p. 67.
52. Imatani Akira, *Sengoku ki no Muromachi bakufu* (Tokyo, 1975), p. 21.
53. "Tsuikahō," arts. 216, 223, 242, 319, 325, 402, 530, 537, *CHS II*, pp. 79, 80, 86, 105, 107, 128, 149, 150.
54. Fujioka Daisetsu, "Zen'in nai ni okeru tōbanshū ni tsuite," pp. 27–28.
55. Imaeda Aishin, *Chūsei Zenshūshi no kenkyū* (Tokyo, 1970), pp. 408–413.
56. Ibid., pp. 419–420.
57. Imatani Akira, *Sengoku ki*, p. 45.

4. THE BAKUFU SYSTEM: BUREAUCRACY AND ADMINISTRATION

1. The provincial house laws of the Ōuchi (cited in note 3 of Chapter Three), whose articles date from as early as 1439, clearly reveal the extent to which the Muromachi Bakufu set the pace for the rest of the country, and the degree of imitation of Bakufu institutions at the provincial level. In the realm of etiquette as well, great *shugo-daimyō* like Ōuchi Yoshioki and Ōtomo Yoshikane sought the instruction of Bakufu officials; in their particular case that official was the *mandokoro shitsuji* Ise Sadachika. Futaki Ken'ichi, "Kojitsuke Ise shi no seiritsu," *Kokugakuin zasshi* 68.12:16–17 (December 1967).
2. Satō Shin'ichi dated the writing of the *Busei kihan* between 1471 and 1490. (*CHS II*, pp. 431–432.) Ishii Ryōsuke gave an earlier estimate, dating it "after the Eikyō period," i.e., after c. 1440. Ishii Ryōsuke, *Nihon hōseishi gaisetsu* (Tokyo, 1971), p. 291.
3. *CHS II*, p. 429.
4. Ibid., pp. 376–377.
5. Stealing harvests (*karita rōzeki*) was shifted from civil to criminal jurisdiction by Kamakura Bakufu "Tsuikahō," art. 713, 1310, in *CHS I*, p. 312.
6. *CHS II*, pp. 387–388.
7. Ibid., p. 389.
8. Kobayashi Yasuo, "Jikata tōnin kō," *Shirin* 58.5:137 (September 1975).
9. *CHS II*, p. 390. One scholar has suggested that the *monchūjo's* loss of its other duties may have resulted from the need for a specialized bureau to handle just the increasing volume of paperwork and accumulation of documents by the Bakufu at this time. See Kasamatsu Hiroshi, "Muro-

machi bakufu soshō seido 'iken' no kōsatsu," *Shigaku zasshi* 69.4:27, n. 15 (April 1960).

10. *Suiko* loans were the subject of earlier legislation as well, having been mentioned in the *Goseibai shikimoku* "Tsuikahō," art. 20, 1231/3rd month/19, and art. 55, 1233/8th month/15, *CHS I*, pp. 70, 85–86.

11. *Honmotsu kaeshi* took various forms: in some contracts the pawned land could be bought back from the creditor at any time; in some the right to repurchase was forfeit after a specified time limit; in others the right to repurchase began after a specified waiting period, and so on.

12. *CHS II*, p. 391.

13. An English translation of the *Kemmu shikimoku* (1336) and of the Muromachi Bakufu *Tsuikahō* may be found in Kenneth Grossberg, ed., *The Laws of the Muromachi Bakufu* (Sophia University, Tokyo, 1981).

14. Marc Bloch, *Feudal Society*, vol. 2, p. 422.

15. Satō Shin'ichi, "Muromachi bakufu kansōki no kansei taikei," in *Chūsei no hō to kokka*, pp. 484–485 lists the following Ashikaga-related and vassal families: Kira, Hosokawa, Ishibashi, Uesugi, and Kō. Kamakura Bakufu families included: Nikaidō, Nagai, Sasaki, Utsunomiya, Chūjō, Gotō, Machino, Hatano, Ota, Mizutani, Settsu, Azuma, and Shimazu. For Ashikaga-related houses, see also Appendix C in this volume.

16. There were 70 of these decisions (*saikyojō*) issued between 1338/8th month and 1349/2nd 6th month, all of which were Tadayoshi decrees of the *gechijō* format. See Haga Norihiko, "Ashikaga Tadayoshi no tachiba—sono ni, saikyojō o tsūjite," *Shiron* 26–27:2 (1973).

17. Ibid., p. 9.

18. Itō Kiyoshi, "Muromachi bakufu to buke shissō," *Nihonshi kenkyū* 145: 30 (September 1974).

19. Ibid., p. 32.

20. Shiba Takatsune's career is the subject of Ogawa Makoto, "Ashikaga (Shiba) Takatsune no bakusei un'ei," *Kokugakuin daigaku kiyō* 11.1–34 (March 1973).

21. Ogawa Makoto, *Hosokawa Yoriyuki*, p. 97.

22. Satō Shin'ichi, *Nambokuchō*, pp. 349–350. Ibid., pp. 350–352, summarizes the reasons for Shiba Takatsune's sudden fall from power.

23. The first law decreed by Yoriyuki as regent was in the area of sumptuary legislation and demanded parsimony of all members of the shogun's court. "Tsuikahō," arts. 86–90, 1367/12th month/29, *CHS II*, p. 41.

24. *Kaei sandaiki*, 1368/4th month/15, *Shinkō gunshoruijū* vol. 20, pp. 181–182.

25. Ibid., 1368/4th month/27, p. 182.

26. Ibid., 1372/11th month/22, p. 194. Land confirmation (*shoryō ando*) began to be granted by means of the shogun's order (*gohan no mikyōjo*)

rather than the emperor's *(rinji)* or the cloistered emperor's *(ingen)* decree from just before Yoshimitsu became shogun, that is, during Yoriyuki's regency. See Kurokawa Naonori, "Muromachi bakufu gechijō to gohan no mikyōjo," *Nihonshi kenkyū* 117:99 (March 1971).

27. "Tsuikahō," art. 106, 1371/1st month/22; art. 107, 1372/2nd month/9; arts. 108–109, 1372/4th month/15, *CHS II*, pp. 46–47.

28. *Onchichi no shoku*, mentioned in *Kojiruien–Kan'i bu 2 (Buke myōmokushō–shokumyō 14)*, p. 1,222.

29. Ichikura Kiyoshi, "Mandokoro shitsuji to shite no Ise shi no taitō ni tsuite," *Nihon rekishi* 104:16 (February 1957). Briefly during the Bunmei period (c. 1486) the Ise also were shugo of Yamashiro province. Gomi Fumihiko, "Kanreisei to daimyōsei–sono tenkan," *Kōbe daigaku bungakubu kiyō* 4 (January 1975), p. 35.

30. Momose Kesao, "Tansen kō," pp. 9–10.

31. Ibid., p. 14.

32. Kobayashi Yasuo, "Nambokuchō–Muromachiki no kasho hakkyū ni tsuite–Muromachi bakufu shikiseishi no kisoteki kōsatsu," in Nagoya Daigaku Bungakubu Kokushigaku Kenkyūshitsu, ed., *Nagoya daigaku Nihonshi ronshū 1* (Tokyo, Yoshikawa Kōbunkan, 1975), pp. 391–392.

33. According to Itō Kiyoshi, the *kuge densō* were absorbed into the Bakufu c. 1392–94. Itō Kiyoshi, "Ōei shoki ni okeru ōchō seiryoku no dōkō–densō o chūshin to shite," *Nihon rekishi* 307:77 (December 1973).

34. "Tsuikahō," arts. 146–150, 1393/11th month/26, *CHS II*, pp. 59–60.

35. Kuwayama Kōnen, "Muromachi bakufu keizai kikō no ichi kōsatsu," p. 18. The *kurabugyō*, who also handled certain public documents, became the hereditary office of the Ashikaga-related Momonoi family.

36. Ibid., pp. 26–27, discusses three examples of *kubō okura*–the *kurabugyō* family Momonoi, the *nōsenkata* Shōjitsubō, and Zenjubō, the latter two of whom were originally under the authority of the Sanmon temples on Mt. Hiei.

37. Ibid., p. 6.

38. Gomi Fumihiko, "Kanreisei to daimyōsei," p. 31.

39. Nagahara Keiji, *Gekokujō*, p. 147, cited an entry in the diary of the Board of Administration's *shitsuji-dai* Saitō Mototsune (*Saitō Mototsune nikki*), 1447/3rd month/2, *Zoku shiryō taisei* vol. 10, p. 6, attesting to the existence of a *nōsenkata* office in the Bakufu.

40. Kuwayama Kōnen, "Chūki ni okeru Muromachi bakufu mandokoro no kōsei to kinō," in Hōgetsu Keigo Sensei Kanrekikinenkai, ed., pp. 137–139 and passim. A document of 1488 indicated that the *nōsenkata* were divided into those who collected revenue under the *shitsuji*'s authority, and those who handled disbursement, under the *shitsuji-dai*'s supervision. See Gomi Fumihiko, "Kanreisei to daimyōsei," p. 32.

41. Kawayama Kōnen, "Chūki ni okeru," p. 121.
42. Satō Shin'ichi, *Nambokuchō*, pp. 378–379.
43. *Mansai jungo nikki,* 1428/5th month/26, in *Zoku gunshoruijū* vol. 870, part 1, p. 503; cited also by Kasamatsu Hiroshi, "Muromachi bakufu soshō seido," p. 13, and Satō Shin'ichi, "Ashikaga Yoshinori shiritsuki no bakufu seiji," *Hōsei shigaku* 20:8 (March 1968).
44. Kasamatsu Hiroshi, "Muromachi bakufu soshō seido," pp. 15–16.
45. One observer, the *kuge densō* Madenokōji Tokifusa, explicitly compared the two in his diary: *Kennaiki,* 1428/6th month/20, *Dai Nihon kokiroku* vol. 44, p. 199, cited by Satō Shin'ichi, "Ashikaga Yoshinori shiritsuki," p. 9.
46. The first *gonaisho* was issued on 1428/10th month/12. Ōta Junzō, "Shogun Yoshinori to gozen rakkyo hōsho no seiritsu," *Shikan* 91.27 (March 1975).
47. Ibid., p. 29. The *kanrei shohan gechijō* was functionally equivalent to another form of document called the *Muromachi bakufu gechijō*.
48. Ibid., p. 30. This particular document involved land confirmation for a Sanmon branch temple (*matsuji*).
49. Usually two *bugyōnin* countersigned a *gohan (no) mikyōjo* decree, but there were sometimes three or even only one signatory. The names were those of hereditary *bugyōnin* families: Inō, Matsuda, Fuse, Saitō, Ise, Nikaidō, Sei, Settsu, Jibu, Suwa, Saika and others. See Ijichi Tetsuo, ed., *Nihon komonjogaku teiyō 1* (Tokyo, Shinseisha, 1966), pp. 495ff.
50. Ōta Junzō, "Shogun Yoshinori to gozen rakkyo," p. 31. Other members of this bureaucratic family, Inō Tameyuki and Inō Tamenori, were at this time serving as officials in charge of toll barriers on waterways and ports like Hyogo (*Kawakami kasho bugyō*) and on land (*kasho bugyō*). Kobayashi Yasuo, "Nambokuchō–Muromachiki no kasho hakkyū ni tsuite," pp. 403–404.
51. Ōta Junzō, ibid., p. 33. The primary source for these judgments is the *Gozen rakkyo kiroku,* which contains four different types of documents issued by the Bakufu in handing down decisions made under the *gozen gosata* system between 1430 and 1432. By far the most common document was Yoshinori's personally signed decree, the *gohan (no) mikyōjo,* of which twice as many were issued as the second most numerous variety, the *Muromachi bakufu mikyōjo/gechijō,* which was signed by the *kanrei.* The third type was the (*Muromachi bakufu*) *bugyōnin rensho hōsho,* which became more prevalent later in the century. The fourth type of document was the *gonaisho,* Yoshinori's informal directive used for decisions pertaining to *kuge.* These four types are explained in detail in ibid., pp. 36–41.

52. "Tsuikahō," arts. 190–197, especially art. 194, 1429/8th month/30, *CHS II*, pp. 69–71.
53. Imatani Akira, *Sengoku ki*, p. 156. One example of how those two helped to overrule the *kanrei* took place in 1461, when Ise Sadachika and the shogun vetoed Hosokawa Katsumoto's prohibition against the Sōkokuji temple's lumber ships passing through toll barriers duty-free. Kobayashi Yasuo, "Nambokuchō–Muromachiki no kasho hakkyū ni tsuite," pp. 415–416.
54. Momose Kesao, "Ōnin–bunmei no ran," *Nihon rekishi 7 chūsei 3* (Tokyo, Iwanami Shoten, 1976), pp. 181–182.
55. Kobayashi Yasuo, "Jikata tōnin kō," *Shirin* 58.5:137 (September 1975).
56. Imatani Akira, *Sengoku ki*, p. 129. Imatani cites two examples of the extent of *jikata tōnin* (i.e., *jikata bugyō*) jurisdiction recorded in the *Yasutomi ki* and the *Inryōken nichiroku* (Ibid., p. 30.). In 1442 Nakahara Yasutomi visited the mansion of the *jikata tōnin* to request mediation in a case which involved illegal seizure of his family property. *Yasutomi ki*, 1442/11th month/19–*Zōho shiryō taisei* vol. 37, p. 318. In 1466, a famous monk-painter named Oguri Sotan, who requested land on which to build a house and was granted it by the shogun, then sought confirmation of the grant from the *jikata tōnin*. *Inryōken nichiroku* vol. 2, 1466/5th month/26, p. 652.
57. *Yasutomi ki*, 1442/8th month/28, *Zōho shiryō taisei* vol. 37, pp. 276–277.
58. The acceptance of bribes by Bakufu officials was not unknown even before this time. During Yoshinori's reign *bugyōnin* were paid by private parties in return for granting tax exemptions and preferential treatment. See Iikura Harutake, "Ōnin no ran ikō ni okeru Muromachi bakufu no seikaku," *Nihonshi kenkyū* 139–140:150, n. 18 (March 1974). Such venality was especially severe during periods when the shogun tried to rule through his favorites. Kawai Masaharu, *Ashikaga Yoshimasa*, p. 39, refers to Ise Sadachika's extravagance and his accessibility to bribes during his term as *mandokoro shitsuji* from 1460–1471. In later periods, shogunal favorites of the Tokugawa such as Tanuma Okitsugu and Ōoka Tadamitsu were likewise accused of being willing to compromise themselves for a suitable fee. See Bolitho, *Treasures Among Men*, p. 158 and passim, and John W. Hall, *Tanuma Okitsugu, 1719–1788: Forerunner of Modern Japan* (Cambridge, Mass., Harvard University Press, 1955).
59. Imatani Akira, "Kanreidai hōsho no seiritsu–Muromachi bakufu buke monjo hensenshi no hito koma," *Komonjo kenkyū* 7–8:43–44 (February 1975).
60. Ibid., p. 46.
61. Ibid., p. 52.

62. Ibid., p. 54.
63. Ibid., p. 60.
64. Kasamatsu Hiroshi, "Muromachi bakufu soshō seido 'iken' no kōsatsu," p. 19.
65. The *Inryōken nichiroku* vol. 2, 1485/5th month/25, p. 721, records that there were "about sixty" *bugyōnin* and the *Chikamoto nikki,* 1485/8th month/4, gives a figure of 40. My own calculations, based on incomplete data, have yielded a total of 50 *bugyōnin* for the same year (1485). K. A. Grossberg, "Bakufu Bugyōnin: The Size of the Lower Bureaucracy in Muromachi Japan," *Journal of Asian Studies* 35.4:651–654 (August 1976).
66. Imatani Akira, *Sengoku ki,* p. 166.

5. THE BAKUFU SYSTEM: MILITARY ORGANIZATION

1. Gomi Fumihiko, "Zaikyōnin to sono ichi," *Shigaku zasshi* 83.8:18 (August 1974), suggests that the *gobanshū* was probably formed sometime during the Jōji era (c. 1362–1367).
2. Satō Shin'ichi, *Nambokuchō,* p. 411.
3. Tanuma Mutsumi, "Muromachi bakufu–shugo–kokujin," p. 17.
4. Haga Norihiko, "Muromachi bakufu samuraidokoro kō," Ogawa Makoto, ed., *Muromachi seiken* (Tokyo, Yuseido, 1975), pp. 39–40.
5. Ibid., pp. 47–48.
6. *Kojiruien 16–Kan'i bu 2,* pp. 820, 823–825.
7. Fukuda Toyohiko and Satō Ken'ichi, "Muromachi bakufu shōgun kenryoku ni kansuru ichi kōsatsu–shōgun kinjū o chūshin to shite," *Nihon rekishi* 228–229:51–52 (May–June 1967).
8. Fukuda Toyohiko, "Muromachi bakufu 'hōkōshū' no kenkyū–sono jin'in kōsei to chiikiteki bunbu," *Hokkaidō musashi joshi tanki daigaku kiyō* 3:2 (1970/71).
9. Ibid., p. 4. Gomi Fumihiko, "Zaikyōnin to sono ichi," p. 19 and passim, asserts that another component of the early *hōkōshū* were *zaikyōnin,* warriors who had been stationed in Kyoto by the Hōjō regents under the command of the Kamakura Bakufu commissioner in that city, the *Rokuhara tandai.*
10. Fukuda Toyohiko, "Muromachi bakufu 'hōkōshū' no kenkyū," p. 5.
11. Ibid., p. 13.
12. Ibid., p. 18. An example of *kyōsai* special treatment is "Tsuikahō," art. 112, 1372/7th month/11, *CHS II,* p. 49. An earlier example of complete exemption from a tax levied on all other stewards and house vassals (*jitō gokenin*) is "Tsuikahō," art. 43, 1347/3rd month/9, *CHS II,* pp. 24–25.

13. "Tsuikahō," art. 266, 1463/4th month/27, *CHS II*, p. 92.
14. Fukuda Toyohiko, "Muromachi bakufu 'hōkōshū' no kenkyū," p. 19.
15. Ibid., p. 29 (note 21).
16. Fukuda and Satō, "Muromachi bakufu shōgun kenryoku," p. 41.
17. Kobayashi Hiroshi, "Muromachi jidai no shugoshi funyūken ni tsuite," *Hokudai shigaku* 11:40 (September 1966).
18. The shogun even overruled the *Kantō kubō* in his selection of a clan head in a region where the *Kantō kubō's* autonomy was supposed to be unquestioned. See Kawai Masaharu, "Nambokuchō no dōran o keikito suru bushidan seikaku no henka," *Uozumi sensei kokikinen kokushigaku ronsō* (1959), pp. 146–147.
19. Fukuda and Satō, "Muromachi bakufu shōgun kenryoku," p. 55.
20. Fukuda Toyohiko, "Hōkōshū," p. 22. The provincial breakdown of numbers of estates held by *hōkōshū* members is as follows:

Province	Certain	Probable
Omi	21	25
Mikawa	17	44
Owari	16	19
Mino	15	30
Tango	9	18
Etchū	9	10
Kaga	9	10
Wakasa	8	9
Tamba	7	11
Ise	7	9
Inaba	7	9
Bingo	7	7
Settsu	6	7
Mimasaka	5	9
Harima	5	6
Izumo	5	5
Echizen	5	5
Tōtōmi	4	6
Bitchū	3	4
Tajima	3	3
Izumi	3	3
Kii	3	3
Aki	2	4
Noto	2	3
Yamashiro	2	2
Iwami	1	2
Suō	1	2

Province	Certain	Probable
Hida	1	1
Awaji	1	1
Hōki	1	1
Bizen	1	1
Kawachi	0	1
TOTALS	186	270
(for 32 provinces)		

Source: Ibid., p. 21.

21. Morisue Yumiko, "Muromachi bakufu goryōsho ni kansuru ichi kōsatsu—sono keiei jittai o chūshin to shite," Shisō 12:73 (October 1971). A list of hōkōshū samurai and the shogunal estates to which they were assigned as overseers is contained in Kobayashi Hiroshi, "Muromachi jidai no shugoshi funyūken ni tsuite," p. 55.

6. THE MUROMACHI BAKUFU IN COMPARATIVE PERSPECTIVE

1. During Edward's entire reign Parliament was summoned only six times. Edouard Perroy, The Hundred Years War (New York, 1965), p. 341.
2. Of France during this period Martin Wolfe has written, "In perspective . . . the fiscal reforms of the seventeenth century seem like modifications of the greater and more basic changes wrought during the Renaissance. Historians who study the fiscal institutions of Old Regime France without appreciating how much these owe to the Renaissance era are looking through the wrong end of the telescope." Martin Wolfe, The Fiscal System of Renaissance France (New Haven, 1972), p. 251.
3. The English crown exploited the wool Staple both to tax profits by means of a heavy export duty and then to raise loans from the merchants on the security of that duty. See The Cambridge Economic History of Europe, vol. 3 (Cambridge, 1965), pp. 335-336.
4. Harry A. Miskimin, The Economy of Early Renaissance Europe, 1300-1460 (Englewood Cliffs, N.J., 1969), p. 133.
5. Ibid., p. 150.
6. E. M. Carus-Wilson, Medieval Merchant Venturers (London, 1967), p. xx.
7. The edict stated that "the profits from maritime commerce are very great. If properly managed, they can bring a million (strings of cash). Is this not better than taxing the people? We pay attention to this matter because We wish to lighten the burden of the people." Sung-hui-yao chi-pen: Chih-kuan 44/2a-20b (A Draft Collection of the Major Sung

Events), tr. Laurence J. C. Ma, *Commercial Development and Urban Change in Sung China (960-1279)* (Ann Arbor, 1971), p. 34.

8. E. A. Kracke, Jr., *Civil Service in Early Sung China 960-1067* (Cambridge, Mass., Harvard University Press, 1953), p. 14.

9. Michel Mollat, *Genèse médiévale de la France moderne, XIV-XVe siècles* (Paris, 1970), pp. 283-292.

10. Suzerainty approached sovereignty to the extent that the ruler was able to regulate all justice and to tax all men. See Joseph R. Strayer, *On the Medieval Origins of the Modern State* (Princeton, 1970), pp. 42-43.

11. Bloch, *Feudal Society*, vol. 2, p. 422.

12. Eugene F. Rice, Jr., *The Foundations of Early Modern Europe, 1460-1559* (New York, 1970), p. 98.

13. Kracke, pp. 10-11.

14. Denys Hay, *Europe in the Fourteenth and Fifteenth Centuries* (London, 1966), pp. 83-84, offered these as characteristics common to both Commynes and Fortescue.

15. Paul Murray Kendall, *The Yorkist Age* (New York, 1970), p. 164.

16. George Sansom, *A History of Japan to 1334* (Stanford, Stanford University Press, 1958), pp. 376, 416 and passim.

17. Daniel Waley, *Later Medieval Europe: From St. Louis to Luther* (London, 1975), pp. 62-63.

18. Hay, p. 114.

19. Waley, pp. 59-60.

20. E. F. Jacob, *The Fifteenth Century 1399-1485* (Oxford, 1969), p. 596.

21. Hay, pp. 114-115.

22. C. W. Previté-Orton, *The Shorter Cambridge Medieval History*, vol. 2 (Cambridge, England, 1971), pp. 1029-1030.

23. Among the major outbreaks and the shoguns during whose reigns they occurred were: Yoshimitsu—Meitoku (1391) and Ōei (1399) rebellions; Yoshimochi—Uesugi Zenshū (1416-1417) and Shōchō (1428); Yoshinori—Eikyō (1438) and Kakitsu (1441); and Yoshimasa—Ōnin-Bunmei (1467-1477) and Yamashiro kuni'ikki (1485).

24. Hay, pp. 38-39.

25. J. R. Lander, *Conflict and Stability in Fifteenth-Century England* (London, 1969), p. 113.

26. P. S. Lewis, *Later Medieval France* (London, 1968), p. 105.

27. Waley, pp. 61-62.

28. J.M.W. Bean, *The Decline of English Feudalism 1215-1540* (Manchester, 1968), pp. 8-11, 235-236. Bean describes wardship as follows: if a tenant's heir was a child, the lord possessed the rights of wardship, which included both custody of an heir's body and of his inheritance, and the right to marry the heir to a person of the lord's choosing. Wardship lasted

until a male was twenty-one years of age, and the lord's rights of wardship within these terms were absolute. Both wardship and marriage provided the lord with an important source of revenue. The right of marriage could be sold, and, until the heir came of age, the lord could either retain the inheritance in his own hands or sell the right of wardship as a marketable commodity. All lords benefited from wardship, but the king was the chief beneficiary, not only because he was the greatest lord in terms of the extent of his territorial power, but also because of the special right of "prerogative wardship," that is, if a tenant-in-chief died leaving an heir under age, the Crown had the right not only to the wardship of those lands which were held in chief, but also to that of all the lands held by the deceased tenant of other lords.

29. Hay, p. 125.
30. Waley, pp. 241–242.
31. See table, "Average Yearly English Exports of Raw Wool and Woolen Cloth, 1361–1500," reproduced in Carlo Cipolla, *Before the Industrial Revolution* (New York, 1976), p. 257.
32. Jacob, p. 591.
33. S. N. Eisenstadt, *The Political Systems of Empires* (New York, 1969), p. 27, defines free-floating resources as "resources—manpower, economic resources, political support, and cultural identifications—not embedded within or committed beforehand to any primary ascriptive-particularistic groups."
34. Waley, p. 67.
35. Lander, p. 53.
36. George Holmes, *Europe: Hierarchy and Revolt, 1320–1450* (New York, 1975), p. 25.
37. Ibid., p. 27.
38. Hay, pp. 101–102.
39. Ibid., p. 102.
40. Ibid., p. 103.
41. Ibid., p. 104.
42. Kendall, *The Yorkist Age*, p. 491. Hay, pp. 108–109.
43. Hay, p. 105.
44. Lewis, *Later Medieval France*, p. 103.
45. Hay, p. 99.
46. Lander, p. 109.
47. H. H. Gerth and C. Wright Mills, eds., *From Max Weber: Essays in Sociology* (New York, Oxford University Press, 1958), pp. 180–194 discusses these two concepts.

Bibliography

DOCUMENTS, DIARIES, CHRONICLES

Aragoyomi 荒曆.

Buke myōmoku shō 武家名目抄 (8 vols.).

Busei kihan 武政軌範.

Chikamoto nikki 親元日記 (6 vols.).

Dai Nihon shiryō 大日本史料, series 6 and 7.

Goseibai shikimoku 御成敗式目 (Satō Shin'ichi and Ikeuchi Yoshi-suke, eds.).

Gozen rakkyo kiroku 御前落居記録.

Gozen rakkyo hōsho 御前落居奉書.

Inryōken nichiroku 蔭涼軒日録 (5 vols.).

Jinten'ainōshō 塵添壒囊抄.

Kaei sandaiki 花営三代記.

Kana nendaiki 仮名年代記.

Kanenobu kōki 兼宣公記.

Kanmon gyoki 看聞御記 (2 vols.).

Kemmu shikimoku: Kemmu irai tsuikahō 建武式目：建武以来追加法 (Sato and Ikeuchi, eds.).

Ken'naiki 建内記 (5 vols.).

Kojiruien–Kan'i bu 2 古事類苑 — 官位部二.

Kugyō bunin 公卿補任.

Mansai jungo nikki 満済准后日記 (2 vols.).

Muromachi ke gonaisho an 室町家御内書案.

Nanzenji monjo 南禅寺文書 (Sakurai Kageo and Fujii Manabu, eds.).

Nejime monjo 禰寝文書 (Kawazoe Shōji, ed.).

Ninakawa ke monjo 蜷川家文書.
Nochikagami 後鑑 (4 vols.).
Ōuchi shi okitegaki 大内氏掟書 (Satō, Ikeuchi, and Momose, eds.).
Rokuon'in dono Itsukushima mōdeki 鹿苑院殿厳島詣記.
Saitō Mototsune nikki 斎藤基恒日記.
Sappan kyūki 薩藩旧記.
Shitsuji bunin shidai 執事補任次第.
Teikin ōrai 庭訓往来 (Ishikawa Matsutarō, ed.).
Tōji hyakugō monjo 東寺百合文書.
Wakan reikyō 和簡礼経.
Yasutomi ki 康富記.
Yoshida ke hinamiki 吉田家日次記.

BOOKS AND ARTICLES

Abe Takeshi 阿部猛. "Tanmai–tansen no kenkyū" 段米・段銭の研究 (Research on *tanmai* and *tansen*), *Shichō* 64–65:55–69 (1958).

——. "Muromachi jidaishi no shomondai" 室町時代史の諸問題 (Problems in Muromachi history), *Rekishi hyōron* 108:41–47 (August 1959).

Akamatsu Toshihide 赤松俊秀. "Kemmu irai tsuika ni tsuite" 建武以来追加に就いて (The supplementary laws after Kemmu), *Rekishi to chiri* 歴史と地理 28.3:17–32 (August 1931).

—— and Yamamoto Shirō 山本四郎, eds. *Kyōto fu no rekishi* 京都府の歴史 (The history of Kyoto). Tokyo, Yamakawa Shuppansha, 1971.

Amino Yoshihiko 網野善彦. "Chūsei ni okeru gyoba no seiritsu" 鎌倉時代の太良庄をめぐって (The establishment of fish markets in the medieval period), *Shigaku zasshi* 72.7:34–59 (July 1963).

——. "Akutō, daikan, yūryoku myōshu–Kamakura, Nambokuchōki no Harima no kuni Yano no shō o chūshin ni" 悪党・代官・有力名主 － 鎌倉・南北朝期の播磨国矢野荘を中心に (*Akutō, daikan,* and powerful *myōshu* in the Kamakura and Nambokuchō periods, with special reference to Yano *shōen* in Harima province), *Rekishigaku kenkyū* 298:18–29 (March 1965).

Bean, J. M. W. *The Decline of English Feudalism, 1215–1540.* Manchester, University of Manchester, 1968.

Bloch, Marc. *Feudal Society,* vol. 2. Chicago, University of Chicago Press, 1964.

Brown, Delmer. *Money Economy in Medieval Japan: A Study in the Use of Coins.* New Haven, Yale University Press, 1951.

Burckhardt, Jacob. *The Civilization of the Renaissance in Italy,* vol. 1. New York, Harper & Row, 1958.

The Cambridge Economic History of Europe, vol. 3. Cambridge, Cambridge University Press, 1965.

Carus-Wilson, E. M. *Medieval Merchant Venturers.* London, Methuen, 1967.

Cipolla, Carlo. *Before the Industrial Revolution.* New York, W. W. Norton, 1976.

Eisenstadt, S. N. *The Political Systems of Empires.* New York, Free Press, 1969.

Elvin, Mark. *The Pattern of the Chinese Past.* Stanford, Stanford University Press, 1973.

Fujioka Daisetsu　藤岡大拙. "Zen'in nai ni okeru tōbanshū ni tsuite—toku ni Muromachi bakufu no zaisei to kanren shite"　禅院内に於ける東班衆について　－　特に室町幕府の賊政と関連して　(The eastern ranks in Zen temples and their relationship to Muromachi Bakufu finances), *Nihon rekishi* no. 145: 19-28 (July 1960).

Fukuda Toyohiko　福田豊彦. "Kokujin ikki no ichi sokumen—sono jōbu kenryoku to no kankei o chūshin to shite"　国人一揆の一側面　－　その上部権力との関係を中心として　(The power of the leadership in *kokujin* leagues), *Shigaku zasshi* 76.1:62-80 (January 1967).

——. "Muromachi bakufu 'hōkōshū' no kenkyū—sono jin'in kōsei to chiikiteki bunpu"　室町幕府「奉公衆」の研究　－　その人員構成と地域的分布　(The composition and territorial distribution of the Muromachi Bakufu's *hōkōshū*), *Hokkaidō musashi joshi tanki daigaku "kiyō"*　北海道武蔵女子短期大学「紀要」, 3:1-52 (1970/71).

——. "Muromachi bakufu no 'hōkōshū'—gobanchō no sakusei nendai o chūshin to shite"　室町幕府の「奉公衆」－　御番帳の作成年代を中心として　(Dating the membership rosters of the Muromachi Bakufu's *hōkōshū*), *Nihon rekishi* 274:46-65 (March 1971).

—— and Satō Ken'ichi　佐藤堅一. "Muromachi bakufu shōgun kenryoku ni kansuru ichi. kōsatsu—shōgun kinjū o chūshin to shite"　室町幕府将軍権力に関する一考察　－　将軍近習を中心として　(The shogunal army and shogunal power in the Muromachi Bakufu), *Nihon rekishi* 228:37-53 (May 1967); 229:48-56 (June 1967).

Fukumoto Jun 福本潤. "Nambokuchō Muromachiki ni okeru kikujin sō no dōkō" 南北朝・室町期における国人層の 動向 (Trends among *kokujin* during the Nambokuchō and Muromachi periods), *Jōchi shigaku* 16:64-82 (October 1971).

Fukuo Kyōju Taikan Kinenjigyōkai 福尾教授退官記念事業 会 ed. *Nihon chūseishi ronshū* 日本中世史論集 (Essays on the history of medieval Japan). Tokyo, Yoshikawa Kōbunkan, 1972.

Fukuo Takeichirō 福尾猛一郎. *Ōuchi Yoshitaka* 大内義隆 (Ōuchi Yoshitaka). Tokyo, Yoshikawa Kōbunkan, 1969.

Furushima Toshio 古島敏雄. *Nihon nōgyō gijutsushi 1* 日本農 業技術史 上巻 (History of agricultural technology in Japan, vol. 1). Tokyo, Jichōsha, 1947.

——. *Nihon nōgyō shi* 日本農業史 (History of Japanese agriculture). Tokyo, Iwanami Shoten, 1956.

Futaki Ken'ichi 二木謙一. "Kojitsuke Ise shi no seiritsu" 故実 家伊勢氏の成立 (Establishment of the Ise family as experts on rites and etiquette), *Kokugakuin zasshi* 68.12:12-24 (December 1967).

——. "Muromachi bakufu kyūba kojitsuke Ogasawara shi no seiritsu" 室町幕府弓馬故実家小笠原氏の成立 (Establishment of the Ogasawara family as Muromachi Bakufu experts on archery and horsemanship), *Kokugakuin daigaku nihon bunka kenkyūjo kiyō* 国学院大学日本文化研究所紀要 24:29-60 (September 1969).

——. "Shōgatsu no busha girei—Muromachi bakufu matohajime o chūshin to shite" 正月の歩射儀礼 - 室町幕府的始を中 心として (The Muromachi Bakufu's archery ceremony of the new year), *Kokugakuin zasshi* 72.2:31-45 (February 1971).

Gernet, Jacques. *Daily Life in China on the Eve of the Mongol Invasion, 1250-1276*. Stanford, Stanford University Press, 1970.

Gomi Fumihiko 五味文彦. "Shichō no kōsei to bakufu—12-14 seiki no ryakuchū shihai" 使庁の構成と幕府 - 12-14 世 紀の洛中支配 (Court and Bakufu rule of the capital between the 12th and 14th centuries), *Rekishigaku kenkyū* 392:1-19 (January 1973).

——. "Zaikyōnin to sono ichi" 在京人とその位置 (The position of the *zaikyōnin*), *Shigaku zasshi* 83.8:1-26 (August 1974).

——. "Kanreisei to daimyōsei—sono tenkan" 管領制と大名制 - その転換 (The transition from *kanrei* system to daimyo system), *Kōbe daigaku bungakubu kiyō 4* 神戸大学文学部紀 要 (January 1975), 27-54.

Grossberg, Kenneth A. "Bakufu Bugyōnin: The Size of the Lower Bureaucracy in Muromachi Japan," *Journal of Asian Studies* 35.4:651-654 (August 1976).

——, ed. *The Laws of the Muromachi Bakufu.* Tokyo, Sophia University, 1981.

Haga Norihiko　羽下德彦. "Echigo ni okeru shugo ryōkoku no keisei—shugo to kokujin no kankei o chūshin ni"　越後に於る守護領国の形成 — 守護と国人の関係を中心に (The formation of the shugo domain in Echigo province and *shugo-kokujin* relations), *Shigaku zasshi* 68.8:29–57 (August 1959).

——. "Muromachi bakufu samuraidokoro tōnin, tsuketari, Yamashiro shugo, funin enkaku kōshō kō"　室町幕府侍所頭人，付山城守護，補任沿革考証稿 (An inquiry into the history of appointments to the post of head of the Board of Retainers and Yamashiro shugo within the Muromachi Bakufu), *Tōyō daigaku kiyō, bungakubu hen* 東洋大学紀要，文学部篇　16:77–97 (1962).

——. "*Nochikagami*—sono shiryōteki kachi"　後鑑 — その史料的価値 (The *Nochikagami*'s value as a historical document), *Nihon rekishi* 194:114–147 (July 1964).

——. "Ashikaga Tadayoshi no tachiba—sono ichi, gunzei saisokujō to kanjō o tsūjite"　足利直義の立場—その一，軍勢催促状と感状を通じて (Ashikaga Tadayoshi's position as seen in military requisitions and commendations), *Komonjo kenkyū* 古文書研究 6:1–20 (October 1973).

——. "Ashikaga Tadayoshi no tachiba—sono ni, saikyojō o tsūjite"　足利直義の立場 — その二，裁許状を通じて (Ashikaga Tadayoshi's position as seen in dispensations granted), *Shiron* 26–27:1–18 (1973).

Hall, John W. *Government and Local Power in Japan, 500 to 1700.* Princeton, Princeton University Press, 1966.

—— and Marius B. Jansen, eds. *Studies in the Institutional History of Early Modern Japan.* Princeton, Princeton University Press, 1968.

—— and Toyoda Takeshi, eds. *Japan in the Muromachi Age.* Berkeley, University of California Press, 1977.

Harada Tomohiko　原田伴彦. "Chūsei shajiryō shihai no seikaku to sono hensen—shaji kenryoku to monzen toshi to no kankei o chūshin to shite"　中世社寺領支配の性格とその変遷 — 社寺権力と門前都市との関係を中心として (The nature and change of rule in the medieval temple and shrine domain, with particular reference to the relationship between temples and their adjoining towns), Itō Tasaburō 伊東多三郎, ed. *Kokumin seikatsushi kenkyū 1—seikatsu to seiji* 国民生活史研究1—生活と政治. Tokyo, Yoshikawa, Kōbunkan, 1957.

——. *Nihon hōken toshi kenkyū* 日本封建都市研究 (Studies on the feudal city in Japan). Tokyo, Tōkyō Daigaku Shuppankai, 1967.

——.*Chūsei ni okeru toshi no kenkyū* 中世における都市の 研究 (Studies on cities in the medieval period). Tokyo, San'ichi Shobō, 1972.

Hatai Hiromu 畑井弘. *Shugo ryōkoku taisei no kenkyū* 守護領 国体制の研究 (Studies on the shugo domain system). Tokyo, Yoshikawa Kōbunkan, 1975.

Hay, Denys. *Europe in the Fourteenth and Fifteenth Centuries.* London, Longman, 1966.

Hayashiya Tatsusaburō 林屋辰三郎. *Chūsei bunka no kichō* 中世文化の基調 (The basis of medieval culture). Tokyo, Tōkyō Daigaku Shuppankai, 1953.

——.*Machishū* 町衆 (Townsfolk). Tokyo, Chūō Kōronsha, 1964.

——."Higashiyama bunka" (Higashiyama culture) 東山文化, *Nihon rekishi 7 chūsei 3* (1971), 303–337.

Hōgetsu Keigo Sensei Kanrekikinenkai 宝月圭吾先生還曆 記念会 ed. *Nihon shakai keizaishi kenkyū–chūsei hen* 日本 社会経済史研究 – 中世編 (Studies in Japanese social and economic history–Medieval). Tokyo, Yoshikawa Kōbunkan, 1967.

Holmes, George. *The Later Middle Ages, 1272–1485.* New York, W. W. Norton, 1962.

——.*Europe: Hierarchy and Revolt, 1320–1450.* New York, Harper & Row, 1975.

Ichihara Yōko 市原陽子. "Muromachi jidai no tansen ni tsuite" 室町時代の段銭について (*Tansen* in the Muromachi period), *Rekishigaku kenkyū* 404:1–19 (January 1974); 405:14–30 (February 1974).

Ichikura Kiyoshi 一倉喜好. "Bun'ichi tokuseirei to Muromachi bakufu no zaisei" 分一徳政令と室町幕府の財政 (Partial debt-cancellation decrees and Muromachi Bakufu finances), *Shichō* 52:10–22 (1954).

——."Mandokoro shitsuji to shite no Ise shi no taitō ni tsuite" 政所 執事としての伊勢氏の抬頭について (The rise of the Ise family as head of the Board of Retainers), *Nihon rekishi* 104:7–18 (February 1957).

——."Tamba no kuni Kirinokawachi ni okeru Muromachi bakufu kenryoku no shittsui" 丹波国桐野河内における室町幕 府権力の失墜 (The decline of Muromachi Bakufu power in Kirinokawachi of Tamba province), *Nihon rekishi* 132:73–90 (June 1959).

——."Chūsei kōki no kinai no jōsei–Muromachi bakufu no zaisei" 中世 後期の近畿の状勢 – 室町幕府の財政 (The situation in the Kinai region in the late middle ages: Muromachi Bakufu finances), *Rekishi kyōiku* 7.8:40–45 (August 1959).

Iikura Harutake　飯倉晴武．"Ōnin no ran ikō ni okeru Muromachi bakufu no seikaku"　応仁の乱以降における室町幕府の性格 (The nature of the Muromachi Bakufu after the Ōnin War), *Nihonshi kenkyū* 139–140: 140–151 (March 1974).

Imaeda Aishin　今枝愛真．"Tamba Sasamura ni okeru Ashikaga Takauji no kyohei to sono negaibumi"　丹波篠村における足利尊氏の挙兵とその願文 (Ashikaga Takauji's recruitment of fighting men in Sasa village of Tamba province), *Shigaku zasshi* 70.1:34–43 (January 1961).

——.*Chūsei Zenshūshi no kenkyū*　中世禅宗史の研究 (Studies in the history of the Zen sect in medieval times). Tokyo, Tōkyō Daigaku Shuppankai, 1970.

Imatani Akira　今谷 明．"Hosokawa–Miyoshi taisei kenkyū josetsu–Muromachi Bakufu no kaitai katei"　細川・三好体制研究序説 － 室町幕府の解体過程 (The Hosokawa and Miyoshi clans and the dissolution of the Muromachi Bakufu), *Shirin* 56.5: 1–73 (September 1973).

——.*Sengoku ki no Muromachi bakufu*　戦国期の室町幕府 (The Muromachi Bakufu in the Sengoku period). Tokyo, Kadokawa Shoten, 1975.

——."Kanreidai hōsho no seiritsu–Muromachi bakufu buke monjo hensenshi no hito koma"　管領代奉書の成立 － 室町幕府武家文書変遷史の一齣 (The establishment of the *kanreidai hōsho* order: one step in the transformation of Muromachi Bakufu documents), *Komonjo kenkyū* 7–8:43–64 (February 1975).

——."Muromachi bakufu saimakki no Kyōto shihai–monjo hakkyū o tsūjite mita Miyoshi seiken"　室町幕府最末期の京都支配 － 文書発給を通じて見た三好政権 (Ruling Kyoto at the end of the Muromachi Bakufu: the Miyoshi regime as seen in documents), *Shirin* 58.3:69–105 (May 1975).

Inagaki Yasuhiko　稲垣泰彦　and Nagahara Keiji　永原慶二 , eds. *Chūsei no shakai to keizai*　中世の社会と経済 (Society and economy in medieval times). Tokyo, Tōkyō Daigaku Shuppankai, 1969.

——."Ōnin–Bunmei no ran"　応仁・文明の乱 (The wars of Ōnin and Bunmei), *Nihon rekishi 7 chūsei 3*　日本歴史 7, 中世 3 (1971), 163–202.

Ishihara Michihiro　石原道博．*Wakō*　倭寇 (Japanese pirates). Tokyo, Yoshikawa Kōbunkan, 1964.

Ishii Ryōsuke　石井良助．*Nihon hōseishi gaiyō*　日本法制史概要 (A summary of Japanese legal history). Tokyo, Sōbunsha, 1969.

——.*Nihon hōseishi gaisetsu*　日本法制史概説 (An outline of Japanese legal history). Tokyo, Sōbunsha, 1971.

Ishii Shirō　石井紫郎．*Nihon kokuseishi kenkyū 1–kenryoku to tochi shoyū* 日本国制史研究 1 — 権力と土地所有 (History of the Japanese national system, vol. 1: power and land ownership). Tokyo, Tōkyō Daigaku Shuppankai, 1966.

Ishii Susumu 石井進. *Nihon chūsei kokkashi no kenkyū* 日本中世国家史の研究 (Studies in the history of the medieval Japanese nation). Tokyo, Iwanami Shoten, 1970.

——.*Kamakura bakufu* 鎌倉幕府 (Kamakura Bakufu). Tokyo, Chūō Kōronsha, 1971.

——."Kamakura bakufu ron" 鎌倉幕府論 (On the Kamakura Bakufu), *Nihon rekishi 5 chūsei 1*, pp. 87–133.

——et al. *Chūsei seiji shakai shisō 1* 中世政治社会思想 上 (Medieval political and social thought, vol. 1). Tokyo, Iwanami Shoten, 1972.

Itano Tetsu 板野哲. "Muromachi bakufu no seitōkaron to sono seikaku" 室町幕府の正当化論とその性格 (The theory of legitimacy of the Muromachi Bakufu), *Shigaku kenkyū* 110:72–97 (1971).

Itō Akihiko 伊藤旭彦. "Ashikaga Yoshimitsu no kugeka" 足利義満の公家化 (The aristocratization of Ashikaga Yoshimitsu), *Shoryōbu kiyō* 書陵部紀要 21:23–40 (1969).

Itō Kiyoshi 伊藤喜良:"Ōei shoki ni okeru ōchō seiryoku no dōkō—densō o chūshin to shite" 応永初期における王朝勢力の動向 — 伝奏を中心として (The *densō* officials and trends in court power during the early Ōei era), *Nihon rekishi* 307:66–85 (December 1973).

——."Muromachi bakufu to buke shissō" 室町幕府と武家執奏 (The Muromachi Bakufu and *buke shissō* officials), *Nihonshi kenkyū* 145:23–51 (September 1974).

Itō Kunio 位藤邦生. "Fushiminomiya Sadafusa tai Ashikaga Yoshinori—'Kanmon nikki' e no bungakuteki apurōchi" 伏見宮貞成対足利義教 — 「看聞日記」への文学的アプローチ (Fushiminomiya Sadafusa versus Ashikaga Yoshinori: a literary approach to the Kanmon diary), *Hiroshima daigaku bungakubu kiyō* 広島大学文学部紀要 32.1:86–103 (January 1973).

Itō Tasaburō 伊東多三郎. "Shōgun, Nihon kokuō to shōsu—sono shiteki igi" 将軍日本国王と称す — その史的意義 (The historical significance of calling the shogun "King of Japan"), *Nihon rekishi* 60:2–6 (May 1953).

Itō Teiji 伊藤鄭爾. *Chūsei jūkyoshi* 中世住居史 (History of medieval dwellings). Tokyo, Tōkyō Daigaku Shuppankai, 1968.

Iwahashi Koyata 岩橋小弥太. *Hanazono tennō* 花園天皇 (Emperor Hanazono). Tokyo, Yoshikawa Kōbunkan, 1969.

Jacob, E. F. *The Fifteenth Century 1399-1485*. Oxford, Oxford University Press, 1969.

Kanamoto Masayuki 金本正之 . "Chūsei Ōmi shōnin no seikaku" 中世近江商人の性格 (The Ōmi merchants in medieval times), *Shigaku zasshi* 70.8:58-80 (August 1961).

Kasamatsu Hiroshi 笠松宏至 . "Muromachi bakufu soshō seido 'iken' no kōsatsu" 室町幕府訴訟制度「意見」の考察 (The *"iken"* procedure in the litigation system of the Muromachi Bakufu), *Shigaku zasshi* 69.4:1-28 (April 1960).

Kawai Masaharu 河合正治 . *Nanchō to hokuchō* 南朝と北朝 (The Northern and the Southern Court). Tokyo, Bun'eidō, 1970.

——.*Ashikaga Yoshimasa* 足利義政 (Ashikaga Yoshimasa). Tokyo, Shimizu Shoin, 1972.

——.*Chūsei buke shakai no kenkyū* 中世武家社会の研究 (Studies on medieval warrior society). Tokyo, Yoshikawa Kōbunkan 1973.

——."Higashiyama bunka to bushi kaisō" 東山文化と武士階層 *Nihon chūseishi ronshū* 日本中世史論集 Fukuo Kyōju Taikan Kinenjigyōkai ed., 175-199. (Tokyo, Yoshikawa Kōbunkan, 1972).

——. "Nambokuchō no dōran o keiki to suru bushidan seikaku no henka" 南北朝の動乱を契機とする武士団性格の変化 (Change in warrior bands precipitated by the disturbances of the Nambokuchō period), *Uozumi sensei kokikinen kokushigaku ronsō* 魚澄先生古稀記念国史学論叢 (1959), 141-153.

——with Kenneth A. Grossberg. "Shogun and Shugo: The Provincial Aspects of Muromachi Politics," John W. Hall and Toyoda Takeshi, eds. *Japan in the Muromachi Age*. Berkeley, University of California Press, 1977.

Kawazoe Shōji 川添昭二 . "Muromachi bakufu seiritsuki ni okeru seiji shisō—Imagawa Ryōshun no baai" 室町幕府成立期における政治思想 — 今川了俊の場合 (Political thought in the early Muromachi Bakufu: the case of Imagawa Ryōshun), *Shigaku zasshi* 68.12:37-66 (December 1959).

——.*Imagawa Ryōshun* 今川了俊 (Imagawa Ryōshun). Tokyo, Yoshikawa Kōbunkan, 1969.

Kendall, Paul M. *The Yorkist Age*. New York, W. W. Norton, 1970.

Kishida Hiroshi 岸田裕之 . "Shugo shihai no tenkai to chigyōsei no henshitsu" 守護支配の展開と知行制の変質 (The development of shugo rule and changes in the system of proprietorship), *Shigaku zasshi* 82.11:1-42 (November 1973).

Kobata Atsushi 小葉田淳 . "Chūsei kōhanki ni okeru nissen kingin bōeki no kenkyū" 中世後半期に於ける日鮮金銀貿易の研究 (Gold and silver trade between Japan and Korea in the later medieval period), *Shigaku zasshi* 43.6:1–25 (June 1932) and 43.7:71–110 (July 1932).

——.*Chūsei Nisshi tsūkō bōekishi no kenkyū* 中世日支通交貿易史の研究 (Studies in the history of Sino-Japanese trade and diplomatic relations in the medieval period). Tokyo, Tōkō Shoin, 1969.

——.*Nihon kahei ryūtsūshi* 日本貨幣流通史 (History of currency circulation in Japan). Tokyo, Tōkō Shoin, 1969.

Kobayashi Hiroshi 小林宏. "Muromachi jidai no shugoshi funyūken ni tsuite" 室町時代の守護使不入権について (The right to exclude shugo envoys from lands during the Muromachi period), *Hokudai shigaku* 11:39–65 (September 1966).

——. "Nambokuchō–Muromachiki ni okeru Aki no kuni Kikkawa shi no dōkō ni tsuite–Muromachi bakufu no gokenin sei" 南北朝・室町期における安芸国吉川氏の動向について ‐ 室町幕府の御家人制 (The Muromachi Bakufu housemen system as seen in the activities of the Kikkawa clan of Aki province during the Nambokuchō and Muromachi periods), *Hokudai shigaku* 13: 25–35 (August 1971).

Kobayashi Yasuo 小林保夫. "Jikata tōnin kō" 地方頭人考 (The head of the Office of Urban Property), *Shirin* 58.5:134–145 (September 1975).

Kōsaka Konomu 高坂好. *Akamatsu Enshin–Mitsusuke* 赤松円心・満祐 (Akamatsu Mitsusuke). Tokyo, Yoshikawa Kōbunkan 1972.

Kotani Toshihiko 小谷俊彦. "Nambokuchōki ni okeru Kokuga" 南北朝期における国衙 (Kokuga estates during the Nambokuchō period), *Shigaku* 36.2–3:259–272 (1963).

Kurokawa Masahiro 黒川正宏. "Chūsei Imabori shōnin ni kansuru hitotsu no shiryō ni tsuite" 中世今堀商人に関する一つの史料 (The Imabori merchants in the medieval period), *Nihon rekishi* 273:102–107 (February 1971).

Kurokawa Naonori 黒川直則. "Shugo ryōkokusei to shōen taisei–kokujin ryōshusei no kakuritsu katei" 守護領国制と荘園体制 ‐ 国人領主制の確立過程 (Shugo and *shōen* in the formation of the *kokujin* domain system), *Nihonshi kenkyū* 57:1–19 (November 1961).

——. "Chūsei kōki no ryōshusei ni tsuite" 中世後期の領主制について (Proprietorship in the later medieval period), *Nihonshi kenkyū* 68:53–63 (September 1963).

——."Chūsei kōki no nōmin ikki to tokuseirei" 中世後期の農民一揆と徳政令 (Peasant uprisings and debt-cancellation decrees in the later medieval period), *Nihonshi kenkyū* 108:9–24 (November 1969).

——."Muromachi bakufu gechijō to gohan no mikyōjo" 室町幕府 下知状と御判御教書 (*Gechijō* and *gohan no mikyōjo* decrees of the Muromachi Bakufu), *Nihonshi kenkyū* 117:97–100 (March 1971).

Kuwayama Kōnen 桑山浩然 . "Muromachi bakufu no sōsōki ni okeru shoryō ni tsuite" 室町幕府の草創期における所 領について (Lands in the formative period of the Muromachi Bakufu), *Chūsei no mado* 中世の窓 12:4–27 (April 1963).

——."Muromachi bakufu keizai kikō no ichi kōsatsu—nōsenkata kubō okura no kinō to seiritsu" 室町幕府経済機構の一考察 ― 納銭方・公方御倉の機能と成立 (*Nōsenkata* and *kubō okura* officials in the economic machinery of the Muromachi Bakufu), *Shigaku zasshi* 73.9:1–33 (September 1964).

Kyōto shi 京都市 . ed. *Kyōto no rekishi 2 chūsei no mei'an* 京都 の歴史 2，中世の明暗 (History of Kyoto, vol. 2: light and dark in the medieval period). Kyoto, 1975.

Lander, J. R. *Conflict and Stability in Fifteenth-Century England.* London, Hutchinson University Library, 1969.

Lewis, P. S. *Later Medieval France.* London, Macmillan, 1968.

Ma, Laurence J. C. *Commercial Development and Urban Change in Sung China (960–1279).* Ann Arbor, University of Michigan Press, 1971.

Matsumoto Shinpachirō 松本新八郎 . *Chūsei shakai no kenkyū* 中世社会の研究 (Studies on medieval society). Tokyo, Tōkyō Daigaku Shuppankai, 1968.

Matsuoka Hisato 松岡久人 . "Ōuchi shi no hatten to sono ryōkoku shihai" 大内氏の発展とその領国支配 (The rise and regime of the Ōuchi clan) in Uozumi Sōgorō 魚澄惣五郎 , ed., *Daimyō ryōkoku to jōkamachi* 大名領国と城下町 . Kyoto, Yanagihara Shoten, 1957.

——.Ōuchi shi no Buzen no kuni shihai" 大内氏の豊前国支 配(Ōuchi rule of Buzen province), *Hiroshima daigaku bungakubu kiyō* 23.2:1–30 (August 1964).

——."Ōuchi shi no Aki no kuni shihai" 大内氏の安芸国支 配 (Ōuchi rule of Aki province), *Hiroshima daigaku bungakubu kiyō* 25.1:67–87 (December 1965).

——.Ōuchi Yoshihiro 大内義弘 (Ōuchi Yoshihiro). Tokyo, Jinbutsu Ōraisha, 1966.

——."Nambokuchō Muromachiki Iwami no kuni to Ōuchi shi" 南北 朝室町期石見国と大内氏 (The Ōuchi in Iwami province during the Nambokuchō and Muromachi periods), *Hiroshima daigaku bungakubu kiyō* 32.1:1–23 (January 1973).

Miki Yasushi 三木靖 . Nambokuchō nairanki no ikki—*Taiheiki* o chū-shin ni" 南北朝内乱期の一揆 ― 太平記を中

心に (Leagues during the Nambokuchō period as represented in the *Taiheiki*), *Nihon rekishi* 276:42-77 (May 1971).

Miskimin, Harry A. *The Economy of Early Renaissance Europe, 1300-1460.* Englewood Cliffs, N. J., Prentice-Hall, 1969.

Mizuno Kyōichirō 水野恭一郎 . "Shugo Akamatsu shi no ryōkoku shihai to Kakitsu no hen" 守護赤松氏の領国支配 と嘉吉の変 (The Kakitsu rebellion and the Akamatsu's rule of their shugo domain), *Shirin* 42.2:102-129 (1959).

——."Ōnin Bunmeiki ni okeru shugo ryōkoku—Yamana shi no ryōkoku o chūshin ni" 応仁文明期における守護領国 – 山名氏の領国を中心に (The Yamana shugo domain during the Ōnin-Bunmei era), *Okayama shigaku* 岡山史学 10:208-229 (December 1961).

——.*Buke jidai no seiji to bunka* 武家時代の政治と文化 (Politics and culture in the age of the military houses). Osaka, Sōgensha, 1975.

Molho, Anthony. *Florentine Public Finances in the Early Renaissance, 1400-1433.* Cambridge, Harvard University Press, 1971.

Mollat, Michel. *Genèse médiévale de la France moderne, XIV-XVe siècles.* Paris, Arthaud, 1970.

Momose Kesao 百瀬今朝雄 . "Bunmei jūninen no tokusei kinzei ni kansuru ichi kōsatsu" 文明十二年の徳政禁制に関 する一考察 (The prohibition on debt cancellation of Bunmei 12), *Shigaku zasshi* 66.4:1-26 (April 1957).

Momose Mitsu 百瀬美津 . "Eiryōchi ni kansuru zeninushi kaeshijō ni tsuite" 永領地に関する銭主返状について (Creditors' contracts for lands held in perpetuity), *Nihon rekishi* 175:47-56 (December 1962).

Mori Shigeaki 森茂暁. "Kō ichizoku to Muromachi bakufu" 高一族と室町幕府 (The Kō family and the Muromachi Bakufu), *Shien* 113:1-31 (March 1976).

Morisue Yumiko 森末由美子 . "Muromachi bakufu goryōsho ni kansuru ichi kōsatsu—sono keiei jittai o chūshin to shite" 室町幕府御料所に関する一考察 – その経営実態 を中心として (The administration of the shogun's estates in the Muromachi Bakufu), *Shisō* 12:46-76 (October 1971).

Murata Masashi 村田正志 . "Kemmu chūkō to kokugaryō" 建武中興と国衙領 (The Kemmu Restoration and the imperial estates), *Rekishi chiri* 75.2:1-14 (February 1940).

Murdoch, James. *A History of Japan,* vol. 1. London, Kegan Paul, 1925.

Nagahara Keiji 永原慶二 . *Nihon no chūsei shakai* 日本の中世社会 (Japan's medieval society). Tokyo, Iwanami Shoten, 1968.

——.*Daimyō ryōkokusei* 大名領国制 (The daimyo domain system). Tokyo, Nihon Hyōronsha, 1969.

——.*Nihon hōkensei seiritsu katei no kenkyū* 日本封建制成立過程の研究 (Studies on the establishment of the feudal system in Japan). Tokyo, Iwanami Shoten, 1969.

——, ed. *Nihon keizaishi taikei 2 chūsei* 日本経済史大系 2，中世 (Outline of Japanese economic history, vol. 2: medieval period). Tokyo, Tōkyō Daigaku Shuppankai, 1969.

——and Inagaki Yasuhiko 稲垣泰彦 , eds. *Chūsei no shakai to keizai* 中世の社会と経済 (Medieval society and economy). Tokyo, Tōkyō Daigaku Shuppankai, 1969.

——.*Gekokujō no jidai* 下剋上の時代 (The age of the lower superseding the higher). Tokyo, Chūō Kōronsha, 1971.

Nagashima Fukutarō 永島福太郎 . "Hanzei seido no ichi kōsatsu" 半済制度の一考察 (The *hanzei* system), *Kokushigaku* 15:39–57 (June 1933).

——."Kin'yūgyō no ichi sō" 金融業の一僧 (A priest-moneylender), *Nihon rekishi* 13:47–49 (May 1948).

——.*Ōnin no ran* 応仁の乱 (The Ōnin War). Tokyo, Shibundō, 1972.

Nakamura Kichiji 中村吉治 . *Tokusei to tsuchiikki* 徳政と土一揆 (Debt cancellation and peasant rebellions). Tokyo, Shibundō, 1970.

Nihon rekishi 5 chūsei 1 日本歴史 5，中世 1 (Japanese history, vol. 5: medieval vol. 1). Tokyo, Iwanami Shoten, 1971.

Nihon rekishi 6 chūsei 2 日本歴史 6，中世 2 Tokyo, Iwanami Shoten, 1971.

Nihon rekishi 7 chūsei 3 日本歴史 7，中世 3 Tokyo, Iwanami Shoten, 1971.

Nihon rekishi 8 chūsei 4 日本歴史 8，中世 4 Tokyo, Iwanami Shoten, 1971.

Nihon rekishi 6 chūsei 2 日本歴史 6，中世 2 Tokyo, Iwanami Shoten, 1975.

Nihon rekishi 7 chūsei 3 日本歴史 7，中世 3 Tokyo, Iwanami Shoten, 1976.

Nihonshi Kenkyūkai Shiryōkenkyūbukai 日本史研究会史料研究部会 , ed. *Chūsei no kenryoku to minshū* 中世の権力と民衆 (Power and the masses in medieval times). Osaka, Sōgensha, 1970.

Nishio Minoru 西尾実 . *Chūseiteki na mono to sono tenkai* 中世的なものとその展開 (The unfolding of a medieval style). Tokyo, Iwanami Shoten, 1970.

Noda Tadao 野田只夫 . "Chūsei Kyōto ni okeru kōrikashigyō no

hatten" 中世京都に於ける高利貸業の発展 (The development of moneylending in medieval Kyoto), *Kyōto gakugei daigaku gakuhō* 京都学芸大学学報 A.2:31-42 (August 1952).

Ogawa Makoto 小川信. *Yamana Sōzen to Hosokawa Katsumoto* 山名宗全と細川勝元 (Yamana Sōzen and Hosokawa Katsumoto). Tokyo, Jinbutsu Ōraisha, 1966.

——."Hosokawa Kiyouji no taitō" 細川清氏の抬頭 (The rise of Hosokawa Kiyouji), *Kokugakuin zasshi* 69.7:1-14 (July 1968).

——."Hosokawa Kiyouji no botsuraku" 細川清氏の没落 (The downfall of Hosokawa Kiyouji), *Kokugakuin zasshi* 70.8:1-8 (August 1969).

——.*Hosokawa Yoriyuki* 細川頼之 (Hosokawa Yoriyuki). Tokyo, Yoshikawa Kōbunkan, 1972.

——."Ashikaga (Shiba) Takatsune no bakusei un'ei" 足利（斯波）高経の幕政運営 (Ashikaga (Shiba) Takatsune's management of Bakufu administration), *Kokugakuin daigaku kiyō* 国学院大学紀要 11:1-34 (March 1973).

——."Kannō jōran zengo ni okeru Shiba shi—Ashikaga (Shiba) Takatsune no dōkō o chūshin to shite" 観応擾乱前後における斯波氏 — 足利（斯波）高経の動向を中心として (The Shiba family during the time of the Kannō disturbance, with special reference to the activities of Ashikaga (Shiba) Takatsune), *Kokugakuin zasshi* 74.10:1-16 (October 1973).

——, ed. *Muromachi seiken* 室町政権 (The Muromachi regime). Tokyo, Yūseidō, 1975.

Ōiwa Kuni 大岩邦. "Chūsei makki ni okeru bunka kōryū" 中世末期における文化交流 (Cultural exchange in the later medieval period), *Rekishi kyōiku* 7.8:60-65 (August 1959).

Okuno Takahiro 奥野高広. "Muromachi jidai ni okeru dosō no kenkyū" 室町時代に於ける土倉の研究 (The *dosō* in the Muromachi period), *Shigaku zasshi* 44.8:44-95 (August 1933).

——."Zenki hōkensei to erizeni kinrei" 前期封建制と撰銭禁令 (Laws prohibiting coin selection in the early feudal period), in Itō Tasaburō 伊東多三郎, ed., *Kokumin seikatsushi kenkyū 2—seikatsu to shakai keizai* 国民生活史研究 2， 生活と社会経済. Tokyo, Yoshikawa Kōbunkan, 1959.

——.*Ashikaga Yoshiaki* 足利義昭 (Ashikaga Yoshiaki). Tokyo, Yoshikawa Kōbunkan, 1968.

Ono Terutsugu 小野晃嗣. "Muromachi bakufu no sakaya tōsei" 室町幕府の酒屋統制 (Muromachi Bakufu regulation of the sake brewers), *Shigaku zasshi* 43.7:28-70 (July 1932).

——."Oroshiuri shijō to shite no Yodo uoichi no hattatsu" 卸売市場としての淀魚市の発達 (The Yodo fish market's growth into a wholesale market), *Rekishi chiri* 65.5:1-26 (May 1935).

——."Chūsei shuzōgyō no hattatsu" 中世酒造業の発達 (The development of sake brewing in medieval times), *Shakai keizai shigaku* 6.8:1-36; 9:25-47; 10:55-74 (1936).

Ōta Junzō 太田順三. "Chūsei kōki no bakufu kenryoku no tokushitsu to jinmin tōsō—Yoshinori seiken o megutte" 中世後期の幕府権力の特質と人民闘争 — 義教政権をめぐって (Special features and personal conflicts in the late medieval Bakufu: the case of Yoshinori's regime), *Rekishigaku kenkyū* (bessatsu) (November 1973), 53-65.

——."Shōgun Yoshinori to gozen rakkyo hōsho no seiritsu" 将軍義教と御前落居奉書の成立 (Shogun Yoshinori and the establishment of the *gozen rakkyo* order), *Shikan* 91:24-42 (March 1975).

Oyamada Yoshio 小山田義夫. "Muromachi jidai no Mōri shi ni tsuite" 室町時代の毛利氏について (The Mōri family in the Muromachi period), *Rekishi kyōiku* 7.8:23-30 (August 1959).

Perroy, Edouard. *The Hundred Years War*. New York, Capricorn, 1965.

Postan, M. M. *Essays on Medieval Agriculture and General Problems of the Medieval Economy*. Cambridge, Cambridge University Press, 1973.

——.*Medieval Trade and Finance*. Cambridge, Cambridge University Press, 1973.

Previté-Orton, C. W. *The Shorter Cambridge Medieval History*, vol. 2. Cambridge, Cambridge University Press, 1971.

Rawski, Evelyn Sakakida. *Agricultural Change and the Peasant Economy of South China*. Cambridge, Harvard University Press, 1972.

Raz, Jacob. "The Actor and His Audience: Zeami's Views on the Audience of the Noh," *Monumenta Nipponica* 31.3:251-274 (Autumn 1976).

Rice, Eugene F., Jr. *The Foundations of Early Modern Europe, 1460-1559*. New York, W. W. Norton, 1970.

Sagawa Hiroshi 佐川宏. "Chūsei tōgoku ni okeru shōnōmin no sonzai ni tsuite" 中世東国における小農民の存在について (Small farmers in eastern Japan in medieval times), *Nihon rekishi* 278:33-50 (July 1971).

Sansom, George. *A History of Japan, 1334-1615*. Stanford, Stanford University Press, 1961.

Sasaki Gin'ya 佐々木銀弥. *Shōen no shōgyō* 荘園の商業 (*Shōen* commerce). Tokyo, Yoshikawa Kōbunkan, 1964.

——.*Chūsei shōhin ryūtsūshi no kenkyū* 中世商品流通史の研究 (The circulation of goods in medieval times). Tokyo, Hōsei Daigaku Shuppankyoku, 1972.

——.*Muromachi bakufu* 室町幕府 (The Muromachi Bakufu). Tokyo, Shōgakukan, 1975.

Satō Kazuhiko 佐藤和彦 . *Nambokuchō nairan* 南北朝内乱 (The disturbances of Nambokuchō). Tokyo, Shōgakukan, 1974.

Satō Shin'ichi 佐藤進一 . *Muromachi bakufu shugo seido no kenkyū 1* 室町幕府守護制度の研究 上 (The shugo system in the Muromachi Bakufu, vol. 1). Tokyo, Tōkyō Daigaku Shuppankai, 1967.

——."Ashikaga Yoshinori shiritsuki no bakufu seiji" 足利義教嗣立期の幕府政治 (Bakufu politics at the time of Ashikaga Yoshinori's coming to power), *Hōsei shigaku* 20:3-9 (March 1968).

——."Muromachi bakufu ron" 室町幕府論 (On the Muromachi Bakufu), *Nihon rekishi 7 chūsei 3* (1971), 1-48.

——.*Nambokuchō no dōran* 南北朝の動乱 (The wars of Nambokuchō). Tokyo, Chūō Kōronsha, 1971.

——and Ikeuchi Yoshisuke, eds. *Chūsei hōsei shiryōshū 2 Muromachi bakufu hō* 中世法制史料集 2, 室町幕府法 (Medieval legal documents, vol. 2: Muromachi Bakufu laws). Tokyo, Iwanami Shoten, 1969.

——, Ikeuchi Yoshisuke, and Momose Kesao 百瀬今朝雄, eds. *Chūsei hōsei shiryōshū 3 buke kahō 1* 中世法制史料集 3, 武家家法 (Medieval legal documents, vol. 3: military house laws). Tokyo, Iwanami Shoten, 1969.

——and Ikeuchi Yoshisuke 池内義資 , eds. *Chūsei hōsei shiryōshū 1 Kamakura bakufu hō* 中世法制史料集 1, 鎌倉幕府法 (Medieval legal documents, vol. 1: Kamakura Bakufu laws). Tokyo, Iwanami Shoten, 1970.

——and Ishimoda Shō 石母田正 eds. *Chūsei no hō to kokka* 中世の法と国家 (Medieval law and the state). Tokyo, Tōkyō Daigaku Shuppankai, 1971.

Seta Katsuya 瀬田勝哉 . "Chūsei makki no zaichi tokusei" 中世末期の在地徳政 (Local debt cancellations during the late medieval period), *Shigaku zasshi* 77.9:1-52 (September 1968).

Shimada Jirō 島田次郎 . "Hanzei seido no seiritsu—Muromachi seiken seiritsushi no kenkyū" 半済制度の成立 - 室町政権成立史の研究 (The establishment of the *hanzei* system), *Shichō* 58:1-24 (1956).

Shimosaka Mamoru 下坂守 . "Sanmon shisetsu seido no seiritsu to tenkai—Muromachi bakufu no sanmon seisaku o megutte" 山門使節制度の成立と展開 - 室町幕府の山門政策をめぐって (The Muromachi Bakufu's policy with respect to Mt. Hiei: origin and growth of the Mt. Hiei envoy system), *Shirin* 58.1:67-114 (January 1975).

Shinjō Tsunezō 新城常三 . *Kamakura jidai no kōtsū* 鎌倉時代 の交通 (Communications in the Kamakura period). Tokyo, Yoshi-kawa Kōbunkan, 1967.

Steenstrup, Carl. "The Imagawa Letter," *Monumenta Nipponica* 28.3:295–316 (1973).

Strayer, Joseph R. *On the Medieval Origins of the Modern State.* Princeton, Princeton University Press, 1970.

Sugimoto Hisao 杉本尚雄. *Kikuchi shi sandai* 菊池氏三代 (Three generations of the Kikuchi clan). Tokyo, Yoshikawa Kōbunkan, 1966.

Suma Chikai 須磨千穎 . "Dosō ni yoru shōen nengu shūnō no ukeoi ni tsuite—kamo-wake-ikazuchi jinja no shoryō noto no kuni tsuchida no shō no nengu shūnō ni kansuru dosō yasui no katsudō" 土倉による荘園 年貢収納の請負について ― 賀茂別雷神 社の所領能登国土田庄の年貢収納に関 する土倉野洲井の活動 (*Nengu* tax collection by *dosō* tax farmers), *Shigaku zasshi* 80.6:1–43 (June 1971).

——."Dosō no tochi shūseki to tokusei—kamo-wake-ikazuchi jinja keidai ni okeru dosō yasui no tochi shoshiki kaidoku o megutte" 土倉の土 地集積と徳政 ― 賀茂別雷神社境内に おける土倉野洲井の土地所職買得をめぐっ て (Land accumulation by the *dosō* and debt cancellation), *Shigaku zasshi* 81.3:1–40 (March 1972).

Tabata Yasuko 田端泰子 . "Muromachi–Sengokuki no Kobayakawa shi no ryōshusei" 室町・戦国期の小早川氏の領 主制 (The domain system of the Kobayakawa clan during the Muro-machi and Sengoku periods), *Shirin* 49.5:1–29 (September 1966).

——."Chūsei kōki Kinai dogō no sonzai keitai—kawashima shi samukawa shi o chūshin ni" 中世後期畿内土豪の存在形態 ― 革島氏・寒川氏を中心に (Powerful local families in the Kinai during the late medieval period), *Nihonshi kenkyū* 82:15–42 (January 1966).

Takizawa Takeo 滝沢武雄. "Erizeni rei ni tsuite no ichi kōsatsu 1" 撰銭令についての一考察 （一） (On coin se-lection decrees, part 1), *Shigaku zasshi* 71.12:1–21 (December 1962).

Tamaizumi Dairyō 玉泉大梁. *Muromachi jidai no denso* 室町時 代の田租 (The rice field tax in the Muromachi period). Tokyo, Yoshikawa Kōbunkan, 1969.

Tamura Tetsuo 田村哲夫 . "Nagato shugodai no kenkyū" 長門 守護代の研究 (The *shugo-dai* of Nagato province), *Yamaguchi ken monjokan kenkyū kiyō* 山口県文書館研究紀要 1: 1–36 (March 1972).

Tanaka Minoru 田中稔. "Samurai–bonge kō" 侍・凡下考 (On samurai and commoners), *Shirin* 59.4:1–31 (July 1976).

Tanaka Takeo 田中健夫. *Chūsei kaigai kōshōshi no kenkyū* 中世海外交渉史の研究 (Foreign relations in medieval times). Tokyo, Tōkyō Daigaku Shuppankai, 1959.

——.*Wakō to kangō bōeki* 倭寇と勘合貿易 (Japanese pirates and the official tally trade). Tokyo, Shibundō, 1961.

Tanuma Mutsumi 田沼睦. "Jisha ichien shoryō ni okeru shugo ryōkoku no tenkai–Tōjiryō Tamba no kuni Ōyama no shō o chūshin ni shite" 寺社一円所領における守護領国の展開 — 東寺領丹波国大山庄を中心に (The growth of shugo domains and their effect on temple and shrine estates: the case of the Tōji's Ōyama manor in Tamba province), *Rekishi hyōron* 108: 24–40 (August 1959).

——."Kokugaryō no ryōyū keitai to shugo ryōkoku" 国衙領の領有形態と守護領国 (Imperial lands and shugo domains), *Nihonshi kenkyū* 80:27–46 (September 1965).

——."Kōden tansen to shugo ryōkoku" 公田段銭と守護領国 (*Tansen* taxes on public lands and shugo domains), *Shoryōbu kiyo* 書陵部紀要 17:16–33 (October 1965).

——."Chūseiteki kōden taisei no seiritsu to tenkai" 中世的公田体制の成立と展開 (The establishment and growth of a medieval system of public lands), *Shoryōbu kiyo* 21:1–22 (1969).

Thrupp, Sylvia L. *The Merchant Class of Medieval London*. Ann Arbor, University of Michigan Press, 1968.

Toyama Mikio 外山幹夫. "Kemmu seifu–Muromachi bakufu hajime no shugo ni tsuite–Ōtomo shi no baai" 建武政府・室町幕府初の守護について — 大友氏の場合 (The shugo in the Kemmu and early Muromachi periods: the case of the Ōtomo), *Nihon rekishi* 282:38–56 (November 1971).

Toyoda Takeshi 豊田武. "Za to dosō" 座と土倉 (The za and the *dosō*), *Nihon rekishi 6 chūsei 2* (1963), 153–186.

——.*Zōtei chūsei Nihon shōgyōshi no kenkyū* 増訂中世日本商業史の研究 (Studies in the commercial history of medieval Japan). Tokyo, Iwanami Shoten, 1970.

——.*Nihon no hōken toshi* 日本の對建都市 (The feudal city in Japan). Tokyo, Iwanami Shoten, 1972.

Tsunoda Ryusaku and L. Carrington Goodrich, eds. *Japan in the Chinese Dynastic Histories*. South Pasadena, P. D. & Ione Perkins, 1951.

Usui Nobuyoshi 臼井信義. "Ashikaga Yoshimochi no kōkyo to keishi mondai" 足利義持の薨去と継嗣問題 (The succession problem after the death of Ashikaga Yoshimochi), *Kokushigaku* 国史学 57:21–34 (May 1952).

——."Kubō to kanrei" 公方と管領 (The shogun and the *kanrei*), *Nihon rekishi* 60:27-28 (May 1953).

——.*Ashikaga Yoshimitsu* 足利義満 (Ashikaga Yoshimitsu). Tokyo: Yoshikawa Kōbunkan, 1960).

Uwayokote Masataka 上横手雅敬. *Hōjō Yasutoki* 北条泰時 (Hōjō Yasutoki). Tokyo, Yoshikawa Kōbunkan, 1958.

——."Kemmu irai tsuika no seiritsu" 建武以来追加の成立 (The establishment of the supplementary laws after Kemmu), Kobata Atsushi Kyōju Taikan Kinenjigyōkai 小葉田淳教授退官記念事業会 ed., in *Kobata atsushi kyōju taikan kinen kokushi ronshū* 小葉田淳教授退官記念国史論集 (Kyoto, 1970), 499-510.

Wakimoto Jūkurō 脇本十九郎, "Ashikaga Yoshimitsu to sōgen ga" 足利義満と宋元画 (Ashikaga Yoshimitsu and Sung-Yuan painting), *Bijutsu kenkyū* 美術研究 38:1-11 (1935).

Wakita Haruko 脇田晴子. "Chūsei shukōgyōza no kōzō" 中世手工業座の構造 (The organization of handicraft-manufacturing *za* in the medieval period), *Rekishigaku kenkyū* 272:14-24 (January 1963).

Waley, Daniel. *Later Medieval Europe: From St. Louis to Luther*. London, Longman, 1975.

Wang Yi-t'ung. *Official Relations Between China and Japan, 1368-1549*. Cambridge, Harvard University Press, 1953.

Watanabe Yosuke 渡辺世祐. *Kantō chūshin Ashikaga jidai no kenkyū* 関東中心足利時代之研究 (The Kantō region in the Ashikaga period). Tokyo, Shin Jinbutsu Ōraisha, 1971.

Wolfe, Martin. *The Fiscal System of Renaissance France*. New Haven, Yale University Press, 1972.

Yamaguchi Takamasa 山口隼正. "Nambokuchōki no Satsuma no kuni shugo ni tsuite" 南北朝期の薩摩国守護について (The shugo of Satsuma province during the Nambokuchō period), *Shigaku zasshi* 76.6:37-74 (June 1967).

——."Zenki Muromachi bakufu ni yoru Hyūga no kuni 'ryōkoku'ka'" 前期室町幕府による日向国「料国」化 (The conversion of Hyūga province into shogunal domain during the early Muromachi Bakufu), *Nihon rekishi* 329:42-57 (October 1975).

Yanagi Chizuru 柳千鶴. "Muromachi bakufu no hōkai katei–Ōnin no rango ni okeru Yamashiro no kuni no hanzei o chūshin ni" 室町幕府の崩壊過程 — 応仁の乱後における山城国の半済を中心に (*Hanzei* in post-Ōnin War Yamashiro province and the collapse of the Muromachi Bakufu), *Nihonshi kenkyū* 108:25-46 (November 1969).

Yokoi Kiyoshi 横井清. *Chūsei minshū no seikatsu bunka* 中世

民衆の生活文化 (Popular culture and the medieval masses). Tokyo, Tōkyō Daigaku Shuppankai, 1975.

Yonehara Masayoshi 米原正義 . *Ōuchi Yoshitaka* 大内義隆 (Ōuchi Yoshitaka). Tokyo, Jinbutsu Ōraisha, 1967.

Glossary

Akamatsu Mitsusuke
赤松満祐

Asakura Takakage
朝倉孝景

ashigaru　足軽

Ashikaga　足利

—Mitsutaka　満隆

—Mochiuji　持氏

—Motouji　基氏

—Tadayoshi　直義

—Takauji　尊氏

—Ujimitsu　氏満

—Yoshiaki　義昭

—Yoshiakira　義詮

—Yoshihisa　義尚

—Yoshimasa　義政

—Yoshimi　義視

—Yoshimitsu　義満

—Yoshimochi　義持

—Yoshinori　義教

bantō　番頭

bashaku　馬借

bonjin　凡人

bugyō(nin)　奉行(人)

bugyōnin rensho hōsho
奉行人連署奉書

buke densō　武家伝奏

buke shissō　武家執奏

bun'ichi tokusei　分一徳政

bun'ichi tokusei kinzei
分一徳政禁制

bushi　武士

chō　町

chōnin　町人

chūbunsen　抽分銭

daibon sankajō
大犯三箇条

daikan　代官

Da(i)jō Tennō　太上天皇

daijōdaijin　太政大臣

dosō　土倉

Eikyō no ran 永亭の乱
Enryakuji 延暦寺
erizeni 撰銭

fudai 譜代
fudono 文殿
Fujiwara 藤原
Fushiminomiya Sadafusa
伏見宮貞成

gekokujō 下剋上
genpuku 元服
gobanshū 御番衆
Go-Daigo 後醍醐
Go-En'yū 後円融
gohan hajime 御判初
gohan (no) mikyōjo
御判御教書
gokenin 御家人
Go-Komatsu
後小松
gon dainagon 権大納言
gonaisho 御内書
goryōsho 御料所
gozan 五山
gozen gosata 御前御沙汰
gozen rakkyo
御前落居
Hana no gosho 花の御所
hanzei 半済
Hatakeyama Mochikuni
畠山持国

hikan 被官
hikitsukeshū 引付衆
hikitsuke tōnin 引付頭人
Hino Tomiko 日野富子
hizeniya 日銭屋
Hōjō Yasutoki 北条泰時
hōkōshū 奉公衆
honmotsu kaeshi 本物返
honza 本座
Hosokawa Katsumoto
細川勝元
—Mochiyuki 持之
—Takakuni 高国
—Yoriyuki 頼之
hyōjōhajime 評定始
hyōjōshū 評定衆
hyōrōryōsho 兵粮料所

ichimon 一門
ichizoku 一族
Iinoo Tameshige 飯尾為種
ikki 一揆
Imagawa Ryōshun (Sadayo)
今川了俊（貞世）
inryōkenshu 蔭涼軒主
inzen 院宣
Ise Sadachika 伊勢貞親
Iwashimizu Hachimangū
石清水八幡宮

jiguchizeni 地口銭

jikata bugyō 地方奉行
jinushi 地主
jisha honjo 寺社本所
jitō 地頭
jizamurai 地侍
Jōei (Goseibai) shikimoku
貞永（御成敗）式目
jūji 住持
junii 従二位

Kamakura Bakufu
鎌倉幕府
kangō bōeki 勘合貿易
kanmon 貫文
kanrei 管領
kanrei-dai hōsho (soejō)
管領代奉書（添状）
kanrei shohan gechijō
管領署判下知状
kanrinin 管理人
Kantō kanrei 関東管領
Kantō kubō 関東公方
karita rōzeki 刈田狼籍
kebiishichō 検非違使庁
Kemmu shikimoku
建武式目
kenmotsu 献物
kesshochi 闕所地
Kikei Shinzui 季瓊真蘂
kinjū 近習
kirokusho 記録所

kishinjō 寄進状
Kitabatake Chikafusa
北畠親房
kōden 公田
Kōfukuji 興福寺
Koitsumi 肥富
kokugaryō 国衙領
kokujin 国人
kokushi 国司
Kō no Moronao 高師直
Kō no Moroyasu 高師泰
kubariwake bugyō
賦別奉行
kubō okura 公方御倉
kuge densō 公家伝奏
kumon 公文
kurabugyō 倉奉行
Kusunoki Masashige
楠木正成
kyōgen 狂言
Kyōgoku 京極
kyōsai 京済
Kyūshū tandai
九州探題

mabechizeni 間別銭
mandokoro (dai) 政所（代）
Meitoku no ran 明徳の乱
Minamoto no Yoritomo
源頼朝
monchūjo 問注所
mōshitsugi 申次

munebechisen 棟別銭

Muromachi Bakufu
室町幕府

myōshu 名主

Nambokuchō 南北朝
nengu 年貢
nenkichi 年紀地
Nihon kokuō 日本国王
Nikaidō 二階堂
nōdo 農奴
nōmin 農民
nōsenkata 納銭方

Ōei no ran 応永の乱
Ōnin no ran 応仁の乱
onshōkata 恩賞方
ōtabumi 大田文
Ōtomo 大友
Ōuchi Yoshihiro 大内義弘

rakuichi 楽市
rinji 綸旨
Ritsuryō 律令
ryō 領

sadaijin 左大臣
sakaya 酒屋
samuraidokoro 侍所
Sambōin Mansai
三宝院満済

Sanjōbōmon 三条坊門
Sanjūsangendō
三十三間堂
sankin kōtai 参勤交代
Sanmon bugyō 山門奉行
sanmon santō 三問三答
sarugaku 猿楽
sekisho 関所
sengoku daimyō 戦国大名
Sesshū 雪舟
shakusho 借書
Shiba Takatsune 斯波高経
Shiba Yoshimasa 斯波義将
shidōsen 祠堂銭
shiki 職
Shimazu 島津
Shin'e 真恵
shinza 新座
shisetsu jungyō 使節遵行
shitsuji (dai) 執事（代）
Shōchō no tsuchiikki
正長の土一揆
shōen 荘園
shoke 庶家
Shōni 少弐
shoshi 所司
shugo 守護
shugo buninjō
守護補任状
shugo-dai 守護代
shugo daimyō 守護大名

shugo jungyōjō
守護遵行状

shugo shussen 守護出銭

shukurō 宿老

shūto 衆徒

Sōkokuji 相国寺

sōryō (shiki) 惣領（職）

suiko 出挙

Taira 平

taka 高

Takakura gosho 高倉御所

tansen 段銭

Tenryūji 天龍寺

tōbanshū 東班衆

Tōfukuji 東福寺

Tōji 東寺

Tokugawa Ieyasu 徳川家康

tokusei 徳政

tokusei kinzei 徳政禁制

tōnin 頭人

tōryō 棟梁

Toyotomi Hideyoshi
豊臣秀吉

tozama 外様

Uesugi Norizane 上杉憲実

Uesugi Ujinori 上杉氏憲

Uesugi Zenshū no ran
上杉禅秀の乱

utokunin 有徳人

wakō 倭寇

yakubutakumai 役夫工米

Yamana Mochitoyo (Sōzen)
山名持豊（宗全）

yoriai 寄合

yūhitsukata 右筆方

za 座

zaichi ryōshu 在地領主

zakumon 坐公文

Zeami 世阿彌

Zeen 是圓

zōdairiyaku 造内裏役

Index

CORNELL EAST ASIA SERIES

106 Susan Orpett Long, ed., *Lives in Motion: Composing Circles of Self and Community in Japan*

107 Peter J. Katzenstein, Natasha Hamilton-Hart, Kozo Kato, & Ming Yue, *Asian Regionalism*

108 Kenneth Alan Grossberg, *Japan's Renaissance: the Politics of the Muromachi Bakufu*

109 John W. Hall & Toyoda Takeshi, eds., *Japan in the Muromachi Age*

110 Kim Su-Young, Shin Kyong-Nim, Lee Si-Young; Brother Anthony of Taizé & Young-Moo Kim, trs., *Variations: Three Korean Poets*

111 Don Kenny, *Kyōgen Women*

112 Pilwun Wang & Sarah Wang, *Early One Spring: A Learning Guide to Accompany the Film Video* February

113 Thomas Conlan, *In Little Need of Divine Intervention: Scrolls of the Mongol Invasions of Japan*

FORTHCOMING

S. Yumiko Hulvey, *Ben no Naishi Nikki: A Poetic Record of Female Courtiers' Sacred Duties at the Kamakura-Period Court*

Yanghi Choe-Wall, *Vision of a Phoenix: The Poems of Hŏ Nansŏrhŏn*

Samuel Leiter, *Frozen Moments: Writings on* Kabuki, *1966-2001*

To order, please contact the Cornell East Asia Series, East Asia Program , Cornell University, 140 Uris Hall, Ithaca, NY 14853-7601, USA; phone (607) 255-6222, fax (607) 255-1388, ceas@cornell.edu, http://www.einaudi.cornell.edu/bookstore/eap

SB/3-01/.6 M pb